Waltzing Matilda

WALTZING MATILDA

The Life and Times

* * * * * * * * * * * * * * * * * * *

of Nebraska Senator

* * * * * * * * * * * * * * * * * * *

Robert Kerrey

* * * * * * * * * * * * * * * * * * *

IVY HARPER

ST. MARTIN'S PRESS * NEW YORK

*To my mother and father, Royce and
Charlotte Jean, who nourished my
childhood interest in the written
word.*

DESIGN BY DIANE STEVENSON/SNAP·HAUS GRAPHICS

Library of Congress Cataloging-in-Publication Data

Harper, Ivy.
    Waltzing Matilda: the life and times of Nebraska Senator Robert Kerrey
/ Ivy Harper.
        p.   cm.
    ISBN 0-312-07660-6
    1. Kerrey, Robert, 1943–   . 2. Presidential candidates—United
States—Biography.   3. Legislators—United States—Biography.
4. United States. Congress. Senate—Biography.   I. Title.
E840.8.K43H37   1992
973.928′092—dc20
[B]   92-4198
                                                                                  CIP

First Edition: September 1992

10 9 8 7 6 5 4 3 2 1

Contents

Acknowledgments

In 1988, while covering Bob Kerrey's run for the Senate, it became clear to me that his story needed to be told. When research on this book began then, Kerrey was not an announced candidate for President and few expected him to become one in 1992. Presidential campaigns have been known to distort the interview-gathering process and I am grateful that almost all of my work was completed before Kerrey reached his decision to seek the Democratic Party nomination in the fall of 1991. *Waltzing Matilda* is not an authorized biography nor was my progress injuriously impeded.

Still, the journey from the conception of this work to its completion was a road with a few rough passages and I am especially thankful for the support of my sister, Colleen Aagesen, and her husband, Bertil, who provided unfailing encouragement and unerring literary counsel and who opened their doors during my frequent trips to Omaha. I am also deeply appreciative to my other six siblings, Neil, Marla, Mark, John, Valerie, and Steven.

With characteristic patience, many Nebraskans sat through long interviews, and to all of them I express my gratitude and hope that I have earned their respect. I wish first of all to thank Steve Fowler, now of California, for sharing his virtuoso analysis of Kerrey's early gubernatorial years and his unparalleled insight into Democratic politics, Nebraska's in particular. Steve's other contributions to this book were inestimable. I must also single out Marian, Esther, and Larry Price for their help in understanding Kerrey's young years; Bill Lock for sharing his immense knowledge about Nebraska; David Landis for passing on invaluable comments about the Nebraska legislature; John Boyd and John Lee for giving me the opportunity to write for the legendary *Omaha Metropolitan*, James P. (Jim) Cavanaugh for his unwavering optimism, and Forrest (Frosty) Chapman for listening to his gut instinct.

For their hospitality and support, a heartfelt thank you to Professor Joseph Harper, Ph.D., and Mary Beth Grange Harper of Kent, Ohio, and to Washingtonians Janet and Hillel Nachbi, Lori and Jack Ansaldi, Georgia and Grant Stockdale, Nancy Watts and

John Moss, Jennifer Crier Johnston, and Mike Koppel. I want to thank Ozzie Corson for his computer skillfulness and Ralph Atchison for his overwhelming generosity and for his expertise on the S&L industry. A special thank you must go to James Pettus of Hawaii and Winston Pettus of Ireland for showing their faith in me years ago.

My thanks also goes out to Valerie Wilk and Thomas M. McNamara for their transcribing help and thoughtful suggestions to my original manuscript. I am especially grateful to Allan Green and Joan Snyder for their help in editing the final manuscript. And thanks to all the Westbrook Elementary School teachers and parents.

I owe special mention to Nebraskans W. C. Mullan, Dale Mundy, and Natalie Clark for their generous help and to Gail Folda, Tom Plambeck, Susan Ranta, Michelle Armstrong, and Professor George Tuck for their stellar photographs. To my former UN-L journalism professors, Neale Copple, Jim Neal, and Jim Patten, and my political science professors, Philip Dyer and Robert Sittig, I give thanks for their exemplary teaching.

My agent at ICM, Lisa Bankoff, expressed enthusiasm about this book from the beginning, and throughout gave me inspired assistance. I am deeply indebted to my editor at St. Martin's, Bob Weil, whose gifted guidance and passion for "place" was a godsend. I will remain grateful for Bob's vision, which allowed me to realize mine. Also, St. Martin's editorial assistants Geoffrey Kloske, Michelle Levy, and Dan Burrows, publicist Kim Sergio, audio rights manager Erin Collins, and Sloan Harris at ICM deserve kudos for their devotion to details and their willingness to answer my many questions. Also I want to thank associate managing editor Meg Drislane for her incredible tolerance throughout the final phase of this book.

Finally, I thank my husband, Carlos, for sharing his personal recollections of the Cuban Missile Crisis and the Vietnam War era and who, along with my two children, Carlos Jr. and Alina Marie, endured this project with grace, understanding, and humor. And again, a loving thank you to my parents, Royce and Jean, whose wise counsel and unconditional cooperation made their contribution to *Waltzing Matilda* an immeasurable one and who ultimately made publication possible by providing a family atmosphere where ideas and history reigned.

Ivy Harper
Bethesda, Maryland
November 1991

Preface

I n the pristine speaker's theater of Boys Town's sprawling campus, forty teenagers sat in silence, their attention alternating between Nebraska's 1988 Democratic candidate for the U.S. Senate, Robert Kerrey, and the woman nearby who, with manual eloquence, interpreted his message.

"In 1969, I went to Vietnam as a platoon officer for the U.S. Navy. Three months later in a combat operation I was wounded rather seriously. I was flown first to Japan and then to the Philadelphia Naval Hospital. My parents, who were in Lincoln at the time, were flown in to be with me. They arrived right after I was taken out of the operating room. I had a right leg, some of which was traumatically amputated in the field, and some of which was removed during that surgery. When I woke up, my mother and father were sitting against a wall. I asked my mother to come by the bed and answer the question that I had. I wanted her to tell me how much they removed in the operating room. And she looked upon me and said, 'There's a lot left, Bob.'"

At the end of Kerrey's address, his hearing-impaired audience, with arms outstretched, repeatedly fluttered their hands from above their heads to their waists: silent thunderous applause.

Four months later, Kerrey entered Omaha's historic Peony Park Ballroom, this time greeted by an audience of several thousand ecstatic supporters. Returns showed the forty-six-year-old divorced politician far in front of his challenger. He stood before his fellow Cornhuskers that Election Night poised to deliver a victory speech. Flanked by his two children, his brothers and sisters, their spouses, and his Navy SEAL buddies, Kerrey surveyed the cheering masses and decided to fulfill a promise. He turned to his thirteen-year-old son, Ben, and said, "I'm going to do it." Ben grimaced through his braces and pleaded, "Dad, don't." Ignoring his son's entreaty, Kerrey suddenly leaned into the microphone, shifted the weight from his right leg and its prosthesis, and calmly started singing a cappella:

> *When I was a young man I carried a pack*
> *And I lived the free life of a rover*
> *From the Murray's green basin to the dusty outback*
> *Well, I waltzed my Matilda all over*
> *Then in 1915, the country said, "Son*
> *It's time you stopped roving, there's work to be done"*
> *So they gave me a tin hat and they gave me a gun*
> *And sent me away to the war*

For ten minutes, Kerrey struggled through an off-pitch rendition of "And the Band Played Waltzing Matilda," the tale of a young Australian who loses both legs in the World War I Battle of Gallipoli written by contemporary songwriter Eric Bogle. Most in the audience were unfamiliar with Bogle's anti-war masterpiece, but they knew the war history of their newly elected Senator. It took only a few lines to understand that the ballad eerily mirrored Kerrey's odyssey in Vietnam—even to the point of his homecoming.

> *Then they gathered the sick and the crippled and maimed*
> *And sent us back home to Australia*
> *The armless, the legless, the blind and insane*
> *The brave wounded heroes of Suvla . . .*
> *And the band played "Waltzing Matilda"*
> *As they carried us down the gangway*
> *But nobody cheered: they just stood there and stared*
> *Then they turned their faces away*

Bob Kerrey brought America's unfinished war home to Nebraskans that November night—an occasion traditionally reserved for hoopla and forgettable political rhetoric. But he would have none of that. Not the blue-eyed Bethany boy who had faced death at twenty-six, and had thereafter pushed life to the limit. Not the complex restaurateur-turned-politician, the rising political star whose two-decade journey since his enlistment in the Navy SEALS encompassed such passages as bona fide war hero and outspoken antiwar activist; small-town pharmacist and self-made millionaire businessman; divorced father and celebrity-dating bachelor; history teacher and wisecracking, popular Governor. And finally, United States Senator.

Vietnam had steered the course of Kerrey's adult life, and that election night, in singing "Waltzing Matilda," Kerrey honored the memory of the terrible war responsible for his political destiny.

Outsiders might have been surprised by Kerrey's unorthodox victory speech ("We'll waltz tonight and work tomorrow"), but Nebraskans knew that Kerrey was an example of Cornhusker iconoclasm, and they had come to expect the unexpected from him. After all, he had moved from statewide anonymity in 1981 (a survey put Kerrey's name recognition at 1 percent) to dominant force in Nebraska politics just one year later. In Kerrey's first major gubernatorial appointment—a replacement for Nebraska's first attorney general to be removed by impeachment—he picked a Republican, much to the consternation of staunch Democrats, who grumbled that there was no shortage of candidates among them.

A few months after taking office, Kerrey found a soulmate in actress Debra Winger, who alighted in Lincoln to film *Terms of Endearment* and left with a passionate attachment to Kerrey that continues to this day. When Winger returned to the state capital in 1983, it was at the request of Kerrey, who invited the movie star to live in the Governor's mansion whenever her schedule allowed. A poll taken the following year showed that 76 percent of Nebraskans approved of the unmarried lovers' arrangement. Kerrey, whose own approval rating at the time was 74 percent, joked that more of his constituents thought Winger should be in the mansion than thought he should be there. The U.S. Bureau of the Census designated the liaison as partner-roommate.

Later, Kerrey told a roomful of conservative Nebraskans the bravest man he ever met was a SEAL buddy who dropped out of the Navy's special force after their commander gave them the option. The peer pressure was enormous, Kerrey explained, yet this fledging SEAL candidate stood up in front of everyone, after weeks of rigorous training in sabotage and surgical strikes, and announced that he was too frightened to remain a member of the Navy's elite underwater demolition team. "That took true courage," Kerrey said. The Nebraskans rewarded Kerrey's candor with resounding applause.

Within months of his 1982 election, poll takers, pundits, political aficionados, and national journalists labeled Kerrey the John Kennedy of the Plains, a new-breed Democrat who had joined the pack that then included Senators Bill Bradley and Gary Hart, Representatives Richard Gephardt and Albert Gore, and Governors Bruce Babbitt and Bill Clinton. The national spin on the Kerrey story was that the prairie was ablaze with the brilliance of its newest rising star. Republicans consoled themselves with the belief that Kerrey's meteoric rise was a fluke, and that after a term or two as Nebraska's Governor, his star would simply fizzle from sight. After all, such a fate befalls most Governors.

Instead, Kerrey's charmed political life continued. One year after he declined a bid for a guaranteed second stint as Governor, a U.S. Senate seat unexpectedly opened up with the death of Edward Zorinsky. Kerrey was easily elected in 1988, soundly beating a Republican who had been appointed a year and a half earlier to finish out Zorinsky's term.

After just three years in our country's most august political club, Kerrey's candor and his industriousness have earned him laudatory reviews from the press and his colleagues. As a Senator, Kerrey usually ignores invitations from Washington's journalistic, diplomatic, and social circuit, startling for a forty-seven-year-old Celtic charmer who is touted as one of the country's most eligible bachelors. He returns to Nebraska as often as possible, and when he remains in Washington, he immerses himself in agricultural, appropriations, and intelligence committee work. Some Senators are jarred by Kerrey's assiduous work habits because of the Rockin' Bob reputation that preceded him. Because of his relationship with Debra Winger, they expected Kerrey to bring Hollywood to the Potomac. Instead, his colleagues describe him as a diligent, focused, and feisty legislator. Even Nebraskans critical of Kerrey's performance as Governor, and there are some, concede that he has flourished in the Senate, where he has displayed great attentiveness to and enthusiasm for legislative work.

Writers for *The New York Times*, the *New Republic*, the *Washington Post*, the *National Journal*, *Congressional Quarterly*, *Time*, and *Newsweek* concur. They have heaped extraordinary praise on the junior Senator from Nebraska—the kinds of accolades that most politicians only dream of. Most candidates must be content to fantasize about the day when the headline of a *Time* profile begins, as Kerrey's did in the fall of 1991, A SENATOR OF CANDOR MOST RARE, or when a *New Republic* cover declares: "Senator Perfect: Bob Kerrey has a war hero's record, good TV presence, a sense of humor, the vision thing and principles." Most flattering is the way a *Newsweek* writer gushed by way of a Kerrey introduction: "It took years, but the Democratic Party finally located a could-be President with real crackle. This guy is sexy."

Kerrey's fascinating background is such good copy that he has been accused of being a "biography in a suit"—that his political career is simply an extension of his personal drama. But Kerrey's past is a fact. His entrepreneurial success is a fact. His physical handicap is a fact. His heroism and war record are facts—facts that reveal a pattern of courage.

Kerrey's Senate career has shown him to be a leader. After only a few months there, in 1989, Kerrey broke with senatorial protocol and blasted President Bush on the savings and loan crisis. In fact, Kerrey so angered the Administration by his scathing criticism of the handling of the S&L bailout bill that Marlin Fitzwater denounced Kerrey in a nationally televised press conference, thereby also breaking a long-standing tradition against personal attacks from the presidential podium. Not long after, Republicans unveiled a poster during a New Orleans political get-together that showed Kerrey and former Speaker of the

House of Representatives Jim Wright, among others, and fingered them for the S&L debacle. Although Kerrey was furious about the linkage with Wright, he continued his sulfurous criticism of President Bush.

Shortly thereafter, Kerrey confounded conventional wisdom watchers by making a public about-face on the flag-burning issue, one on which he had initially supported the President. Kerrey's eloquent speech on the Senate floor, denouncing both legislation and a constitutional amendment to punish flag-burning, is credited with Senate rejection of the issue.

He refused to join the Quayle-bashing bandwagon in 1988 over the Vice President's National Guard service during the Vietnam War. Kerrey excused Quayle's choice and declared that Vietnam did not provide easy choices for young men.

Kerrey intrigues people by unfailingly speaking bluntly—if that means aligning himself with an opponent and criticizing a comrade, so be it. Kerrey's political ascendancy makes old litmus tests irrelevant. One decade ago, as Governor, Kerrey infuriated Nebraskans who had been instrumental in his election. At the time, observers said, "Well, he isn't aware of the political consequences of his actions," but Kerrey was aware. He was making tough choices. He cares little for labels and dogma and tradition. There are few positions he is adamantly wedded to. Kerrey does what Nebraskans have been doing for more than a hundred and twenty-five years—he sees a problem and he tries to fix it. And while many disagree with his strategies (doctrinaire Democrats were, in fact, incensed by some of his solutions), they're willing to trust him anyway. In the words of Kerrey's 1982 gubernatorial campaign architect, native Nebraskan Steve Fowler, "Kerrey rarely wavers about a direction. He changes points of view, but there is some inner voice that guides him and lets him take these major risks. Bob Kerrey is not guided by an ideology, but there's a philosophy and an ethic underneath that move him."

Should Bob Kerrey ever make it to the White House, he would be the first Medal of Honor holder to earn that honor. Kerrey believes it his calling to be President of the United States someday. He feels he is fulfilling a destiny that was forged in the jungles of Vietnam and molded by the plains of Nebraska.

Introduction

A Nebraska song begins, "There is no place like Nebraska." Nebraskans believe that. You grow up there thinking that you live in the finest state in the country. You play in wide, windy spaces where you can see the sun touch the earth every evening. You grow up in Nebraska reading Willa Cather, John Niehardt, Mari Sandoz, and Loren Eiseley, and watching home-state boys Dick Cavett and Johnny Carson on television. You grow up in Nebraska knowing that Marlon Brando and Henry Fonda received their initiation into the world of acting at the community playhouse in Omaha, the same city that sent Fred Astaire into the world of dance.

As a kid you visit the Nebraska state capitol in Lincoln and you agree with architects who call it the most glorious government building in the world. You grow up in Nebraska feeling proud that the only state in the country with an egalitarian, one-house legislature (called the Unicameral) is yours. And then you study William Jennings Bryan and George Norris, and you learn that President John F. Kennedy, in his Pulitzer Prize–winning book, *Profiles in Courage,* a book shaped and written in large part by Lincoln's native son, Ted Sorensen, recognized Norris as one of the most courageous men ever to serve in the Congress. And then you read Kennedy's speeches and you learn that much of the language you listened to and loved—words that moved a nation—was a Nebraskan's. You discover that, unlike America's other forty-nine states, Nebraska's utilities are entirely owned and governed by the state that also offered the world capitalist extraordinaire Warren Bufett, who singlehandedly managed to shift the focus of finance from Wall Street to Omaha's Dodge Street.

You grow up in Nebraska knowing real farmers. They are

your fathers and grandfathers and uncles and cousins. They are farmers who work the rich soil of eastern Nebraska, and ranchers who tend the north-central and western, grass-covered, rolling sand hills. You grow up in Nebraska feeling blistering winters and blazing summers, and seeing brilliant autumns and springs. You grow up in Nebraska vacationing in Colorado, California, Maine, and Florida, but you always want to come home to the amber waves of grain, to the Platte River, to the sandhill cranes.

And then you grow up. And you find out: People not from Nebraska don't think it is such a fine state; Americans think Nebraska is a place to leave—a boring, tedious expanse of corn and highway. "I drove through Nebraska once," people tell you, "on my way to Colorado, Wyoming, California [take your pick]; it's so flat and goes on forever—is there anything to do out there?" So you question whether any real time was spent in Nebraska and the answer is no. And then you reflect that Nebraskans journey throughout the Midwest and travel to both coasts and you begin to wonder who is provincial. Eventually, you hear pejorative comments about Nebraska so often that you resign yourself to the state's reputation. But you always speak highly of Nebraska; and finally, you figure that maybe you just have to grow up there to appreciate it. And you do.

You have to live in Nebraska to be able to understand the splendor of the plains. You have to give the state more than an interstate drive-through to know the stirring magnificence of a land that appears plain but isn't. You have to kneel on a sandhill and look up to a solitary windmill and a single cottonwood tree etched against the horizon.

And if you are lucky enough to have been raised in Nebraska, you will find that in ways you can't comprehend as a child, the quiet simplicity of the land affects the state of your heart forever.

Writing about Bob Kerrey without knowing the state that produced him would be to miss his essence. Kerrey is connected to the land of his birth in the way that the signers of the Declaration of Independence were to the land that inspired their words. In speeches, Kerrey likes to mention the fact that all but one of the framers of the Constitution were farmers.

"In my judgment, it is not an accident that the drafters of the Constitution make reference to the Divine Being and that there is great awe about the spiritual life," Kerrey said. "The Constitution is not an industrial document. It doesn't clang and bang and make all kind of noise. It is a document that is alive with people who have had that contact with the soil and who understand natural forces."

Was it a coincidence that the compelling vision of our fore-fathers was contemplated and articulated in a day when men and women still had real connection with the land? America's founders pondered the future of their young nation in a time when there was plenty of land and few people—a situation that has existed in Nebraska since its creation. Nebraska, at four hundred and thirty miles across, is almost as wide as Texas and, like Texas, it has a prominent panhandle. Nebraska is home, however, to barely 1 percent of Americans.

And yet the state has offered the country the best and brightest in literature, as shown by Willa Cather and Loren Eiseley, in comedy by Carson, in finance by Buffett, in poetry by John Niehardt and Black Elk, in acting by Brando and Fonda, in politics by Bryan, Norris, and Sorensen, in dance by Fred Astaire.

All of these stellar contributors to America's arts and letters have written that they were deeply affected by Nebraska's plains—land that is denigrated by travelers as plain uninteresting. In a poem for his 1987 Christmas card, Kerrey wrote:

A man said, "I drove across Nebraska once and saw nothing but flat fields of corn! I found nothing and so I left." He smiled and walked away.

Nothing.

But the full moon rising late as the market crashes and men with panic on their faces rush about with answers.

Nothing.

But the harvest moments when on a rope swing at its top we see all pasts at once and say, God! Thanks!

Nothing.

But thankfulness and faith.
Fearsome, wonderful, mysterious
Life and death.
Sweeping the impatient ones away.

Peace on earth.

Growing up in Nebraska means standing under skies so expansive you can see the constellations. You don't need a lookout point or a planetarium. As winter gives way to spring, you can see Orion dip closer and closer to the earth until it's gone. However rudimentarily, Nebraskans see the stars and measure the seasons as the sailors did.

For growing up in Nebraska is like growing up by the sea. Instead of the smell of salt, you smell freshly cut clover and hay. Instead of ships and harbors, you are connected to the world by train or interstate. In 1975, in honor of our nation's bicentennial, Nebraskans dedicated a five-hundred-mile sculpture garden that dovetails the Platte River and I-80 rest stops. A New York artist by way of Texas designed *Crossing the Plains* for the York, Nebraska, westbound stop. Bradford Graves arranged his limestone sculpture to simulate the four points of a compass. Its white spherical shapes suggest sand and the movement of wagons across seas of grass. One great-grandmother from Boston, who came to Nebraska as a child, would lie in the prairie grasses, and when the wind blew, she heard her ocean once again and was comforted.

And the winters. While they are not as long as those of our northern sisters, they are nearly Siberian and often unrelieved by the softness of snow. It is the wind. The wind blows from the Rocky Mountains to the Appalachians and has nothing to stop it or slow it down. Wind-chill indices of fifty below are not uncommon, and schools close to protect children from frostbite.

In summer, the wind acts with similar vengeance—spawning thunderstorms and tornadoes. Growing up in Nebraska means tornado sirens and drills and learning to sense the stickiness, the stillness, and the slight green tinge in the sky that warns of the great, gray funnel. It is a rare Nebraskan who escapes a brush with a tornado. Kerrey did not. His Ralston restaurant was razed when it was right in the path of a tornado in May of 1975.

Nebraska, unlike Vermont, is not home to thousands of maple trees but the few there are, with their burgundy reds, accent the more common cottonwood, which turn golden in the fall. When ordinary afternoon sunlight reflects on the cottonwood's delicate leaves, they look like liquid gold as they tremble and dance, and even sing, as the Indians say. Sumac also splashes the landscape, their red leaves catching the light like stained glass. Easterners who argue that the Nebraska autumn is not spectacular are wrong. Admittedly, the season is short. The wind blows wildly one October night and the next morning, autumn is under your feet. And that's okay too. You still revel in what color is left, and in the crunch of leaves and the poignancy of bare trees with squirrel nests suddenly revealed. Spring moves in and out swiftly. The smell of lilacs and the blossoms of crab apple trees are quickly overpowered by a summer heat wave.

That wild and lonesome wind whipped up a land of romance and ruthlessness, a land of extremes, a land of great paradoxes. The land that was once called the Great American Desert is home to the nation's largest underground reservoir of quality water, the Ogallala Aquifer, and through irrigation the Great American Desert became the Breadbasket of the World. Nebraska's weather tortured the first settlers with dust storms and ravaging tornadoes and then treated them to ocean-blue skies and sundowns so stunning that poetry pales.

The land and the climate evoke both romance and ruthlessness—and no doubt the people who settled the land reflect both. A look at the state and its people, then, cannot fail to focus on the flip side of romance.

Consider that while Nebraska has more than its share of luminaries, Lincoln was also the hometown of our nation's first recognized mass murderer, Charlie Starkweather, a man whose surname is eerily evocative of the elements. Nebraska poet William Kloefkorn, in a poem entitled "Drought," calls the wind "depraved," and adds: "It's no use: Hell has moved her headquarters into Southeastern Nebraska."

In his 1984 state of the state address, "The Promise of the

Prairie," then-Governor Robert Kerrey said: "Nearly every season of the year has brought us new challenges waiting to be addressed. Through blizzards and scorching heat, through parching winds and drenching rainstorms, through floods and droughts and insect infestations, . . . we have historically summoned up our courage and resources to say that on the other side of apparent catastrophe we will be even better and even stronger."

Growing up in Nebraska means feeling central, in the middle of the continent—grounded, in the middle of the country. Some say geography is destiny—that only Ireland could produce a Joyce, only Texas a Lyndon Johnson. If that is true, then it would follow that only Nebraska could produce Bob Kerrey.

For Bob Kerrey, geography truly has been destiny. He was shaped first by the Great Plains and then by a jungle in Vietnam—terrains of great extreme. In his first run for office, Kerrey was ridiculed by an opponent who said the city-bred Kerrey wouldn't know an ear of corn from a ukulele—but Kerrey's boyhood was spent in a sleepy suburb called Bethany, where a few blocks' walk brought you to a carpet of cornfields.

Lincoln writer-humorist-storyteller Roger Welsh and *Lincoln Journal* cartoonist Paul Fell make the connection between the land and the people, in a cartoon that shows a couple of farmers hovering in a field talking about the weather. The caption reads, "You know you're a Nebraskan when you can say with a straight face that bad weather builds character—look at all the characters."

Nebraska has characters. The state has them now and it has produced them in abundance in the past. History also has proven that the state has offered up men and women of great character. And whether Nebraska's unique physical environment (its sand hills exist nowhere else on the continent) has stimulated "individual strength, ingenuity, inventiveness, practicality, buoyancy, and exuberance," in the words of Nebraska historian Frederick C. Luebke, always will be debatable. Professor Luebke writes: "Because Nebraska occupies a unique space and because it has been populated by a unique mixture of different cultural groups, its history is also unique."

Only history will validate the life and character of Bob Kerrey. He has served four years as Nebraska Governor and three years in the United States Senate but it is still too soon to write the final book about him. People who know him believe he is a man of character.

In any case, Kerrey is a metaphor for the land—a land of romance and ruthlessness. And like the land he represents, Kerrey has exhibited great extremes in temperament and action. As a politician, Kerrey presents great paradoxes, and the people of Nebraska respect this. It was Nebraskans who watched a tenderfoot Governor grow into a seasoned politician, allowed him to drop out of politics to follow his heart, then accepted him back and gave him the chance to parlay his politics onto the national stage as a United States Senator. Bob Kerrey is representative of the people of Nebraska—he is not a fluke from Cornhusker country, and that should be remembered as his life, his story, unfolds.

The history of every country begins in the heart of a man or a woman.

—*Willa Cather*

PART I

Chapter 1

HAWK TALK

Senator Bob Kerrey was born and raised in Nebraska, but he grew up in Vietnam. By his own admission, Kerrey went to Southeast Asia an adventure-seeking, beer-drinking frat rat, "gung ho to go at the Viet Cong with a knife in his teeth," as he once told an interviewer. A little more than three months after he arrived, as the leader of a seven-man Navy SEAL unit, Kerrey continued to direct his commando unit on an island in Nha Trang Bay until all his men were safe, despite the explosion of a grenade at his foot. Later, in a 1984 speech introducing Gary Hart at the Democratic National Convention, Kerrey said: "In one explosive moment in Vietnam the physical strength of my youth was blown away." The accident shattered his leg and his unwavering support for American policy in a war he had just begun to learn about firsthand.

Kerrey's pre-1969 sentiments about Vietnam, while not shared by those young Americans and their parents who already opposed the war, reflected those of conservative Midwesterners. Nebraska's two Republican Senators, Carl Curtis and Roman Hruska, were both outspoken Vietnam hawks and unabashed apologists for President Richard Nixon. During the Vietnam War one Congressman is reported to have told a Nebraska audience that America would win in Vietnam because the United States is a nation of meat-eaters and the Vietnamese are a nation of rice-eaters, and carnivores always conquer vegetarians.

Lincoln's American Legion club boasted during the sixties, as it does today, "The Largest Membership of any Post in the World." It makes for great advertising on signs, letters, and fliers, and somehow that claim leaves the impression that Lincoln legionnaires are just a little closer in their comradeship, just a little more organized, and perhaps a little more patriotic than folks from just an ordinary post. In truth, the board of directors, right after World War II, conspired to develop a single post with maximum amenities rather than several smaller ones as was customary in other cities. Lincoln's five thousand vets flock to their spacious Legion club at 56th and O Streets to an expansive dining room, a first-rate kitchen, and an excellent chef who serves Nebraska beef to the boys who banter about Big Red football and huddle over hawk talk.

Many members of the American Legion are veterans who never participated in actual combat. Still, they promote the idea that the United States should be willing to send troops anywhere, anytime. It can be argued that belief in American military superiority has been institutionalized since World War II by the American Legion.

In the early 1960s, Lincoln residents were more aware of the cold war than folks in towns of similar size in the United States. From 1960 to 1964, Lincoln was home to a major Air Force base that was located only forty-five minutes from Strategic Air Command (SAC) headquarters in Omaha. Lincoln's air base was the site for the Alert Program, which kept B-47 bombers constantly in the air between Lincoln and Spain and England. Refueled by airborne tankers over the Atlantic, these four-engine bombers would make the ocean run ready to be diverted to Russia, should a retaliatory or preemptive strike become necessary. Pilots at that time were known to slip in conversations about the "nuclear curtain" inside their planes—a device that supposedly would protect them from the blinding flash in the event that they were directed toward a target. Families planned for the possible by continually stocking their basement cellars with canned goods. And schoolchildren, under the direction of teachers, priests, and nuns, practiced atomic bomb drills with even more enthusiasm than fire drills engendered.

Kerrey does not cite his town or his family as influences in his unusual decision to volunteer for the SEALS. Yet both the milieu in which he was reared and the war history of his father, James, and his uncle, John Kerrey, undoubtedly played a part in his youthful patriotism and eagerness for action.

His Uncle John, a feisty child who had been sent to reform school as a young man, joined the Marines before World War II broke out. He was stationed in the Philippines and remained there after the United States entered the war. John had been there for years when Kerrey's father, James Kerrey, received unofficial word that his brother had been killed in action; yet he did not receive any formal verification of his death. After some time, James Kerrey received notice that his brother had been added to the roster of young men listed as missing in action. The Kerrey family assumed John was dead because at that time there were few survivors coming out of the Philippines. Later, while James was stationed in Japan working on logistical operations after the liberation, his wife, Elinor, at home in Lincoln, opened her mail one day to discover a letter from John stating that he had not died. He wrote of his escape in a boat that ferried him to an island away from the one that had been the site where his comrades were killed. John had been fighting with guerrillas all through the period the Kerrey family had thought him dead. Elated, Elinor contacted James in Japan to inform him. Within days, however, Elinor received a third notice about John, this time an official one from the U.S. government stating that he had drowned in a freak boating accident off the islands. The Kerrey kids grew up hearing the story of wild Uncle John and the saga of his World War II heroics.

Bob Kerrey may have inherited his uncle's zest for adventure. In 1986, after announcing that he would not run for a second term as Nebraska Governor, Kerrey, forty-three, said he was looking for action in whatever road he traveled after his term expired.

It was that same sentiment that had motivated Kerrey to join the SEALS two decades earlier. While he was completing his final semester of pharmacy school in the fall of 1965, Kerrey received a pre-induction notice from the Army. He knew his choices included enlisting, seeking a deferment because of asthma, or continuing his studies, which he did for one additional semester. Kerrey received his B.S. in pharmacy in January 1966 and remained at UN-L until May 1966. After college, Kerrey worked briefly in pharmacy in a small Iowa town before he decided to enlist in the Navy. Kerrey later explained that "he loved the ocean," and had favored that branch of the service since reading *The Caine Mutiny* during his senior year in college. He was also a young hawk and an avowed believer in doing one's duty for country.

Nor was he reluctant to leave pharmacy, as he told a Nebraska journalist: "What am I trained to do? I'm a pill counter and one day I was working in this pharmacy and this lady comes up and she points at me and says, 'Young man, what should I take for my sniffles?' and I said, 'Forget your sniffles. I don't give a ——— about your sniffles.' Can you imagine sitting back there going 'Three, six, nine, twelve, fifteen, eighteen, twenty-two, and putting these pills in a bottle!" Kerrey added, "I have to go do something bigger. This is making me nuts."

When Kerrey announced his decision to enlist, most people who knew him well were not surprised. Bethany boyhood chum Forest (Frosty) Chapman says it was understood that young men from Bethany would follow the call of the service. Chapman did not see any inconsistencies between Kerrey's comfortable position in life and his decision to shoot for the SEALS. "Life was too big to let it pass by. Bob loved excitement. He really wanted to live." Some Kerrey friends were shocked. John Gottschalk, publisher of the *Omaha World-Herald*, told a reporter for his paper that Kerrey's decision "stunned him and other close friends because they thought Kerrey was focused on his career."

Of his decision to enlist, Kerrey said, "I feel duty strongly and I take it very seriously. I also don't complain an awful lot. That's not something that I got in a mail-order catalog—that's a typically Nebraskan quality."

Two decades later, in the middle of Kerrey's campaign for the Senate, Gary Parrott, his close friend and SEAL comrade, wrote him of his youthful reasons for entering the service: "In the sixties and seventies, I had opinions valuable enough to step off a sampan and walk into hostile jungle armed with three grenades, two dexadrines, and four hundred rounds of 5.56. I had opinions valuable enough to leave a bride at home and climb up into the carsts of NW Laos. They were solid opinions. They were opinions formed by seeing, feeling, and doing. Opinions formed by ties of love and brotherhood. They were better opinions than the ones I have now, formed by reading editorials and listening to rantings."

In October 1966, Kerrey reported to the Naval Officer Candidate School in Newport, Rhode Island, where he graduated as an ensign in June 1967. Faced with the choice of where to go within the Navy, Kerrey volunteered for the Navy's underwater demolition team (UDT).

At that time the antiwar movement was low-key but would soon gain momentum. But, in 1967, Kerrey strongly supported the war. He certainly was not part of the group that was exploring the possibility of an alternative to service, such as going to Canada.

Johnson's draft drew Kerrey into the Navy but, given his educational background, he could have obtained an easy assignment as a pharmacist or yeoman. Kerrey was not, however, an enlistee who saw Navy service as a pleasant or safe haven in comparison to a Marine or Army infantry assignment. He volunteered for the SEALS, whose assignments included infantry-type assaults in the mud and jungle in addition to underwater demolition (UDT), parachuting, and a multitude of other hazardous missions. In 1967, the same year that Kerrey became a Navy officer, the antiwar movement had picked up such momentum that activists were being arrested.

By 1968, the nature of the war had changed substantially. It was the year of the Tet offensive, a surprise attack on the Vietnamese New Year, when the North Vietnamese Army and the Viet Cong proved they could mount a countrywide assault without being overrun. But at the same time, it was a grim reminder of the possibility of a stalemate or a continuing war of attrition.

Nineteen sixty-eight was also the year Lyndon Johnson admitted, in a dramatic telecast in March, that he did not know how to win the war—or how to end it—and announced that he would not be a candidate for reelection.

Nineteen sixty-eight was the year that the war protest movement erupted nationwide with its epicenter at the Democratic National Convention in Chicago in August.

Nineteen sixty-eight was the year that Richard Nixon, the Republican candidate, made his first pronouncement that he had a "secret plan for ending the war," the first of his many secrets.

It was during 1968 that Bob Kerrey received his most intensive physical and psychological training in the SEALS. This was the time of preparation for the hazardous missions for which SEALS volunteer. This was the time when morale should have been high, and it was high in the SEALS. But it should be remembered that SEALS are different from other servicemen in that they all volunteer for hazardous duty. As a result, their focus is on a singular mission. Other members of the service, enlisted personnel or draftees, are more likely to reflect the morale of the populace at home, be it positive or negative. Others are more likely to consider their own position or plight in terms of what is "fair." A soldier lying in the mud under fire might think of friends taking refuge in Canada or high-draft-number classmates frolicking with sweethearts at a rock concert. Not so likely with the SEALS.

The year that Kerrey finished his SEAL training, Richard Nixon ran for the presidency with a pledge to end the commitment of U.S. troops in Vietnam. On November 1, 1968, it was agreed that peace talks in Paris would take up a substantive agenda that month and that North Vietnam, the U.S., South Vietnam, and the National Liberation Front would be represented. It was the middle of January 1969 when the U.S. and North Vietnam finally reached an agreement on the shape of the conference table. The last week of January 1969 saw the first substantive peace talks at which each side listened to the demands of the other. There was an expression of hope for peace throughout the country but it was unwarranted, given the realities of the war. Kerrey, at that time, had been in Vietnam four weeks and was wholeheartedly enthusiastic about his life as a SEAL.

Later, as Governor, in response to a question about why he had chosen the UDT and eventually the SEALS, Kerrey joked that all he wanted to do was "learn how to scuba dive with a Rolex on and meet women in the process." Kerrey often suggests a certain naïveté about the SEALS, although he knew their reputation precisely—the SEALS were the Navy's answer to the Army's Green Berets. Despite Kerrey's cavalier responses about his enlistment in the SEALS, the question remains an important one. Why would a young man, who had scores of options during an unpopular war, seek out service in a group whose every mission would be considered extrahazardous? For that matter, what kind of person would volunteer for extrahazardous duty in any branch of the service? Studies indicate certain personality types seek out dangerous duty.

One common quality is a competitive attitude, a desire to stand out and to win. Men and women who engage in dangerous duty often are active in sports. One component of the competitive psyche undoubtedly is the desire to excel among peers and to take center stage, and sports is an appropriate forum.

Another facet of the SEAL psyche is a desire for action. Many times, Kerrey has stated that he loves adventure and danger. SEALS are fast thinkers who like challenges—men who abhor taking the path of least resistance. Although they are intelligent and do well in school, rarely are they considered intellectuals by their peers. They may in fact be intellectual, but that quality does not show on the surface as much as their restlessness for adventure. SEAL types, especially in the early days, had that kind of reputation. They might sport camouflage jackets showing skull and crossbones with sayings like "Swift, Deadly and Accurate."

Many hazardous-duty types consciously or unconsciously seek brotherhood. They know that by joining an extra special unit, they automatically become members of a brotherhood. They form bonds that last lifetimes; they share experiences that transcend social, economic, geographic, or class differences. A story that made the rounds during World War II has a paratrooper being questioned: "Aren't you afraid when you jump with nothing holding you but a few panels of silk?" The paratrooper responds that he is scared to death every single time he jumps. "Why do you do it, then?" he is asked, to which the trooper replies, "I like to be around men who are willing to jump out of airplanes."

After completing UDT training, Kerrey was selected for the Navy SEALS. Out of the one hundred seventy-seven young enlistees who enrolled in UDT training, only sixty-eight would actually complete it. Of these, only Kerrey and thirteen others were chosen and agreed to continue as SEALS. As part of general SEAL training, Kerrey attended Army Airborne and Ranger schools, where one observer noted, "Your life is just on a shit stick. It's terrible." Kerrey likes to tell the story of his response to a flight instructor who razzed him about his parachuting efforts. "At least I jumped," Kerrey replied to the critic.

Next, Kerrey was placed in predeployment training at Coronado, California, the home base of SEAL Team One. SEAL Team Two was stationed on the East Coast. Kerrey was one of two officers—the other was Tim Wettack—in a platoon of fourteen men preparing for duty in Southeast Asia. The men trained in all phases of combat using the necessary weapons. They practiced night landings on California beaches and made forays into mountains and deserts for additional training.

Kerrey has said that he frequently thought of quitting the SEALS. Those who stay with it must endure ferocious training that includes grueling routines like running fifteen miles in heavy sand and performing water exercises in the cold Pacific. Candidates must be exceptionally fit, although often the young men who make it are less the superjock Rambo types, and more the average athletes armed with an overriding will to make it to the end.

Bob Kerrey, at a hundred and fifty-two pounds, had remained in shape throughout his life but he still found SEAL training rough. Kerrey is not an imposing person physically, but he possesses remarkable tenacity that more than makes up for his size and weight. As a high school football player, he was labeled scrappy and stubborn, qualities that gave him an extra edge. Kerrey talked about SEAL training in his 1982 gubernatorial announcement, the most personal of all Kerrey's addresses:

"At the beginning of my training, I wondered if I could complete it. During training, there were many times I thought it might be best to quit. But I finished the training and when it was over, I had a tremendous new self-confidence. I believed I could do the things which had earlier appeared impossible. I believed that if I kept trying I would succeed." In an interview with the *Lincoln Star*, brother Bill Kerrey said, "When he was in SEAL training in the Navy, he used to come in last in the swims. He would write and tell me that he would barely make it. But he kept at it. That's the way he does things."

Kerrey also exhibited his propensity to challenge authority as a SEAL. When two trainees drowned during an exercise, a commanding officer announced that the others must resume work. Kerrey asked for time for reflection and argued for a break. His request could easily have drawn a reprimand. Instead, the officer acquiesced and Kerrey was not punished for speaking out.

Kerrey signed on with the SEALS right after the program had been reenergized by new commanders eager to expand its role in Vietnam. From their inception until the mid-sixties, the extent of the SEALS' role in Vietnam had been to train South Vietnamese counterparts in their image and likeness and to prepare them for secret missions in North Vietnam. At that time, Lieutenant Jim Barnes, the second commanding officer of SEAL Team One, received permission to use SEALS in a Viet Cong–occupied zone known as The Forest of Assassins. It was the turning point for the elite group that would later be called "the most effective fighting force in my command" by General William Westmoreland.

The men of SEAL Teams One and Two were close to being the most broadly trained troops in military history because they combined all of the disciplines of the specialized units of World War II. Americans became widely aware of special units during the Second World War when the need was demonstrated for specially trained or "elite" forces that could operate secretly and effectively behind enemy lines.

In 1942, the Army formed the Rangers, a select group trained to make amphibious landings or parachute assaults. The

Marines organized the Raiders to raid Japanese strongholds in the Pacific. The Navy created the Frogmen to carry out underwater exploration of enemy-occupied areas, obtain intelligence information, blow up shore installations, defuse harbor mines, or attach explosives to the sides of enemy ships. Later the Army organized the Green Berets.

Two decades after the first full-scale introduction of special elite troops, a rare combination of circumstances led to the creation of the SEALS: evolving interservice rivalry, the awareness of the need for hit-and-run tactics in all branches of service, and longing of the Marine Raiders and the Frogmen for a broader range of utilization. The Department of Defense and the Navy combined the units into a single, more versatile one that would operate on the sea, in the air, and on the land. That unit would become the SEALS. If any group merits the designation "elite," it is the Navy SEALS. The Vietnam War had approximately five hundred thousand officers and sailors and two hundred SEALS.

Retired senior chief quartermaster James Dennis Watson, now of Fort Pierce, Florida, was in the first training class when the SEALS were founded on January 8, 1962, at 1300 hours. Thirty years later, he is still associated with the organization; he works at the SEAL Museum, which is located on the beach where the first class trained. Watson has a wealth of general information about the SEALS but, in keeping with SEAL tradition, is reluctant to talk about his own experiences, which span the entire history of the Vietnam War. Since he was present at the birth of the SEALS, he has a father's pride in the organization. He is proud of their record, proud of the individuals who have served, and proud of former SEAL, Senator Bob Kerrey. "Bob Kerrey is very well respected by all retired and active SEALS."

Kerrey's missions in Vietnam, which have been reviewed by Watson, were to capture important Viet Cong and gather intelligence. Intelligence gathering is vital in all wars but it was especially so in Vietnam. The North Vietnamese and the Viet Cong circulated through U.S.-occupied territory disguised and undetected. While the United States and the South Vietnamese controlled most of the countryside, enclaves of Viet Cong still conducted terrorism and political indoctrination. As in any war with fluid lines, there was a political contest alongside the military one. In this setting, SEALS were directed to go after the political as well as the military leadership to disrupt the chain of command or the delegation of specific orders.

Before deployment, all SEALS are screened in rigorous training that tests their physical and psychological strength. Even so, the men who stand out in relationship to their peers are the men chosen for the most important missions. The lieutenant in charge determines the optimum number of men for a specific raid and selects those whose talents best fit the mission. An officer is not required to join his men for every mission; nor is he required to accept all assignments. Kerrey, in fact, turned down missions because they appeared to him to be too risky.

If a SEAL officer does not go, he monitors the mission from a ship or a land base. In this stance, the officer can order the mission to be aborted and the helicopters sent in for either backup or rescue. SEAL standard operating procedure requires one-half of the platoon, a squad, to remain at base while the other squad conducts the mission.

On the day of his fateful assignment, Kerrey had only been in Vietnam two and a half months and he had had little contact with the enemy. He had taken part in a score or so of missions but had witnessed only limited gunfire. Nonetheless, he was chosen to lead a mission that his superiors considered critical.

Mike Ambrose from Cherokee, Iowa, and now of Houston, Texas, joined the SEALS in 1966 and, in 1969, became Kerrey's point man in Vietnam. The point man is the man out in front of the unit, calling out observations to the officer in charge. He is often the first one to see the enemy, the first one to be seen, and the first one to draw enemy fire. On the frontier, in the Civil War and in World War II, the trooper in that position was referred to as a scout. Ambrose was an experienced second-class petty officer who had already pulled one tour as a SEAL in Vietnam, and he had been a roommate of Kerrey's in predeployment training at Coronado, California. The two young men developed a bond of trust and mutual respect that began in training and continued through Vietnam; they remain close today.

Ambrose recalls Kerrey as sincere and truthful—qualities
that led to a close relationship with his men. He remembers Kerrey going to great effort to share the nature of the risk with each
man on the fire team as they planned a mission, something not
every officer did. Kerrey conveyed an attitude of strength to his
men, and he was protective in his willingness to alter plans or
even, if necessary, abort a mission.

Dwight Daigle of New Orleans was an enlisted man in the
fourteen-man platoon; his seven-man fire team was led by Lieutenant Wettack, who was also close to Kerrey. Daigle describes
the SEAL officer as unique in comparison with other naval officers in that he lives, works, fights, and trains very closely with
his men. SEAL officers in training and in combat perform every
job required of an enlisted man.

Daigle viewed Kerrey as a "good operator." From the outset, Kerrey's leadership was evident. "He had the ability to organize chaos," Daigle said, an absolute necessity in clandestine
operations, and in Vietnam in particular. Even before a mission,
chaos can arise out of conflicting intelligence reports and competition between branches of service. Kerrey was considered superior in his attention to detail, something that can save lives in
secret raids. Prior to an operation, the men in the platoon are
brought in and given a warning order, an explanation of the mission by the officer in charge. Daigle recalled that the briefings
by Kerrey were exhaustive, covering ammunition, mapping, alternative radio frequencies, water, fuel, and all the multitude of
details necessary for a clandestine operation. Daigle, who was
older than Kerrey, already had pulled two full tours in Vietnam
before being assigned to predeployment with Kerrey and Wettack. As a veteran SEAL, Daigle was energized by Kerrey's
leadership and recalled that even while preparing for the most
hazardous operations, Kerrey kept the men laughing, a facet of
Kerrey's personality that impresses Daigle to this day.

In Vietnam, most SEAL forays into enemy territory were
"waterborne insertions." Teams were usually delivered to inland
sites by boats from riverine detachments of the Navy and by
Navy patrol boat river. When there was a mission or insertion
along the coast, SEALS were often delivered by the Navy's swift
boats.

Before Kerrey's March 14, 1969, final mission, naval intelligence had obtained information that there was to be a meeting of high-ranking political and military leaders of the North Vietnamese Army and the Viet Cong on Hon Tre Island off the coast of South Vietnam. It was clear to U.S. officers that the meeting was an important one, considering the site that was chosen. Hon Tre Island was, in traditional Navy terms, a "rock," an apparently inaccessible island. Three sides had open areas for clear fields of fire by the defenders and the remaining area was protected by a sheer three-hundred-and-fifty-foot cliff that rose from the ocean. A command decision was made to attack Hon Tre Island while the meeting was taking place.

At 6 P.M. on the night of the mission, Kerrey's SEAL team was watching a John Wayne movie at the naval base at Cam Ranh Bay. The SEALS were called out of the movie and taken along the coast to Nha Trang, where they were briefed for an hour and a half by naval intelligence and members of the Army's Green Berets. The intelligence officers had secured general information from two defectors about the terrain and defense of the island, reputed to be a secret conference site of Viet Cong and North Vietnamese Army strategists. Kerrey's mission was to obtain all written intelligence items, plans, maps, and directives, and to capture prisoners, if possible.

Kerrey and Ambrose had misgivings. Their briefing had been short, and there were no maps or photographs giving the details of the terrain. Still, they accepted the assignment and considered this to be one time when they would have to just go for it. With the briefing over, Kerrey and his men checked their weapons and gear. Soon, a Navy mobile crew put them on a swift boat and took them on the thirty- to forty-minute ride to Hon Tre Island for the midnight mission.

En route, Kerrey led discussions of immediate plans, strategy and alternatives. Since they had learned that three sides of the rock would be guarded with an open field of fire for the defenders, they were delivered to the base of the cliff on the unprotected side. At Kerrey's direction, they decided to split into two groups for their approach to the summit since enemy troops were reported to be sleeping in two separate areas. Kerrey led one group composed of three SEALS accompanied by a South Vietnamese frogman, and Ambrose led the other group, also made up of three SEALS and one Vietnamese frogman.

The teams scaled the cliff and began to move across the thicket and jungle-covered crest along two separate paths. As Ambrose moved his group forward, they looked for a flashlight signal from Kerrey to show that he was in place. Ambrose was still approaching surreptitiously when he and his team heard the sound of an explosion some distance to the side in Kerrey's area.

It was the explosion of the grenade that had hit Kerrey, and then Ambrose heard automatic weapons firing from Kerrey's area. At the same time, the North Vietnamese defending guards rolled out of their bunks and hammocks and started firing in Ambrose's area. He and his men suppressed the fire of the defenders and then they could see the tracer bullets from Kerrey's group shooting into the night.

As they fired into the general area, Ambrose and his team crossed over to the scene, where they found Kerrey wounded but still conscious and directing fire. There is some dispute as to who put a tourniquet on Kerrey's leg, and how it was attached to the remaining leg. It is roundly agreed, however, that it was done quickly. He also suffered shrapnel wounds to the face, chest, and hands. Someone called for a medevac helicopter and a gunship. Within a fairly short time, a medevac helicopter neared the island. The pilot, concerned about the safety of his crew, radioed that he was reluctant to come in absent a protecting gunship. Then, as the pilot talked to the men on the ground and learned of Kerrey's need for attention, he decided to give it a try. Ambrose credits the pilot with maneuvering the ship so close to a cliff that the blades were whirling within inches of solid rock as they lowered the basket to pick up Kerrey.

Until they hoisted him into the basket, Kerrey supervised the counterattack that led to the capture of both prisoners and vital information. The mission was successful. Kerrey remained clearheaded during his radio contact with the helicopter, reporting a change in the landing zone and the presence of red-smoke grenades that could be viewed by infrared equipment on the helicopter.

Kerrey's men maintain they knew he wouldn't die despite the fact that he was so severely wounded. His fellow SEALS also say they're not surprised he remained calm. Chief Watson, who has studied the Hon Tre Island mission, said, "He had lost part of a leg. He never lost his cool. He never lost command. And his men got out." Kerrey's was the only serious injury and by the time he made it into the helicopter, he was nearly unconscious from loss of blood.

Two decades later, as Americans debated the legality of burning the American flag, Senator Kerrey said, "I don't remember giving the safety of our flag anywhere near the thought that I gave the safety of my men."

War places individuals in situations that are so uniquely hazardous that no one can be fully prepared to cope with what is happening. But the fact is, some men and women are able to cope in such situations and cope amazingly well. It is noteworthy that even after being wounded, Kerrey exhibited leadership that showed extraordinary concern for his comrades. A reading of his Medal of Honor citation clearly shows Kerrey's devotion to duty:

> *For conspicuous gallantry and intrepidity at the risk of his life above and beyond the call of duty while serving as a SEAL team leader during action against enemy aggressor (Viet Cong) forces. Acting in response to reliable intelligence, Lt. (j.g.) Kerrey led his SEAL team on a mission to capture important members of the enemy's area political cadre known to be located on an island in the bay of Nha Trang. In order to surprise the enemy, he and his team scaled a 350-foot sheer cliff to place themselves above the ledge on which the enemy was located. Splitting his team in two elements and coordinating both, Lt. (j.g.) Kerrey led his men in the treacherous downward descent to the enemy's camp. Just as they neared the end of their descent, intense enemy fire was directed at them, and Lt. (j.g.) Kerrey received massive injuries from a grenade which exploded at his feet and threw him backward onto the jagged rocks. Although bleeding profusely and suffering great pain, he displayed outstanding courage and presence of mind in immediately directing his element's fire*

into the heart of the enemy camp. Utilizing his radioman, Lt. (j.g.) Kerrey called in the second element's fire support which caught the confused Viet Cong in a devastating crossfire. After successfully suppressing the enemy's fire, and although immobilized by his multiple wounds, he continued to maintain calm, superlative control as he ordered his team to secure and defend an extraction site. Lt. (j.g.) Kerrey resolutely directed his men, despite his near-unconscious state, until he was eventually evacuated by helicopter. The havoc brought to the enemy by this very successful mission cannot be overestimated. The enemy soldiers who were captured provided critical intelligence to the allied effort. Lt. (j.g.) Kerrey's courageous and inspiring leadership, valiant fighting spirit, and tenacious devotion to duty in the face of almost overwhelming opposition, sustain and enhance the finest traditions of the U.S. Naval Service.

War is an event that becomes a benchmark in one's life, an event that unquestionably alters personality. War, that is, where there is direct contact with the enemy—not merely being in the service, not only serving overseas in rear-echelon support groups. It means being in harm's way, where the enemy is shooting and the target is close enough for a hit. This was the war of the Thirty-second Infantry of World War II that fought for three years, from the jungles of Buna, New Guinea, in December of 1942 to the jungles of Luzon in the Philippines in 1945. And it was the war of the combat soldiers and Marines who slogged through jungles in Vietnam with the monsoons pouring down thirty inches of rain a month, mud knee- to waist-deep, with leeches dropping from trees to arms and necks.

This was also the war of small counterinsurgency units like the one commanded by twenty-five-year-old Bob Kerrey, who was given an assignment in March 1969 to go ashore in small craft at night and attack a Viet Cong installation. Kerrey's was a do-or-die assignment without direct support. In his 1982 gubernatorial announcement, Kerrey said, "I was part of a fourteen-man platoon with a mission which frightened me. I wondered if

I could pull it off. I found that with the help of detailed planning and teamwork, we were able to accomplish it. We were able to do things which I did not believe possible."

At the end of the skirmish that March morning, Kerrey was helicoptered back to the naval base, where he was stabilized. Later, a heavily sedated Kerrey was flown to an Army hospital in Yokosuka, Japan, where he remained for a time. His family was notified of his injuries and told of his final destination, the Philadelphia Naval Hospital.

Kerrey has often stated that "going home" was the first thought that entered his mind when he realized he was safe in the helicopter. He remembered thinking he now had an automatic ticket out of Asia and home to Nebraska. But before seeing Lincoln, Kerrey would spend the better part of a year recuperating at the Philadelphia Naval Hospital, a time of pain and pranks, introspection, readjustment, friendship forging, and Vietnam War policy examination.

The defining period in Bob Kerrey's life was the time between March and December 1969 that he spent at the Philadelphia Naval Hospital, which he once called a "hellhole." He has often described the place as a garbage can where the refuse from the Vietnam War was thrown. The young innocent Nebraskan landed there, and when he left he was naive no more. Kerrey had never seen such suffering in his sheltered life, let alone endured it and lived with it. In an interview with the *Wall Street Journal*, Kerrey said, "I had no idea that that was what war was producing. I had no idea, period, that there were people out there hurting." Like the naive Pierre Bezukhov in Tolstoy's *War and Peace*, who heads innocently off to war in top hat and tails, Kerrey headed to Vietnam. eager and unaware of war's reality. Philadelphia made him understand. He saw the consequences of unbridled patriotism. Jim Crotty said about their sojourn in Philly, in an interview with *The New York Times Magazine*: "It was, very simply, another war."

All the men now bed-bound had been physical specimens. These were not guys who had spent their service time typing memos and placing orders. The sad part about a visit to a veterans hospital is the before and after lives of the men filling the beds. These were guys who had defined their lives in high school by the sports they loved. These were young Americans with toned muscles and agile limbs and heady feelings that afternoons that begin as romps, be it diving, surfing, or engaging in military combat, simply do not end in quadriplegia and limb amputation. Those who do consider the possibilities consider death the alternative they prefer. ("Never knew there were worse things than dying," goes a line from Bogle's "And the Band Played Waltzing Matilda.") That is, until it happens and then they find, usually after years of anguished struggle, they are thankful for life.

That contrast of life before and after is even more poignant when the conflict is exceedingly ill conceived, as was Gallipoli and, fifty years later, Vietnam. At Gallipoli, young Australians were used as cannon fodder and, in the eyes of many Americans, so were thousands of young men in Vietnam. To many, history has deemed the Vietnam War a conflict unworthy of the price America had to pay. The nobleness of World War II made war injuries easier to accept by the men who were mangled in that effort.

In Philadelphia, Bob Kerrey learned about suffering firsthand by listening to it, watching it, and getting to know it concretely, not abstractly. Again, his 1982 gubernatorial announcement speech is revealing: "At the Philadelphia Naval Hospital I was twenty-five and one of thousands of maimed and disfigured young men. I saw suffering that I did not know existed. All the time that I was pursuing my goals with determination and zeal, there were people who were hurting. And I shall never forget it. I shall never forget that while I am warm there are people who are cold. That while I am working there are people who are not. That while I am comfortable, there are people who are suffering."

Repeatedly, Kerrey also points to his stay at the hospital as an eye-opener in terms of hands-on experience with America's health-care system. Kerrey often felt demeaned there, yet he felt fortunate that his rehabilitation was provided by the government. Kerrey once told Bethany friend Frosty Chapman that it was a "primitive, brutal" environment, an experience beyond comprehension to those who have not endured it. Watching and listening to the agony of other limbless men, dealing with an often diffident and frustrated hospital staff—the reality of being bed-bound was, for the restless, risk-taking Kerrey, absolute torture. In his 1982 gubernatorial speech, he spoke of Philadelphia: "Few of us were prepared for our homecoming. Like all veterans we were happy to be home. We were happy to be alive and we clung together in that hospital in friendships which still endure."

In countless interviews since the time he was Governor, Kerrey has stated variations on the sentiment that it was difficult feeling grateful for life to the same government that had previously just about taken it away.

In later years, as a politician, his mixed emotions would become a Kerrey trademark. Kerrey often talks about the fact that he learned humility and compassion during his stint in Philadelphia. "It is hard to be arrogant," Kerrey said, "when you've got a bedpan under your butt." Compassion was clearly not a quality that described young Bob Kerrey. He was kind enough and even gentle, to some degree, but he was not unerringly compassionate. He was a young man interested in himself and his career who had respect for other people; he had never ached for others as he would after Philadelphia. Philadelphia softened his soul toward society's hurts even as it hardened his heart toward society's leaders. That cynicism remains.

The seeds of Kerrey's love-hate relationship with government were sown during his days on his back in Philadelphia. That is where he mulled over the sense that government isn't necessarily benign; that it can do great violence to a people and that it can be a great force for right. He directly traces his ambivalence about the role of government to the Philadelphia Naval Hospital.

He also learned immediately just how lucky he was to have lost so little of only one limb. The hospital was filled with Vietnam veterans whose bodies were far more riven than his own. One was Lew Puller, the son of the Marine Corps' most decorated hero, Chesty Puller. In a skirmish near Viem Dong in the fall of 1968, Puller lost both legs and most of his fingers and he had been undergoing rehabilitation at the naval hospital since that time. Bob Kerrey was assigned to the room Puller had previously stayed in, and Puller writes of his first encounter with Kerrey in his moving autobiography, *Fortunate Son*:

> *When I first met Lieutenant (jg) Bob Kerrey, he had just been assigned the bed space I had formerly occupied, and the doctors were evaluating his injured right leg to determine the level at which it would be amputated . . . and the scuttlebutt in the hospital had it that he was about to be recommended for the Medal of Honor.*
>
> *The morning I entered my old room and discovered Bob, he was listening to an Aretha Franklin tape played several decibels above what the ward rules allowed, and he was trying to take pictures of his mangled leg with an Instamatic camera. He seemed oblivious of pain and, after I introduced myself, he handed me the camera and asked me to snap a few pictures of his leg for the American Legion folks back in his home state of Nebraska. Jim (Crotty) and I exchanged glances, but neither of us could tell if Bob was delirious or just marching to the beat of a different drum. I took the pictures while Bob joined Aretha in singing "Respect," and I sensed immediately that life on SOQ (Sick Officers Quarters) 12 was about to undergo a rejuvenation.*

Although he quickly got a reputation as a prankster on the ward, Kerrey's attempt at livening up SOQ 12 belied his bitterness about being there. Kerrey's youngest sister, Nancy, who lives in Milford, Nebraska, with her dairy farmer husband and five children, remembers her first telephone conversation with her brother:

"I hadn't talked with him yet and I was nervous and I didn't plan what I was going to say, so when it came to my turn, we had passed the phone around to different siblings. I said, 'Hey, Bob, how are you?' and the minute I said it, I realized it was a stupid thing to ask, since he had just lost a leg." Kerrey responded in a bitter, sarcastic voice, "I'm just fine, thanks." Frederick Downs, an author and Vietnam veteran, writes in the *Washington Post*: "There is no more devastating blow to the human psyche than to be transformed in microseconds from a healthy robust human being into a cripple. The fear of being disabled is ingrained in us."

Still, Kerrey's irrepressible spirit surfaced in Philadelphia instantly. Bethany buddy Frosty Chapman said, "To Bob, having fun was so important, he would just push back the pain. I don't know what it is but he would never let pain get in the way of having a good time."

Puller goes on to recount his first impressions of Kerrey:

Within days Bob was taken to the operating room, and when he returned, his leg had been removed at mid-calf. During the first few days after the amputation he fought taking the kind of pain shots for which Jim and I had begged, and his stoicism, though unnerving, was a source of amazement to all. Jim and I had learned how to dull the pain with narcotics, and though Bob's wounds were not as severe as mine or his pain as great as Jim's, we wanted to see him more comfortable and to have our view confirmed that morphine was indispensable to recovery. Instead Bob asked for a fungo bat with which to beat back the phantom pains in his missing limb, and Jim and I were left to conclude sheepishly that some people had higher tolerances to pain than others.

Kerrey's high threshold for pain is recalled even by boyhood friends who remember him as a child who resisted expressing feelings about being physically hurt. Throughout his struggle with asthma, Kerrey showed a high tolerance for pain. Early on, he seems to have decided that if he complained about pain, he would be removed from the action, and Kerrey desperately wanted to be where the action was. He watched how physical problems prevented his oldest brother, Jimmy, from participating in organized sports, and he wanted to distance himself from any kind of potential removal. Frosty Chapman said, "I remember one time he had his hand wrapped up and he was in obvious pain, but he would not acknowledge the pain. It was like he had found a way to just mentally block it out; it was like it didn't exist, whereas a normal person would at least say something about it or show some pain. Having fun was always more important to Bob than the pain—he'd just block it out or ignore it."

Puller became a good friend and remains so today, along with Jim Crotty. In his book, Puller describes in detail the excruciatingly difficult healing process that began for the three men at the naval hospital. Kerrey's recovery was not as difficult as Puller's or Crotty's, but was nevertheless an intense period of adjustment and therapy. It took him months to learn how to walk, and still he was slow and ragged. Kerrey spent his time at the hospital reading, attending therapy, listening to music, swapping stories with roommates, and contemplating what effect his injury would have on his life.

Puller writes that Kerrey recognized his blessing and let it be known that "he was only interested in getting the right prosthesis and then getting on with his life." However, Kerrey would not approach life in the same manner ever again. He had stared down death and he lived with men whose physical suffering made his pale in comparison. He was angry that good men had come to such devastation for what he was beginning to believe was an extremely flawed foreign policy. In an interview with the *Washington Post*, Kerrey said, "There were six or seven of us . . . and there were probably fifteen or sixteen limbs between us. And I remember the President said, 'I've seen the ugly face of war. I've seen the boys in the hospital,' and thinking, 'This guy is lying. Man, he hasn't seen the ugly face of war at all. For political reasons he's willing to protect this thing. . . . I mean the deal is done, but thousands more people are going to die.'"

Bob Kerrey was intensely angry, but it would not be until much later that he would realize the extent of his rage. He felt betrayed by a country that had pushed patriotism over the reality of war. Later, June Levine, a professor who befriended Kerrey after Vietnam, said, "I realized from talking with him that he had believed everything he had been told by politicians. I remember thinking how naive he was and that there were men a lot younger than he was who knew what the war was about without having to go there and discover it."

Jamie Obrecht, a Vietnam veteran from Bethany's high

school, Lincoln Northeast, said, "A lot of our teachers were World War II veterans. They passed down a lot of the John Wayne stuff. Every value that I had, my self-image, my image of a warrior, my image of masculinity, my image of patriotism and authority—these were all shaped by our fathers, our teachers, and television. The same is true of Bob Kerrey."

Vietnam was a constant topic of conversation on the ward but few residents during their rehabilitation had crystallized their own feelings about their role in the conflict, their injuries, and U.S. policy. For most, it would take reentering the civilian world for them to know how polarized the country had become and how isolated they would feel in it. While they were all still a part of the brotherhood of amputees, they could not understand the extent to which they had been set apart from their increasingly fractured generation.

Kerrey's therapy went smoothly and he was discharged in the fall of 1969. He left with crutches and a prosthesis. Later Bob Kerrey would remember information and emotions gleaned from his days as a California serviceman, a SEAL leader, a wounded soldier, and a handicapped vet, and would move audiences with his empathy and the breadth of his experience. And if Bob Kerrey is examined against his generational times, he is a reflection of the Vietnam era. So many youth experienced it unidimensionally—they went to war or they protested. Like Ron Kovic, author of *Born on the Fourth of July*, Kerrey did both. Were it not for his injury, Bob Kerrey might have completed his tour of duty in Vietnam unharmed, returned home to Lincoln, and, if he ever entered the political arena, he probably would have done so as a Republican.

Nothing in Kerrey's upbringing would suggest a future as a Democratic activist and leader. Vietnam marked not just Kerrey's physical transformation from a healthy young man to a wounded veteran; it also was the turning point for his ideological transformation from nebulous Republican to unorthodox Democrat.

Bob Kerrey had been wounded at twenty-five. He had celebrated his twenty-sixth birthday in August in the hospital. No longer young, no longer naive, no longer physically whole, he now was ready to come home. The gung ho golden boy of the Great Plains returned to Lincoln in great psychic and physical pain—a young man grappling, like thousands of other Vietnam veterans, with a physical handicap and with mental anguish over the necessity of it all.

Still, he thought that life would be pretty normal except that he was missing part of a leg. He wanted to get back in good physical shape. He hoped he could run again. He thought he might speak out against U.S. policy in Vietnam. He wanted to get his master's degree in business. He wanted to write. He wanted to go to a Cornhusker football game. He wanted to find a woman to love. He wanted to figure out what to do with the rest of his life.

Chapter 2

A BETHANY
BOYHOOD

ike most Midwestern cities, Lincoln was built on a simple grid with O Street dividing the town into north and south sections. Legend has it that poet Allen Ginsburg howled when he discovered that the main street of Nebraska's capital was what he dubbed "zero street," and he later immortalized it in a poem of the same name. Reputed to be the longest straight street in the world, it runs the full length of Lincoln and beyond for fifty miles without a jog, curve, or a turn. Within the city, however, O Street divides the classes: South of O Street is one city and north of O Street is another.

The south side is home to Lincoln's wealth, of which there is a great deal, and the north side is home to Lincoln's industry. The city is known to the rest of the country mostly as a center of education and government, but that reputation belies the diversity in the university town of 180,000. It is true that nearly one-quarter of all Lancaster County residents are employed by the government, many in clerical and secretarial jobs, and that professors, many reared on the coasts, populate Lincoln in relatively large numbers. Still, Lincoln has many factory workers employed by the Goodyear Tire and Rubber Company, the Kawasaki Motor Corporation, and the Burlington Northern Railroad among others.

South Lincoln has tony country clubs, stately mansions, acres of landscaped lawns, even marbled swimming pools. North Lincoln is home to Lincoln's small minority population, made up mostly of blacks and native Americans and Hispanics. It also has communities like University Place, home to Nebraska Wesleyan University, and Bethany, Bob Kerrey's boyhood home.

Bethany began in the mind of a Lincoln businessman and his colleagues who, in the late 1800s, saw the potential of the golden land that crested in a hill only five minutes from Nebraska's thriving capital city. They felt that they could make easy, fast money by buying the land and then selling it to a church organization interested in expansion. Many churches at that time had emissaries out scouting locations for Bible schools, colleges, and seminaries. The land, owned by Nebraska farmers, was sold to farsighted speculators who immediately turned around and offered it to officials of a Baptist church. When the Baptists rejected the offer, the group presented it to representatives of the Nebraska Christian Missionary Alliance, who purchased it with the idea of building a Midwestern version of West Virginia's Bethany College. Other northeast landowners donated land and, eventually, Bethany Heights, the college's first building, was completed in 1890. But from the outset the college had fiscal woes so great it would have collapsed without a transfusion of money and fifty acres of additional land donated by Omaha entrepreneur Samuel V. Cotner. The church school was renamed Cotner College and it limped along anemically until 1933 when it was closed, a victim of the depression.

Over the next four decades the church land would be developed, in part by a young man from Chicago, James Kerrey, who, like the businessmen before him, saw opportunity in the wide-open spaces of the sleepy little suburb called Bethany.

To reach Bethany heading east on O Street, travelers must veer left at 56th Street, and the gentle curve of Cotner Boulevard leads visitors into an area where, almost immediately, the pace gets slower, the houses get smaller, and the people are older and more likely to know one another.

That the majority of residents are elderly is a change from the forties through the sixties, when Bethany was home to hun-

dreds of families with young children. Evidence of this demo-
graphic change was the fate of the Bethany Elementary School,
closed in 1981 and turned into condominiums for senior citizens.
In the sixties, more than seven hundred children attended the
same school that had less than two hundred and thirty students
by 1980.

But back in the 1940s, Bethany was a community in transition from a sleepy little village beyond the limits of the bustling
state capital to a development-oriented American suburb. During that era much of Bethany was still fields of flaxen grasses and
young families moved in for one of two reasons or both, as
would be the case with the James Kerrey family: They were eager to escape the higher real-estate prices in south Lincoln; they
wanted to join the Bethany Christian Church community. From
its inception Bethany was different from other villages-turned-
suburbs of Lincoln because so many of its residents were devout
Christians whose lives revolved around church activities. The
saying was "If you don't go to Cotner College or belong to the
Bethany Christian Church, you have no business being in Bethany." The Bethany Christian Church, located on Cotner Boulevard, sits in the heart of Bethany and was the drawing card for
hundreds of followers of the Disciples of Christ. By the
buttoned-up standards of Bethany residents, the next-door suburb, Havelock, which encompasses the Goodyear plant and the
Burlington railroad yard, was "Sin City," where drinking and
carousing were a way of life for some of the workers. Bethany
was a dry community until recently, and still it is next to impossible to buy liquor anywhere in the Bethany area. Go to Havelock, though, and the main street, on both sides, is filled with
pubs. While Bethany is described as a working-class suburb, in
fact parts of it resembled a middle-class enclave filled with fathers who worked as small-business and insurance men and
women who stayed home and raised children.

James Kerrey had never been to Bethany before he was as-
signed to Lincoln's Air Force base as a captain during World
War II. He had spent most of his life in Michigan, Illinois, and
Iowa.

James Kerrey's parents died within a year of each other, his mother from what family members suspect was diabetes and his father from pneumonia. Little is known of James Kerrey's mother, Anis Potts, except that she was sickly most of her life and "probably shouldn't have had any children to begin with but she had the two boys anyway," according to relatives. Anis Potts had been married before, and on her deathbed she asked that she be buried beside her first husband in Tennessee. "I guess that just really killed my grandfather when she told him that," Nancy Kerrey Swarts said, but he nonetheless agreed. Six months later he caught pneumonia, died, and was buried in Michigan. James Kerrey was not yet one, and his brother, John, was a toddler. They were sent to live in Michigan with an aunt and her daughters, Eva and Jessie. The cousins were much older than the Kerrey boys and, as their mother aged and they matured, the women took over the care their mother had been providing. The women had moved to Chicago's South Side and eventually, the youngsters moved in with them. So while the aunts were, in fact, cousins of James Kerrey, out of respect for their role the Kerrey clan always referred to them as aunts.

The sisters both taught in Chicago public schools. After retiring, both gave lectures at the Museum of Science and Industry until they were well into their eighties. Eva Potter lived to witness her "great-nephew's" gubernatorial inauguration in 1982, when she was one hundred years old. She traveled to Lincoln from Connecticut for the event, attended the ball at the Governor's mansion in a wheelchair, and told a reporter for the *Omaha World-Herald* that the navy print dress she had commissioned for her one hundredth birthday, September 25, "now commemorates two momentous occasions. The inauguration is the topper."

Neither woman ever married or dated during the time James Kerrey spent with them, so he did not have the benefit of a male influence. Later, one friend of the senior Kerrey speculated that it was the absence of any day-to-day male ties as a child that made James Kerrey a somewhat detached personality—a man difficult to befriend as an adult. His was not an easy childhood. He grew up without parents or any male role model and with a brother who, early on, was tagged a troublemaker. By James Kerrey's account, his brother, John, was a fighter, always in the middle of a tussle. "If Uncle John saw somebody who was going to cross him," Nancy Kerrey Swarts said, "he'd make sure that he was there to take him up on a fight, whereas Dad was always avoiding a fight." In high school, John would be shipped away to live with another male relative in the family (in hopes that a father figure might calm down the hard-to-handle child) and eventually on to a military-reform school. Being separated from his only brother as a young man must have produced difficult times for James Kerrey, although he told his daughter he could not remember a single unhappy day as a child. "I was asking him some questions when he was on his deathbed. I had a Grandfather Remembers book and one question was, What was the unhappiest recollection of your childhood? and he couldn't think of anything; he thought awhile, but he just couldn't come up with one. Then I asked him what was the happiest time of your childhood or happiest memory and he said, 'Mmm, well, I guess it was when I got my first new pair of shoes—I was about twelve years old.' He had always worn these holey old hand-me-downs and here he didn't have any unhappy memories but yet he came up with that for his happiest. I *know* he had some unhappy memories."

James Kerrey died during the summer of 1987, just four months before his son was elected to the United States Senate. In the last few months of his life, when he lived in a complex across the street from Omaha Methodist Hospital, Bob Kerrey visited him frequently and read poetry at his bedside. James Kerrey told Marian Price, a longtime family friend from Bethany, that he knew his son would become a Senator and that he wished he could live to see it. "To each of my children, I give my love," James Kerrey wrote to his children in his one-line will.

Elinor Kerrey, who died in 1978 of Lou Gehrig's disease, was raised in rural Iowa in a family of seven. Her memories as a young girl were of a mother who enjoyed the routine rituals of farm and family life: babies, canning, animals, cotton clothes on a line blowing in the breeze, quilting, and cooking. She attended Iowa State University and graduated in 1935, first in her class, in home economics. Another student at ISU was James Kerrey, who was pursuing a degree in engineering. The two met there and married shortly after graduation. Both Elinor and James Kerrey had siblings and other relatives who were college educated. They lived in Ames, Iowa, the first few years of their marriage. Jobs were scarce but James landed one selling insurance.

In wartime service, Kerrey moved his family to the Lincoln air base. In Lincoln he forged a friendship with a man who would not only help him in business but who would also be instrumental in Bob Kerrey's restaurant and political ventures three decades down the line.

Larry Price, now a legend in Nebraska for getting rich in the restaurant business, created King's Food Host USA restaurants, a chain of fast-food outlets that preceded today's McDonald's and Burger King. In many ways, Price is to the Lincoln business scene what Warren Buffett is in Omaha business circles. He possessed similar vision, creativity, and business acumen, all the while resisting the trappings and pitfalls of wealth. When Price met James Kerrey, he was not yet well established in the Bethany community.

Apartment leases in Bethany that accepted children were hard to find during the war but, after an exhausting search, James and Elinor settled in the neighborhood a couple of blocks down from the large home on Lexington Circle where they would rear their seven children, four boys and three girls. Bob Kerrey was born Joseph Robert Kerrey in Lincoln on August 27, 1943, the third Kerrey son. He was called Bob almost from birth, after a favorite relative and because James Kerrey preferred the name Bob over Joe. The Kerreys joined Bethany Christian Church and were invited to sign up with a newly formed group for churchgoers with children. It was at one of these meetings that James and Elinor Kerrey met Larry and Esther Price, a couple who would become a major influence on the Kerreys for the next thirty years. James liked Price instantly and believed that he was an astute businessman. When they met, Price owned a small grocery store and meat locker which he had bought with money saved while he was one of a handful of policemen in Bethany. James saw that Price could help him out and confided to him that he did not want to return to the world of insurance, while Larry discovered that James "was sharp, real quick—he was a quick study." The two men talked about Bethany's business possibilities and Lincoln's great potential because of its colleges: the University of Nebraska–Lincoln, Nebraska Wesleyan, and the Seventh-Day Adventist–sponsored Union College. James repeatedly talked about owning his own business—any business. "He didn't care what kind it was—he just wanted to be a businessman," Price said.

The Kerreys lived in Lincoln for only three or four months the first time they were stationed there. Soon after settling in, James Kerrey was transferred by the Air Force to the University of Chicago for a crash course in Japanese. "It's very demanding and James did very well at it," Price said.

Larry Price remembers clearly the last conversation he had with James Kerrey before he left for Chicago with Elinor and his sons in an old, rattletrap car.

"If there is any kind of a business that comes up for sale in Bethany, buy it, and when I come back, I'll run it because this is where we want to live. I don't know anything about any business, but I'll run it for you and I'll do well by you," James Kerrey boasted confidently. So when a lumberyard came up for sale shortly after James Kerrey had been sent to Japan, Price mortgaged his house and bought it. "It was a bargain. For the whole thing, the yard, the acres of ground, and the entire inventory, I only paid ninety-five hundred dollars," reports Price.

Meanwhile, Elinor Kerrey and the kids moved back to Lincoln after James was sent to Asia. The United States needed American military personnel who could handle logistical operations after the war's end.

After a little more than a year overseas, James returned to Lincoln, to a growing family, and to a new business. He paid Price back for the lumberyard with the ten-thousand-dollar life insurance policy he had collected after his brother's death in the Philippines. Ten thousand dollars was a handsome amount of money back in the forties, and it provided an unexpected financial boost for James at a time when he needed capital. For the next few years, James Kerrey ran the lumberyard, but after a time, lost interest in the business, which was not doing well. He then moved into the hardware scene, a business that, once again, Larry Price helped him get off the ground.

As an entrepreneur, James Kerrey did not endear himself to everyone. Some residents perceived him as an overly shrewd businessman. A few of his fellow church members would not speak to him in protest of his perceived ruthlessness; they equated developers with hustlers. James Kerrey was a dreamer and a deal maker and he viewed Bethany as open territory to be developed. The construction business, particularly post–World War II, had a frontier mentality and Jim Kerrey delighted in negotiating, bartering, and haggling. In almost any other area of town his persona would have been more accepted. It was a time when the roller-coaster development business pitched more than a few riders, while others, like Jim Kerrey and Larry Price, did well, engendering plain, old-fashioned jealousy. Even in the face of several business failures, the senior Kerrey remained one of the wealthiest men in the area.

James Kerrey really didn't care what people thought of him. He had been raised as an orphan with no money, and his main concern was providing the kind of life for his kids that he had been denied growing up. He knew he could do it in business. Also, he believed that Bethany fostered too many folks who were overly righteous and pious. Some residents maintain that Price himself was eventually put off by Kerrey and that their long-standing friendship soured when James Kerrey left Price owing him money on a real-estate deal that had been mishandled by James Kerrey and his second son, John, who moved to California after the deal unraveled.

In comparison with Larry Price, James Kerrey was not successful, but in relation to other Bethany businessmen, he was extraordinarily so. Certainly he had business vision, as it was James Kerrey who came up with the idea of developing a segment of Cotner Boulevard that later turned out to be a brilliant real estate purchase.

Unlike her husband, Elinor Kerrey was admired by everyone who knew her. That she held the family together is a sentiment expressed by those who knew the Kerreys intimately. Family members and close friends alike rave about Elinor's ability to handle the chaos inherent in large families.

James's upbringing as an orphan did not prepare him for the role of nurturer and confidant to such a large and independent group as his progeny. As witty and irrepressible as he could be, overall, James Kerrey was not a warm, outgoing person; he was gone much of the time the children were growing up, and they understood his role as that of family provider.

Elinor was strong and extremely capable; however, from the outset the Prices noticed she seemed vulnerable, because she carried the entire domestic burden of the family. "I remember Mom doing a lot of work that the gals or the guys should have done," Nancy Kerrey Swarts said.

Esther Price recalls being upset with Elinor when she mowed the yard. Price would chide her: "Elinor, with all those sons you've got, it just isn't right that you're mowing the lawn, in addition to everything else you do." But Price stressed that Elinor Kerrey never did the work like a martyr. "She didn't pout and fume as she worked—she did it all without complaining."

Larry Price remembered two occasions when Elinor fell asleep at the Price home during a game of couples' bridge, so exhausted was she from her workday. Both times the Prices covered her up and let her stay at their house. James Kerrey agreed, commenting that if she was tired enough to fall asleep, she should not be awakened and escorted home. "And they really didn't have seven kids—it was eight kids—the dad was one of them. Not that Jim wasn't a provider, but the kids and Jim never did have to work because Elinor did everything. It was easy for her because she never expected it any other way, I guess. But she could get on her hands and knees and get the floor spotlessly clean and Jim might walk across the muddy yard and go right on through the house with his muddy shoes. He was just another one of the kids. It's hard to explain something like that or how somebody thinks like that because he could be real caring."

Jessie Kerrey Rasmussen, the Kerreys' eldest daughter, was elected to the Nebraska legislature in 1990 from a prosperous West Omaha suburb. In a National Women's History Month tribute to her mother, Rasmussen wrote: "I remember her up early in the morning, fixing breakfast for her brood, getting them all off to school, and then joining her husband at work for most of the day and then back home again nurturing the family and doing laundry till wee hours of the morning."

When her youngest child was in third grade, Elinor attended the University of Nebraska–Lincoln, where she completed her master's in home economics. Later, she became a professor of food and nutrition at UN-L's east campus, just a couple miles from her home. Elinor's knowledge of cooking and food practices later would be instrumental in the success of Bob Kerrey's first restaurant business, Grandmother's.

Elinor and James Kerrey were a good match in that they each possessed in abundance what the other was missing. Elinor lacked the edge that was provided by James. He was not affectionate and she was extremely so. James was driven and restless. Elinor was relaxed and patient. She created structure and routine; his business hours were erratic. He was moody; she was consistent. She was pragmatic but wrote poetry and played the piano. He was a dreamer who nonetheless was a practical man. They were devoted to their children, to whom they passed down a wide range of qualities, though in different ways.

Having seven children was highly unusual for Protestant families in the fifties. The majority of Bethany parents had two, three, or at the most, four children. Later, Jessie Rasmussen would declare that her parents were "just passionate Protestants."

"If it was Jim doing the planning, it wouldn't have been [planned]," Price said, "and I don't think Elinor cared—not that she didn't care about the kids—she was an excellent mother." "Elinor loved babies," Esther Price said.

Esther Price recalled one shared vacation when all the kids were roughhousing in the backseat of the car; Elinor remained as unruffled as if they were all behaving like little cadets.

One time Kerrey and boyhood chum Frosty Chapman took a mattress, placed it under a window, and jumped from the window onto the mattress. "My mom remembers me coming home and exclaiming that Bob's mom never even got mad at us," Chapman said.

Esther Price remembers Elinor losing her equanimity only once and the incident involved her third son, Bob. As a toddler, he wandered away from the house one day. "Elinor was frantic," Price said, "she was a wreck. All of us were going up and down the block screaming for Bob and he really was nowhere. Larry, trying to reduce the tension, put his arm around her and said, 'Don't worry, Elinor, you can always get another one.' Elinor didn't think that remark was funny." Kerrey turned up only minutes before his parents were poised to bring in the Bethany police. "Bob showed his independent streak even at the age of three," Price said.

As a child Kerrey lived in a modest home just down the block from the Bethany library and around the corner from the more exotic cul-de-sac ranch home of Larry Price. After several years, James Kerrey bought the land next to Price and oversaw the building of the house that the Kerrey kids lived in until they all graduated from high school. The homes that lead into the cul-de-sac are simple, one-story, working-class structures. Only the Price and Kerrey homes suggest middle-class money.

The house James Kerrey commissioned on the forty-two-hundred-square-foot lot was a modest ranch home with a low roof and a large backyard, but by working-class Bethany standards the house edges toward upper class. Nancy Kerrey Swarts said, "It was sort of embarrassing to me to have a house that was so big, and I was singled out at school—my friends called me rich. If you think about it in the late sixties and early seventies, everybody was worried about peace and not worried about material things. I was raised in the hippie era when it wasn't cool to be rich and I was considered the richest kid at school."

Bob Kerrey, on the other hand, came of age in what Robert Lowell called the tranquilized fifties. He entered kindergarten at Bethany Elementary School in 1948 and, like most Bethany boys, sailed through the elementary years with little on his mind but learning, sports, food, and fun. Although he was bright and always got good grades, he wasn't exceptionally precocious. Slightly built, with a large forehead and big blue eyes, Kerrey was a sweet, sometimes ornery kid who, when he was having a good time, flashed a wide engaging grin. Esther Price remembered him as mischievous and a child who could move from being angelic to being "a little devil" fairly quickly. Shirley Wenzel,

Kerrey's fifth-grade teacher, told a writer for the *Omaha World-Herald* in 1988 that even as a ten-year-old, Kerrey left a strong impression on her. "First, he was a really inquisitive boy," Mrs. Wenzel said, "and I recall that Bob never seemed to want to take no for an answer." He is remembered as stubborn, scrappy, and adventurous. Between the fourth and sixth grades, Kerrey was a Boy Scout and when he was in junior high school, he played midget football.

Kerrey had serious asthma as a child and he seemed more fragile than the other Kerrey boys because of it. Elinor worried about his condition and made sure he was monitored by their family doctor. Elinor's brother, Maurice Gonder, a physician in upstate New York, told Nancy Kerrey Swarts that he remembered several visits when Kerrey's wheezing was so bad it could be heard all over the house.

In their Lexington Circle home, the four Kerrey boys roomed in the basement and the three girls slept upstairs. James Kerrey felt strongly that each boy needed his own space so, because the basement was not big enough for four standard-size bedrooms, he had workers carve out four small dormitory-type rooms.

Kerrey, like most kids in the late forties and fifties in Bethany, roamed the neighborhoods and followed two rules: one, to be home for meals, and two, to be home before dark. He and Frosty Chapman and a couple of other Bethany boys played in a homemade treehouse in the Kerrey family backyard. "It was a neat clubhouse; it hadn't been built by kids; it was a very nifty treehouse. I think maybe his dad had someone come in and build it." During his treehouse days, Kerrey, Chapman, and another youngster formed a club called the Cardinals and created rules while they held powwows. Kerrey enjoyed building forts and finding junk to examine and take apart.

A fair number of tough kids lived in working-class Bethany and Chapman remembered that "Bob Kerrey was not a bully. I remember that well—he was a very friendly kid."

The Prices recall that the Kerreys did not talk in detail about the condition of their oldest son, James, who was born slightly mentally retarded. Jimmy was a toddler when Larry and

Esther Price noticed he was a little slow. "Back then we called
him a spastic child," Price added. Elinor once reflected that she
thought Jimmy's condition was caused by lack of attention during a critical stage of labor and that with modern technology, his
condition would have been prevented.

Both parents worked with Jimmy, although, as he grew
older, more of his care fell on Elinor. For a few years he attended Bethany Elementary School, but after a while, he could
no longer keep up and his parents let him stay at home. Jimmy
was never institutionalized. Once, when asked to describe
Jimmy, Bob Kerrey said, "He is slightly mentally retarded." He
emphasized the word *slightly*.

James and Elinor Kerrey were wonderful with Jimmy, according to observers. They included him in all family activities,
shepherded him around Bethany, tutored him to help him keep
up with the taxing demands of grade school until he could attend
no longer, and monitored him closely when he began to venture
out in Lincoln by himself. It was James Kerrey who beseeched
Frosty Chapman to place Jimmy Kerrey in a job. The younger
Kerrey children were supportive of their older brother, but the
situation was painful and confusing, especially for the boys, who,
at young ages, outdistanced their oldest brother, their father's
namesake. By witnessing their parents' unswerving devotion to
Jimmy, however, the Kerrey children learned to cope with the
conflicting emotions about Jimmy that ranged from love and pro-
tectiveness to embarrassment and pity.

When Bob Kerrey went to Northeast, Lincoln had three
other high schools—Lincoln High School, Southeast High
School, and Pius X High School, each with a reputation. Southeast students were the rich kids; Pius X students were Catholic;
Lincoln High students were eclectic and drew more from the
city's artistic community; all the schools were situated in the
southern part of Lincoln's grid, south of O Street, except
Northeast.

Certainly, Northeast had a diverse student body, as children
of professors attended, but the bulk of the student body came
from working-class families. They were a cohesive lot. Northeast
High students were intensely proud of their school, and while

Southeast students may have been smug about their lot in life, Northeast kids wouldn't have dreamed of trading places.

Kerrey was the son of one of Bethany's most prominent families, but he did not flaunt that fact. His clothes were standard, his cars were clunkers, and he didn't act stuck-up, to use the word of the day. "Bob Kerrey had money but he never acted rich," Frosty Chapman recalled. "Nobody in his family ever made you feel as though they had money but we all knew they did. He wasn't like some guys who bought expensive cars and things. Bob was just real ordinary." Kerrey did not date any young women steadily. Several classmates remember him as shy around girls.

He was not an athletic standout, although he made the football team as a reserve center, to the surprise of many observers who felt that at a hundred and fifty-two pounds he was too small for a Class A division that included Omaha Central High School, where football great Gale Sayers attended. So determined was Kerrey to play that he once even altered a doctor's certificate that had advised he not play. Kerrey lettered in football, swimming, and golf, and his high school yearbook features his pictures many times. His high school friends remember his competitiveness most of all, recalling that he enjoyed the challenge sports provided, that winning was not as important for him as participating, but that he displayed an aggressiveness that was noticeable.

Some intimates believed that James Kerrey played his two sons against each other in an effort to hone their physical and mental skills. Larry Price disagreed with that assessment and said that James encouraged normal competition among his boys and that he did not push them needlessly. In fact, Price feels that James displayed little attention to discipline and applied it so erratically that he never could be called strict. In any event, rivalries evolve naturally in big families and the Kerrey boys exhibited their fair share throughout their days together.

Academically, Bob Kerrey did well, always remaining in the top 10 percent of his class. School was easy for him and that allowed him to concentrate on sports, extracurriculars, and part-time jobs. Barry Moore, a high school teacher, once told the *Omaha World-Herald* that "you either liked Bob or you didn't. But he wasn't a kid who just showed up."

Kerrey graduated from high school in 1961, the year the first significant U.S. troop contingent was sent to Vietnam under the direction of President Kennedy. Still, the average citizen was not really conscious of the jungle war. Even to a history or social studies teacher, it was little more than a place in Southeast Asia where the French had been forced to abandon their colonial policy, a nation humbled and defeated.

In 1961, Americans had many other areas of concern. The cold war was at its height. President Kennedy had inherited the awesome task of leading the free world against the perceived growing Communist conspiracy that, unchecked, would produce the domino effect. Khrushchev told Eisenhower: "We'll bury you," and Eisenhower countered with his policy of "massive retaliation."

Castro controlled most of Cuba, and Kennedy inherited the Eisenhower Administration plans for the infamous Bay of Pigs operation. Some have argued that it was the 1961 Bay of Pigs fiasco that led to, or at least exacerbated, this country's involvement in Vietnam. Following the invasion, Kennedy made statements and decisions that reflected his regret for failing to take a stronger stance. In his inaugural address, John Kennedy had declared that the United States would make any sacrifice necessary in the cause of freedom. Nineteen sixty-one was the year Kennedy sent the first troops to Vietnam to supplement those advisers assigned earlier by Eisenhower. One year later, as commander in chief, Kennedy oversaw the formation of the Navy SEALS. Kerrey's focus at the time was on fraternities.

When Bob Kerrey marched on to college in the fall of 1961, it was still a time of lockstep scheduling for children of middle-class families. One finished high school, entered college, and graduated without dropping out for identity searches. It was assumed that with the help of family, friends, and a few professors, the discovery of one's true self would be achieved easily.

Tradition in Nebraska, as elsewhere, has provided the fraternity as a vehicle for young men to integrate their identities into a large group of like-minded peers and mentors. Bob Kerrey was pledged to Phi Gamma Delta, or the Fijis, as they are commonly called, a well-known and highly regarded social fraternity with a national charter. Both Kerrey's Republican gubernatorial opponent, Charley Thone, and the longtime publisher of the *Omaha World-Herald*, Harold Anderson, were Phi Gamma Deltas. One other Phi Gamma Delta pledge that fall of 1961 was John Gottschalk, who in 1989 succeeded Harold Anderson as publisher of the *Omaha World-Herald*, and who remains a close friend of Kerrey's.

Frosty Chapman recalled feeling a touch of envy that Kerrey was able to both join a fraternity and live on campus. Lincoln students who remained at home were unable to experience college in the same way as campus students. "Kerrey's family had money," Frosty said. "Not many of the rest of us could afford it."

A glance at the UN-L yearbook for his first year, 1961–62, shows Kerrey well on his way toward obtaining social recognition. One photo shows him in pajamas, relaxing at the Fiji house, in front of a fireplace and surrounded by young women from a sorority. Although he did not get much coverage during his sophomore year, by his junior year, 1963–64, he was recognized as an effective student in pharmacy college and he had good press coverage again. Another photo shows Kerrey and another young man, wearing white pharmacy jackets, thoughtfully studying the growth of a plant. Those who shot the photos and those who edited the yearbook saw him as representative of the pharmacy college, from which he managed to graduate in four and one-half years instead of the usual five. Desmond Gibson, UN-L pharmacy college dean from 1961–72, said of Kerrey in an interview with the *Daily Nebraskan*, the campus newspaper, "Bob was the kind of kid that just about anything he did he was successful. . . . Inherently, he had a drive that was somewhat uncharacteristic for someone his age."

When Bob Kerrey declared his major of pharmacy in the early sixties, it was the beginning of a transition era—a movement away from the stable, postwar fifties, the so-called Eisenhower Years, to an era marked by war, civil protest, and economic change that would culminate in a realignment of the values of many of America's youth. But in 1961, Kerrey's freshman year, life in Lincoln had changed little from the early postwar years. It was still the quiet, safe city of 165,000 people with a university enrollment of 21,000 students.

Years later, when asked why he chose pharmacy when nobody who knows him thinks it fits his personality, Kerrey said, "I really don't know." In smaller towns, pharmacists are one part scientist, one part caretaker, and several parts small-business owners, all of which would have appealed to a young Bob Kerrey. What he probably had not considered is just how boring the life of a pharmacist could be for someone who also sought adventure. Nancy Kerrey Swarts said she thought her brothers wanted bona fide professions because their father "had the kind of work where you never could say exactly what he did. He was always doing deals."

As a junior Kerrey ran for student council in 1963 and was elected. That same year was a crisis period in South Vietnam. It was a time of many advances in the countryside by the Viet Cong, and the assassination of the South Vietnamese premier, Ngo Dinh Diem. In November of 1963, John F. Kennedy was murdered in Dallas, and Lyndon Johnson was sworn in as President of the United States. The crisis, the decisions about Vietnam, became Johnson's unfortunate legacy.

That fall Kerrey was enrolled in difficult science courses and was fully occupied with studies, extracurricular activities, and his fraternity social life. Kerrey during college was interested in current events, and his fraternity brothers recall their days watching the Cuban Missile Crisis and the Kennedy assassination unfold on television. "Back then, Bob was a card-carrying Goldwater Republican," Frosty Chapman said, "I remember that well."

Still the war in Vietnam was remote, a conflict one read about in the papers or discussed in classes. After Johnson took office in November 1963, a sustained escalation of the war began. At the time, a large segment of the American people simply could not conceive of failing to keep a commitment and losing a war. Even if Johnson had been inclined to disengage, he would have been subject to ridicule in many camps. As each year went by, the United States increased its troop commitment substantially. By the end of Kerrey's junior year, an additional fifty thousand soldiers, sailors, and Marines were being added to the forces every six months.

By his fourth year, 1964–65, it was clear that Kerrey had joined the ranks of college leaders. He was on the student council and he was chosen to be a member of Kappa Psi, an honorary pharmacy fraternity that recognized students for their intellectual achievement. He was also elected to Interfraternity Council, a group that administered the problems and programs of all of the fraternities.

In his senior year, Kerrey was chosen to be one of only ten members of the Innocents, a select group of campus leaders who must maintain a grade point average of 3.3 or above. The Innocents date back to the early history of the University of Nebraska. The organization is secret to the extent that students cannot apply and are chosen only by a unanimous agreement of current members. It is a service fraternity made up of recognized campus leaders who are dedicated to the service of fellow students and the university. Although the word has little or no meaning outside the state of Nebraska, it does have indisputably positive meaning to UN-L students and alumni. Kerrey's induction as an Innocent was fitting because the word accurately sums up his college days.

He had not traveled extensively. He had not been involved in any heartbreaking liaisons (he dated quite a bit but he never suffered a soul-wrenching relationship). Bob Kerrey had moved from the nest of home to the cocoon of a fraternity house without incurring any serious responsibilities. He went from a nurturing life with his mother to being tended to by a fraternity house mother.

After college and his pharmacy days, Kerrey returned to Lincoln one holiday weekend on leave from the Navy. The place seemed calmer even than California, quieter than he remembered. It was a Friday night and he stopped by Duffy's tavern on O Street for a drink. Frosty Chapman, on leave from the Army, had the same idea. "Frosty!" Kerrey roared when he recognized him. "Bob Kerrey!" Chapman yelled back. They looked at each other's cropped haircuts, shorter by far than most of the male patrons'. The specter of Vietnam was looming for both young men.

"We didn't have to say anything to each other. There was this unspoken bond. At that point, things were grim and we didn't know what our fates would be."

Chapter 3

"WALTZING MATILDA"

After convalescing in Philadelphia, a thin and bitter Bob Kerrey returned to Lincoln in December of 1969. The contrast between the full face and the muscled body he had possessed before his enlistment and the image he presented when he returned home was striking. But what was most notable was the change in Kerrey's personality. Family and friends were concerned with the sadness they saw in his eyes and were anxious to support his efforts to rebuild his life. His parents still lived in his boyhood home on Lexington Circle. Kerrey's youngest sister, Nancy, who had not yet graduated from high school, was the only Kerrey child still living there. "We were all a little nervous," Nancy Kerrey Swarts said. "No one knew what he wanted to do."

Bethany neighbors stopped by to visit and talk with him. Larry Price, who had a mangled hand from his World War II service, remembered a time when Kerrey spoke with him about his amputation in which Kerrey asked how long it had taken him to regain his dexterity. Frosty Chapman's mother wrote to him in Sandia Base, New Mexico, telling him that "Bob Kerrey was hurt very badly over in Vietnam. He lost a leg. You should contact him." Old friends sent letters and some stopped over to see if he needed help. After he had been home a while, John

Gottschalk recalled in the *Omaha World-Herald* that "the call went out that Kerrey was in bad shape, not so much physically as mentally. It was one of those calls to drop everything, we needed to get together." Since those days, Kerrey, in speeches, has credited his friends, family, and the government collectively for saving his life. "I was angry and searching. I know I was a very unpleasant person to be around, but I was fortunate that my friends and family stuck by me anyway," Kerrey said in an interview as Governor.

His plans were to remain at his parents' home until he was more comfortable on his prosthesis, then to rent an apartment in Lincoln and find a job. Again, Larry Price helped a Kerrey by giving him work in the management office of his King's restaurant. Kerrey remained there briefly and then worked as a pharmacist at Bryan Memorial Hospital for several months. Again, he found pharmacy unsatisfying and in addition, it was physically painful because of his prosthesis. By this time, he had already had several operations on his leg and his hand, which had received some shrapnel. Kerrey would undergo operations for the next eight years and be fitted for new prostheses each time technology improved prosthetic design. The government paid for all of Kerrey's medical bills, and it covered the cost of his later trips to the Cooper Clinic in Dallas, where Kerrey went for stamina and fitness tests.

Almost immediately Kerrey began to work out, pushing himself to continue the therapy and exercises he had learned in Philadelphia. While working on his physical recovery Kerrey renewed his friendship with Frosty Chapman, who had finished his Army stint. "When I first saw him after his injury, he was still getting used to his prosthesis," Chapman said. One of their first conversations stands out in his memory. Kerrey told Chapman that he had recently been warned by a doctor that he never could drive a stick-shift car. "Bob went right out and bought a car with a stick shift," Chapman said.

"They told him he couldn't run and I remember him distinctly at the YMCA trying to run on an indoor track in absolute agony but not letting anyone know except by his facial expression."

In 1970, Kerrey's prosthesis was not a high-tech, lightweight artificial limb—back then, he strapped on a heavy, inflexible plastic and balsa wood limb everyday. According to California writer Gary Richards, whose leg was amputated above the knee for cancer, until the last five years, amputees attempting strenuous activity were subjected to "blisters and bleeding on their stumps, pinching with each step and fatigue after a stroll around the block."

Chapman recalls urging Kerrey once to take it easy because he was sweating and in great pain. "I stopped him and I said, 'Bob, what are you doing?' and he said, 'Frosty, have you ever had a doctor tell you that you can't run,' and of course, I said, 'No' and he responded, 'Well, I have and I'm not going to let anybody tell me that—I'm gonna run.' And he did." A little more than one decade later, Bob Kerrey ran the Lincoln Marathon. Chapman, who also ran that May of 1981, and who watched a triumphant Kerrey complete the race, could not help but conjure the memories of his buddy's tenuous and tortuous days at the YMCA and reflect on Kerrey's promise that he would indeed run someday.

"Bob would come over every Thursday night and we would lift weights in the basement," Chapman said of Kerrey's post-recovery period in 1970. "Afterwards, we'd drink beer and play cards. You know, Bob says that he was not much fun to be around then, that he was so bitter. That's not true. He was always great to be around and I think it was his spirit of adventure and the fact that he was so incredibly interesting. He enjoyed doing fun things. We had shared a childhood. At that point, he had no medal, nothing, he was just a wounded veteran, hobbling around on one leg."

Kerrey soon found out that he had, indeed, been chosen to receive the Medal of Honor; rumors to that effect had surfaced at the Philadelphia Naval Hospital. Initially, Kerrey had been recommended for the Navy's Silver Star by his SEAL comrade, Mike Ambrose. Later, superior officers, after evaluating his act of heroism, determined that he should be awarded the Medal of Honor, a medal that fourteen Navy men received during the Vietnam War. Because the Medal of Honor is technically granted by writ of Congress, it is called the Congressional Medal of Honor, but peers and superior officers choose recipients and the President actually makes the award.

Kerrey, however, was troubled by the news. His scrutiny of the war during time spent in Philadelphia and the ensuing months at home in Lincoln had dramatically altered his feelings about American policy in Vietnam. He thought seriously about refusing it. The whole concept of a medal was anathema to him at that point in his life. Kerrey began asking intimates whether they thought he should accept it and go to the award ceremony, given the depth of his antiwar sentiment. Kerrey did not talk about his war experience, but he talked a great deal about accepting the medal and, from those discussions, intimates realized the intense pain he was experiencing.

"He never talked about his feelings about Vietnam," Nancy Kerrey Swarts said, "except he talked about the Medal of Honor. He did not want to accept it. I remember him saying, 'When a man loses a life over there, nobody should walk away from it and get a medal. Nobody alive should get a medal when all these guys are dying over there'—he couldn't understand it." His family urged him to accept it. James Kerrey, a World War II veteran, knew of the medal's significance, but his son did not fully appreciate it then. One Medal of Honor recipient reflected that you know about the medal but that it is impossible to really *know* about the medal until you receive one—that the respect a recipient is accorded is overwhelming.

To put his Medal of Honor, our nation's highest military award, in some historical perspective, consider that General Douglas MacArthur, a hardened combat veteran, pouted for years that he was only given the second-highest medal, the Distinguished Service Cross, for leading "over the top" charges against the Germans in World War I. President Truman's remark—"I'd rather earn one of these [a Medal of Honor] than be President of the United States"—is also revealing.

A few individuals familiar with the medal's history shared their knowledge with Kerrey and told him of the incredible honor he would be passing up if he refused. His SEAL buddies, most of whom had learned of the news, encouraged him to accept it in the name of his fallen comrades. One persuasive argument, to do it for his teammates, made by a former SEAL instructor, convinced a hesitant Kerrey. That rationale propelled him to Washington to face a President with whose policies he thoroughly disagreed: It would be a tribute to the men with whom he had served, both those who made it back and those who didn't. Today, he is not ambivalent about the honor. In an interview with the *Wall Street Journal*, Kerrey said, "People feel proud of me because of that and I don't have any misgivings about people feeling that pride."

Ten days before Kerry was to receive his medal, four students at Kent State University were gunned down by National Guardsmen who panicked during an antiwar protest on the Midwestern campus. In the week after the deaths, Nebraskans stepped up their antiwar efforts. On May 6, more than ten thousand students streamed into the Nebraska sports colliseum and voted for a three-day strike. Kerrey supported them, but one week later he left Lincoln to pick up his medal.

Navy personnel arranged the Kerreys' trip to Washington, D.C. As is customary, the entire family was accorded first-class treatment throughout their stay in the nation's capital. Limousines were dispatched and they were picked up in Lincoln, driven to the airport, and again picked up in Washington, where they were squired around the city.

Nancy Kerrey Swarts recalled, "From the very moment we walked out the door to the very end, the Navy escorted us everywhere. It seemed like Bob got a lot of press and that people were really interested in it. In D.C., they taxied us all over and wined and dined us. They took us to the nicest restaurants, and our hotel rooms had baskets of fruit and flowers. We got to tour the city. I got to shake President Nixon's hand. We all did. It was a moment to remember. Bob had a lot of fun on the trip. Once he got into something, he always did, but the purpose of the trip still bothered him." And so, on May 14, 1970, a solemn and troubled Robert Kerrey was presented with the blue-and-bronze medal in a White House ceremony.

In Lew Puller's masterful autobiography, *Fortunate Son*, he tells about a party he and his wife, Toddy, and former Philadelphia Naval Hospital roommate Jim Crotty threw for Kerrey. "Bob came up to Philadelphia after the ceremony. . . . Bob regaled us with White House anecdotes, including comments on President Nixon's bad breath and Secretary of Defense Melvin Laird's diminutive size, but I noticed that he did not allow his medal and its silk-lined box out of his sight for the entire night. . . . The medal had elevated Kerrey from the ranks of ordinary mortals, and I remember thinking that it could eventually prove to be a heavy burden to carry through life."

And indeed, men who have been awarded (they recoil over the use of the word *won*) the Medal of Honor often speak with other recipients of the unusual burdens they bear. In a 1985 history of the medal, *Above and Beyond*, an essayist writes:

> *The spotlight of the medal can also expose the human shortcomings of ordinary men when they are thrust suddenly into the extraordinary role of war hero and public figure. Some have broken under pressures, the demands and the intrusions that fame can bring. The Medal of Honor can be, in the words of one recipient, "a lot harder to wear than it is to earn."*

Puller went on to write that

> *before he had actually received any of his medals, he had made a trip back to Nebraska. He had worn his uniform because it got him a reduced air rate, and he had considered borrowing my ribbons to wear. At our party, as I thought about the incident in light of what Bob Kerrey had just experienced, I had to smile, but beneath the smile I realized that we both were searching for any evidence that might validate our war experience and the terrible beating we had taken.*

Kerrey returned from Washington, D.C., a war hero. People from Bethany came by to congratulate him. Gubernatorial candidate James Exon sent him a letter of congratulations. Members of his family's church posted notice of his award in the bulletin, and various civic and community groups requested speaking engagements. Lincoln newspapers ran a large photograph of him and excerpted portions of his citation.

Still, Vietnam recipients of the Medal of Honor did not receive the unconditional adulation given to those who were awarded the medal for service in other wars, most especially World War II. Kerrey's medal was given for valor in Vietnam which, in 1970, was an unfinished, unpopular, and unexamined war. In the aftermath of the 1991 Gulf War victory, Senator Robert Kerrey reflected on the difference in the public attitude toward the Desert Storm veterans. "There were no homecomings for us," he said. In a January 6, 1991, interview with the *Los Angeles Times*, Senator Kerrey said, "I must tell you that even in my case [a Medal of Honor holder] there was no parade. . . . Nobody wanted their picture taken with the Medal of Honor recipient in 1970. The only congratulatory letter I got was from a guy running in a gubernatorial primary."

Nevertheless, pockets of people in Lincoln were extremely impressed with the fact that a hometown boy had been awarded the Medal of Honor, and they told him so. As the years unfolded, as the wounds of war healed, Nebraskans, especially Kerrey's peers, many of whom could not summon interest in the medal while young men still served in Southeast Asia, began to view his achievement in a new light. Kerrey, like most Medal of Honor holders, did not bring up the medal in casual conversations, but it is an honor that people talked about and knew that he had received. People in Lincoln who had never heard of the Kerreys knew there was a young man from Northeast who still lived in town and who had been awarded the Medal of Honor.

The time between his return from the medal ceremony in Washington in 1970 until his marriage in early 1974 was a time of intense emotional struggle for Kerrey. In Philadelphia he had become a different person, and throughout the next four years Kerrey worked to reconcile his newfound philosophical and humanistic yearnings with his old self and his familiar surroundings.

Kerrey became intellectually driven and devoured all he could on history, politics, and literature. He knew that he had glided through college without taking up the intellectual opportunities available on campus. He wanted to return to school armed with this new awareness, and broaden his historical perspective, previously limited by his right-leaning conservative upbringing. He was a born-again idealist looking for a vision.

Kerrey also decided to work against the war in Vietnam. For the next four years he was active in the antiwar movement, but always in a somewhat erratic way. He was single-minded and aimless at once. He was not like activists who put their lives on hold during the war, and yet he worked hard to seek its end. Frosty Chapman recalled, "He was obsessed by the war, in a way, but he was unfocused. And there was always this playful fun side of him that was totally separate from his Vietnam activities. If you talked about Vietnam, he was very, very serious, and his face would just cloud over. He would change instantly—we'd be having a good time and then if he thought of Vietnam, it would be like a switch and you could see dark thoughts of the war dominating his mind."

One of the first places disenchanted veterans headed to in Lincoln during the Vietnam War was the University of Nebraska–Lincoln, in particular, the student union. Kerrey gravitated there shortly after arriving home. Located in the center of the campus, directly across from Frat Rat Row, the student union saw great activity during the late sixties and early seventies. Hundreds of students converged there every day to follow the war on television, discuss it with other students and professors, plan antiwar activity, and generally hang out.

By 1970, students at UN-L mirrored young men and women in other cities. Many were virulently against the war; others were mildly opposed—only a small fraction of students actually supported U.S. policy. The union building seemed to draw liberal students whose interest in Southeast Asia was as great as their interest in academia, and activists practically lived in the building during the height of the antiwar movement. UN-L alumni who knew the union then hardly recognize the place today with its fast-food outlets, electronic banking windows, and snappy gift and book stores. Back then, more conservative students often decried the fact that the Union had been taken over by "hippies"—it was a time of long hair, short tempers, and strong passions.

Kerrey sought out kindred souls at UN-L and met a senior English professor, June Levine, the wife of David Levine, who before his death in 1976 was the chairman of the university's psychology department. Levine recalled, "Bob, at that point, was very much at loose ends. He did not know what he wanted to do. That's the Bob I really knew." Periodically, Kerrey would pop into her office to see her, and usually he spoke of his desire to write. One day he questioned whether she would take him on as an independent student in creative writing. Customarily, Levine requests samples of a student's writing before she agrees to such work, but in Kerrey's case she made an exception; she knew he needed a boost. She thought his subject matter would be compelling and she could help him polish it. She made a suggestion that he write about his war experience because that was the cause of his turmoil, but he responded that he wasn't ready to do that. Five years later, when Kerrey and Professor Levine met in the air on a trip to the West Coast, Kerrey brought up writing again and Levine questioned him. "Bob, years ago you told me you weren't ready to write about your war experience—do you think you're ready to write about that now?" He responded, "I've been writing and I don't like it, I save some, I tear some up. I don't like it."

But one month after he was in Levine's office making the request for independent study, she received a call from him. Levine recalls their conversation clearly. "'I'm in San Francisco, June,' he announced. 'I'm thinking of going to San Francisco State College, taking courses there; they have a good arts program.'" Kerrey had traveled to San Francisco in the summer of 1970 to stay with Bethany boyhood friend Peter Darlington, who was a graduate student at SFSC. One month later, Levine received another call from Kerrey and he opened the conversation with, "Well, now I'm at Stanford and I'm thinking of taking an MBA." Levine responded, "An MBA, Bob? You want to go into the business world?" He said, "Well, I'd like to reform the business world from within. I think if you want to have a reforming impact, you have to do it from the inside." Levine wished him well and hung up the phone, assuming she would not see or hear from Kerrey for a while.

Not long after that, he was back in Lincoln permanently. No Stanford, no San Francisco State, although Kerrey did attend liberal arts classes at the University of California at Berkeley for a time before returning home in the spring of 1971. He missed Nebraska. He wanted to go back to a place where everybody knew his name, as the song says. Although Kerrey had let his hair grow from his SEAL days and he sported a mustache, he was not a hippie and he felt lifetimes removed from the rebellious radicals who dominated the California campus scene back then.

"One of the appeals of Berkeley in '71 for me was that it was a quieter campus than most," Kerrey told an interviewer. "Believe it or not, it was. I was very angry and not in the best condition physically. I didn't know what I was doing. I thought people on both sides of the Vietnam issue were rejecting me, but the truth of it was I just didn't give a damn about either side. I was in a lot of physical pain. I'd just been fitted with an artificial limb and gone through a number of operations."

Once again, Kerrey headed to the UN-L campus. Throughout the early seventies, antiwar speakers were featured at the student union, where they spoke to overflow crowds of students, parents, legislators, and anyone else interested in the effort to end the war in Vietnam. All of the leading national antiwar protesters, from Dr. Benjamin Spock to Tom Hayden, traveled to Lincoln to fire up the cornfed kids of the Great Plains who were as angered by the war in Vietnam as the students of Berkeley or Boston.

During this time, New York Congressman Allard Lowenstein made one such appearance before a packed crowd of rapt students. Lowenstein was seeking to register eighteen-year-olds to vote so that their young voices, protesting the war in Vietnam, would be heard at the ballot box. One listener who was inspired by what he heard was Bob Kerrey. Lowenstein, known for his passionate speaking style, urged the eager students before him to participate in the process that had only recently enfranchised young voters. Kerrey was moved. He would often tell friends that Lowenstein was a seminal influence in his political development, and he once called him "the finest patriot I ever met." Kerrey signed up with him and spent time on the project, which mobilized legions of young voters across the country. He also campaigned for Lowenstein-backed candidates in other states, including Minnesota and California. Kerrey set up meetings with UN-L campus leaders to encourage them to form campus voter registration drives and to help orchestrate the campaigns. By this time, in 1971, Kerrey was at least six years older than the average student.

Steve Fowler, who would later be one of the architects of Kerrey's successful gubernatorial campaign, recalled his first meeting with him when Kerrey was promoting Lowenstein's agenda and criticizing Nixon's foreign policy. "Kerrey's argument was more that it was bad strategy, rather than a mistake, to get involved in the conflict. There were some people who were strongly anti-American and Kerrey wasn't approaching it from that point of view but just from the angle that he'd been there, saw that it was a wrong strategy, and didn't believe that we could succeed." Down the line, Kerrey would say that he was uneasy with many protestors and much of the stridency of the antiwar movement because it felt antiveteran to him.

The fact that Kerrey had served in Vietnam and had turned against the war gave him immeasurable credibility, and gradually he realized that he should begin speaking out against the war. "As soon as he was pretty much healed up, he started doing speeches. He got a lot of requests for speeches from churches and groups like that; all different kinds of groups wanted him. It seemed like he had become pretty popular," Nancy Kerrey Swarts said. His disillusionment with U.S. war policy was full-blown at that point, and he put his name out in Lincoln as someone who would be willing to lend his luster to the antiwar movement. "In those early years back in Nebraska, I developed an anger that persists today at a government which deceived all of us," Kerrey said in his 1982 gubernatorial speech. "A government which was so concerned with getting reelected that it would not trust us with the truth. A government which instead chose to deceive us and to get us to fight amongst ourselves."

Professor June Levine shared the podium with Kerrey several times in those days. "It was so important to have a veteran and a veteran with a Medal of Honor talking against the war. Later, of course, this would come back and haunt Bob when he ran for Governor. The Republicans tried to make ammunition out of his antiwar days."

Periodically, peaceful demonstrators gathered at Lincoln's Terminal Building at 9th and O Streets, the site of the state selective service office. Once, Bob Kerrey gave an impassioned speech there criticizing U.S. policy. One Nebraskan who listened to him was Dan Ladely, curator of the Sheldon Film Theater located on campus. Ladely recalled that Kerrey's performance was compelling, not because of his personal biography, which he shared with the crowd, but because he delivered an impressive speech. "I was a conscientious objector and here was a person who was a Medal of Honor winner who had been in the war and who was now making a very rational, very good argument against U.S. policy. It was one of the two best arguments against the war that I had ever heard anyone make. I went up to him afterward and introduced myself and told him I was moved by the speech, and he was very friendly. He had charisma back then, but it was his argument that was persuasive." The two men gradually developed a friendship that continues.

Kerrey was committed to the antiwar movement but searching for some structure in his life. Before, Bob Kerrey had always had a project, whether a college crusade, a vacation, or the mission of the SEALS. Suddenly, he had no sustaining interest other than the war, and there weren't enough rallies in a given month to keep him busy. He did return to the East Coast during this time to visit his friend Lew Puller and other amputees. He felt a loyalty and linkage to his fellow amputees. In *Fortunate Son*, Puller, who lost both legs and parts of his hands, wrote: "Crotty, and Kerrey, like me, . . . had arrived at the hospital flat on their backs and almost totally helpless, yet each was now walking. I understood that my wounds were more extensive than those of any other officer . . . but it was still demoralizing. . . ."

Kerrey routinely visited Lincoln's veterans hospital and spent time talking with patients and posing for pictures with his medal. Chapman recalled Kerrey often speaking of his visits with disabled vets as "extremely rewarding." He added, "Kerrey was drawn to those men." After Philadelphia, Kerrey became "a part of other people's lives," as he told the *Wall Street Journal.*

He also worked for civic organizations. In 1971, he signed on to work for the Easter Seals and worked as a fund-raiser for five months. He was instrumental in the development of a camp for handicapped children near Agnew, Nebraska. In an interview with the *Lincoln Journal* that year, Kerrey said, "You can't legislate something like that [the camp], you just have to begin to do it."

Kerrey discovered that he possessed the rare gift of giving real comfort to people in pain. Later, as Governor, he would quietly visit amputee victims, telephone new amputees, buy prosthetic devices for the underprivileged, and give special counsel to young male amputees who often felt that their days as virile men were over. In essence, Kerrey would tell them not to worry—it doesn't matter to women. When he was Governor, one of the legislature's leading lobbyists, a Republican, lost a leg, and Kerrey's personal contact thoroughly buoyed his spirits. Kerrey always made his visits without fanfare. Still, hospital visits and antiwar activities took only a fraction of his time, and he bounced around trying to figure out what to do with the rest of it.

Professor Levine remembered a time when Kerrey showed up unannounced at a film class she was teaching at Farmhouse fraternity on UN-L's east campus. Kerrey, who was not enrolled in the class, simply sat in on the lecture, then lingered afterward and invited himself over to her house to talk. He followed her in his car, a small yellow convertible, but didn't arrive at her house for a long time. "I got a speeding ticket on the way," he said when he finally showed up. Always restless. The incidents with Professor Levine were typical of Kerrey during the drifting days between his release from the Philadelphia Naval Hospital and his marriage and restaurant ventures.

"One day you'd run into him and he'd say he was learning to play the harmonica. The next time you'd hear that he was going to go to business school; then he'd tell you he had decided to become a teacher," Frosty Chapman recalled.

Kerrey continued his involvement in Lincoln's antiwar movement and became an active member of Nebraskans for Peace. In the spring of 1971, the Nebraska legislature had voted against a resolution that would have granted a public hearing on the Vietnam War. Kerrey was incensed and, with the help of activist Leroy Shuster, drafted an editorial that was printed in the campus newspaper, the *Daily Nebraskan*:

> *An apparent anomaly of the Vietnam War is that Americans acquiesced so easily in the demands of their national government. If federal agents came into Nebraskan homes and took our sons to fight a war, we would probablyobject. . . .*
>
> *However, the federal government takes our young men under the guise of the draft, and selective service has been so steeped in patriotism we hardly dare resist for fear of being called a traitor. . . . The great physical distance between us and the war, the patriotic slogans, and the memory of pre–World War II aggressor activities have also contributed to our having been so easily persuaded that our country was justified in its actions.*
>
> *The American people have been isolated and have become little more than spectators to this war. If we try to get into the game as individuals, our energy is quickly consumed in a confrontation with federal forces. In addition, the physical and emotional gap between us and the fighting tends to prevent a direct association of the war's horrors with our actions.*
>
> *Legislative Resolution 32 would have accomplished two things. First, it would have enabled Nebraskans to overcome the predicament of the individual when he tries to confront something as large and complex as our federal bureaucracy. When this state agreed to abide by our national Constitution we did not sign away our right to disagree with federal policy either singly or as a group.*
>
> *Perhaps more importantly the resolution would have allowed for a public hearing. The most effective way of combating the tendency to forget and to ignore what is going on in Vietnam is through open discussion. We can bring the war closer to us and thus help us to understand*

*it better only if we force ourselves not to tire of talking
about it.*

On May 5, 1971, two days after his editorial was printed,
Kerrey appeared at a major antiwar rally scheduled to protest
the legislature's actions. He had agreed to present a speech.
Hundreds of Nebraskans opposed to the war marched to the
state capitol and gathered on the steps to listen to the speakers.
One was Terry Carpenter, an aging and venerable Vietnam War
critic from Scottsbluff and one of the legislature's most impassioned opponents of Nixon's policies. Another was Ernie Chambers, a young, controversial, T-shirt-clad, black legislator from
Omaha who needles Nebraskans with summations like "Nebraska, number one in football, number *nothing* in anything
else."

Eventually, it came time for Kerrey's speech. He was described as a Medal of Honor holder who now opposed the war.
Protesters in the audience soon saw two men heading toward the
microphones with one man stepping up to it. Those unfamiliar
with Kerrey assumed that the man at the mike was Kerrey until
they realized what he was saying: Kerrey had recently undergone
oral surgery, and his mouth was wired shut. The man at the mike
would read his speech for him. (Earlier Kerrey had undergone
functional tooth alignment surgery, the result of which was a less
prominent chin.) Omahan John Green recalled the speech as eloquent and wished that Kerrey had been able to deliver it himself. Kerrey's spokesman referred to "the honor which results in
having had the courage to admit the extent of your errors."
Green did not hear of Bob Kerrey again until a decade later, in
1982, when Kerrey stood inside the capitol building and announced that he was running for Governor.

During his antiwar days, Kerrey widened his circle of friends
to include left-leaning, liberal professors and students, groups
with which he would not have connected were it not for Vietnam. Later, as he began his political quest, he gradually distanced himself from these activists, humanists, and leftists who
had been the support group for his transition from SEAL to deal
maker.

PART II

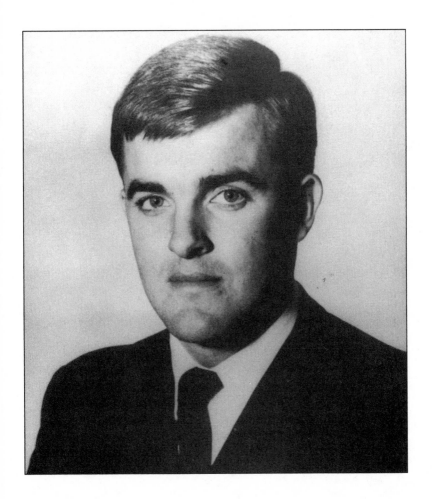

Chapter 4

MARRIAGE, CHILDREN, AND GRANDMOTHER'S

That Bob Kerrey would be drawn to the world of business is not surprising, given the influence of his father. It was because of business that James Kerrey, an orphan from Chicago, could prosper and provide seven children with a solid middle-class, all-American upbringing. Nancy Kerrey Swarts said: "My dad had meetings all the time and he was working all these business deals. He never stopped thinking about business, and guys were always coming around at dinnertime or in the evening or on the weekends. Bob and Dad were kind of similar that way."

The business scene was the primary environment in which Bob Kerrey was raised. By the time his mother, Elinor, returned to college to complete her master's degree, Kerrey was a young man. After selling off his lumber and hardware businesses, the senior Kerrey had a decade-long relationship with Larry Price during the height of his King's Food Host USA expansion. "Jim loved to put together deals and he was very good at it," according to Price, who employed Kerrey as an officer in the company. Along with his father, Bob Kerrey watched as Larry Price became a millionaire and the kids were reared knowing that the restaurant world could make you rich. James Kerrey always wanted to be rich.

He would die, however, owing bank loans that Bob Kerrey quickly paid off. In an interview shortly after his father's death in 1988, Kerrey spoke of his father's generosity and said that he died with so little because "he gave money away, he'd give you the shirt off his back."

Nineteen seventy-two was a year of great change for Kerrey. The idea of opening a restaurant in Omaha was broached by Kerrey's brother-in-law, Dean Rasmussen, who had been managing a King's restaurant in Indiana for two years. Married to the eldest Kerrey daughter, Jessie, Rasmussen was ready to open his own restaurant and wanted to try his luck in the western Omaha suburbs. Rasmussen had learned the restaurant business from the ground up, having worked at King's since high school.

For teenagers growing up in Nebraska during the sixties and seventies, King's was an institution. For some Lincoln kids, King's was a way of life and Northeast students felt a special kinship with the chain since founder Price hired more students from his part of town than any other. Long before the domination of the golden arches, Nebraska kids flocked to the neon crowns—the logo of King's.

Rasmussen planned to ask Larry Price to cosign a start-up loan. Later, Price recalled that he didn't even know of Bob Kerrey's involvement in the project in the beginning when he agreed to sign a note but that when he heard about it, the idea made sense to him. "I knew Bob was really smart and that he needed something to do, some direction," Price said. Rasmussen also felt that Kerrey would be a natural in the business and he was eager to have a family member as a partner.

Earlier, Kerrey thought of opening a pharmacy. Although he had found being a pharmacist unsatisfying and painful two years earlier in Lincoln, he thought that he could hire pharmacists to work for him. Also, by this time he felt more comfortable standing for long periods on his prosthesis and more confident about his physical challenge in general. Kerrey was tired of working for companies and wanted to do something concrete for himself.

Rasmussen and Kerrey made tentative plans to open both businesses but gave up on the pharmacy when a commissioned study showed that west Omaha already had plenty. Kerrey moved to Omaha and landed a job as a part-time pharmacist at University Hospital, where he would remain for nine months while he worked on the restaurant.

Both Kerrey and Rasmussen were aware of the many success stories of Nebraska restaurant entrepreneurs. They knew the restaurant business was a roller coaster ride, but they also knew that if owners were willing to hang on, the rewards could be considerable. In addition to their familiarity with King's, they were aware of Omaha wunderkind Willie Thiesen, who, during the 1970s, parlayed a little pizza dive into the trendsetting and highly lucrative Godfather's Pizza. Omaha and Lincoln were filled with other no-money-to-millionaire restaurant success stories, and Kerrey and Rasmussen were ready to add another one to the list.

Kerrey and Rasmussen held many meetings to discuss the details of their new enterprise. They bandied about names for the new place and finally settled on Grandmother's Skillet.

Since Rasmussen was the real restaurant pro, the plan was for him to be the detail man and Kerrey to be the big-picture man. As it turned out, however, Kerrey showed a flair for administration, just as he had earlier with the SEALS. Later, in speeches as Governor, Kerrey repeatedly complained about the amount of paperwork required by the government to run small businesses.

In November 1972, Kerrey voted for President just as construction was beginning on his new restaurant. He was still a registered Republican and he was still intermittently active in the antiwar movement. In January 1973, a long-sideburned and intense-looking Kerrey appeared at a town meeting on Vietnam filmed by the Nebraska Educational Television Network and broadcast nationwide. He was interviewed by public television moderator Jim Lehrer, who asked, "Do you think this war was worth the cost?" "No," Kerrey responded. "Do you have any personal bitterness about the price you paid?" Lehrer questioned. "Right now I don't," Kerrey said, "but there are times when I do." Kerrey went on, "At the same time, certainly, there are some good things that it did for me, but the good things aren't worth it. I've seen people get those things without paying those kinds of dues."

With the Vietnam War winding down, Grandmother's opened in Ralston, an Omaha suburb, at 82nd and L Streets in June 1973, and was successful almost from the start. Restaurants come and go continually in Omaha and Lincoln and there certainly was no guarantee that Rasmussen and Kerrey's would make it, but both men were determined. They worked over every detail and told their ideas to friends and family members, encouraging anyone who was interested to make suggestions. Both men solicited advice from Larry Price, who passed on what words of wisdom he felt he could offer. James Kerry also worked tirelessly to help his son and son-in-law become established.

Kerrey had a hand in every facet of the restaurant and he is fond of saying that he did everything from wash dishes to pay vendors. In fact, so much of his energy was taken up by his restaurant ventures that he was fired from his hospital pharmacy job for missing work.

As it turned out, Kerrey was energized by the restaurant business. He finally had found a project tailor-made for his workaholic tendencies. One friend remembered how animated he was when talking about the restaurant, and how he loved to go to other eating establishments and see what the competition was doing.

One of Kerrey's strong points as a restaurant owner was his affability. He had the ability to motivate people who worked for him. He also liked being the boss. Since high school, Kerrey had exhibited a preference for hierarchical relationships in which he was at the top of the hierarchy.

"I thoroughly enjoy what I do," Kerrey wrote later, "recruiting and working with partners and managers who set difficult goals for themselves and can inspire and motivate the people with whom they work; being profitable, having learned how to conserve my own resources and save; and investing those savings in Nebraska to create jobs for people I admire." Today, Kerrey holds a 35 percent partnership in the enterprise, which in 1992 includes eight restaurants and three health clubs.

When the restaurant began to show a profit, one friend recalled Kerrey slamming his fist down on a table, settling into a chair, and announcing how well the business was doing. "I'm going to be a millionaire soon," Kerrey crowed.

About the time that Grandmother's opened, Kerrey interrupted a relationship with Lincoln native Beverly Defnall, a fellow Northeast High School graduate whom he had been dating off and on for nearly two years. Some mutual friends had introduced them during her senior year of college at the University of Nebraska–Lincoln, where she earned a degree in elementary education in 1971. After graduation, she taught school in Louisville, Nebraska, a small town outside Omaha. Kerrey was still living in Lincoln when they began their relationship. She knew from her first formal date that she enjoyed the company of Bob Kerrey. Like most other Northeast residents, Bev knew the Kerrey name, had graduated from the same schools, and grew up in north Lincoln not far from the Kerrey home.

Bev, a statuesque, raven-haired, strong-tempered young woman, felt from the start that Kerrey was special and she appreciated him most for his sense of humor. Before their marriage, she told Nancy Kerrey Swarts that "he is always so much fun to be with," although his levity ended when serious subjects came up. He remained silent about his Vietnam experience, hiding his personal feelings about the war throughout their four-year marriage.

They dated off and on for a while and Bev let it be known that she was ready to get married, but Bob let it be known he wasn't. They broke up, and she quit her job and moved to California. For years, Bev had been interested in the prospects of a modeling or acting career and she decided the West Coast would be the place to make a stab at it. Kerrey telephoned her periodically. Career opportunities moved slowly with her at first. She realized the competition was steep and she was beginning to feel discouraged when the possibility appeared of a modeling job with a major cosmetics company. Bev always had been interested in clothes, makeup, and her appearance, and people had been telling her since childhood that she should pursue some kind of modeling career.

During her stay in California, she returned home once to Lincoln, traveling back with James and Elinor Kerrey, who had been there on a visit. Bubbling with enthusiasm about Bob all the way home, Bev talked openly about her affection for him and her eagerness to see her sometime boyfriend. The foursome arrived at the Kerreys' Capitol Beach home at 2020 Surfside Drive, a home they had moved into just a short time earlier.

Bob walked in, greeted his girlfriend with a "Hi, Bev," and breezed past her into the kitchen to talk restaurant business with his father. A disappointed Bev grimaced at the Kerrey's youngest daughter, Nancy, who recalled: "And we both had been really looking forward to seeing our guys again."

As young lovers often are, however, Bev was blind to his faults. She ignored the signs of Kerrey's workaholism and instead preferred to think about his magnetism. Bev found his charisma evident in the early days of their courtship. "And Bob really enjoyed being around Bev," Frosty Chapman recalled. "I remember one time they were over at our house and he was being real playful with her and you could just tell there was great affection."

The two were married at four o'clock on a Saturday afternoon, April 6, 1974, at Lincoln's First Baptist Church, across from the Nebraska state capitol. Bev immersed herself in traditional first-year marriage activities—decorating, organizing, and entertaining. Their first child, Benjamin was born November 18 of that year, seven months after the marriage. They lived in Ralston so they could be close to their flagship restaurant.

Kerrey joined the chamber of commerce and registered to vote as a Republican, as he had done since age twenty-one. In a state with blurred party identification, it is not uncommon for Nebraskans to vacillate between parties. They never have held party-switching against politicians, as is evidenced by the career of former Senator Edward Zorinsky. After being frozen out by his fellow Republicans, Zorinsky switched parties and won a U.S. Senate seat in 1976 as a Democrat. During his Senate career, Zorinsky threatened to rejoin the Republican Party several times when he was struggling with the Democratic hierarchy.

Years later, in explaining his party switch, Kerrey said: "I was registered as a Republican, but I was a functional Democrat." University of Nebraska political scientist Robert Sittig states that when Kerrey was first confronted in public on the issue, "he had good political instincts. . . . He said he was a Democrat for quite some time before he officially changed."

The Bob Kerrey that Beverly Defnall fell in love with was neither a millionaire nor a politician. In the mid-seventies, he was a struggling and ambitious businessman, and she was a teacher who still harbored other ambitions. When she married him, she loved him for what he was; as yet, there was no hint of what he would become or whether she would fulfill her dreams. Years later, she would bristle over a *People* magazine article about her ex-husband and Debra Winger, that she felt cavalierly dismissed her as a "former schoolteacher."

Stresses in the marriage appeared almost immediately. With a child during the first year of their union and a restaurant business in its infancy, the young couple found little time for themselves during the early stages of their relationship. In an interview with the *Omaha World-Herald*, Beverly (now Mrs. Bev Higby) confided that Kerrey spent part of their honeymoon night tending to his restaurant and that she sensed then that there would be trouble ahead. There was.

Overseeing a restaurant, even once it is running smoothly, exacts a tremendous toll on families, but the burdens placed on people in the initial stages of start-up are the most taxing. They were attempting to tend to a new eatery, a new marriage, and a new family—a task that would be formidable for even the most committed of partners.

Throughout his life, Bob Kerrey had observed his father, a consumed worker, and he emulated that behavior. "Dad didn't ever stop thinking about work," Nancy Kerrey Swarts said. Bob Kerrey wouldn't either. Bev became increasingly distraught with his sixteen-hour days. She complained, but her outbursts did not alter her husband's behavior; it only increased the chasm that was rapidly opening between the two of them. Later, she would argue that he was doing what he had to do to make the business successful and that she didn't realize the necessity of his obsession at the time. She would fix meals—he wouldn't show up. She would make plans with another couple—he would run off to the restaurant for business. He would say he was coming home at a certain time and come in hours later. Nancy Kerrey Swarts observed, "At one point, they had a lot in common, but Bob can be hard to talk to and I think they drifted apart."

The Kerreys tried for two years in Ralston to make a go of the union while Kerrey was tethered to his restaurant. Marian Price, a protective longtime friend and neighbor of Kerrey and a sister-in-law to Larry Price, said: "Bev was happy as a mother and with him. . . . I know how these men just propel themselves into business trying to get ahead and always thinking of business even when they are home. . . . They had just started theirs and were talking about a chain—Bob Kerrey had a lot of big plans and he really threw himself into his work. Being a restaurateur myself and knowing what it can do to your family and your marriage, I related to Bob's side of it, but yet I had empathy and sympathy for Bev."

Adding to his restaurant duties, Kerrey became involved in politics in Ralston. Earlier, he and Rasmussen had befriended Ralston City Council President Jerry Koch, whose support they had enlisted. Before construction could begin on Grandmother's, they needed a zoning change that was spearheaded and approved by the Ralston council at Koch's urging. Kerrey enjoyed Koch's company and said he should run for higher office. In 1974, Koch told Kerrey he was running for the Nebraska legislature and asked him to chair his race. Kerrey agreed and immediately set out raising money, which he was well positioned to do as a member of the restaurant community.

Again, friends recalled Kerrey and Koch brainstorming about strategy at Grandmother's during the days of the campaign. Koch won. Kerrey was elated and first began to consider the idea of running for public office himself. It was during the Koch campaign that many Omahans, who were unfamiliar with Bob Kerrey, first became aware of him. When Koch was settled in at the Nebraska legislature, Kerrey spent time in his office. One Koch legislative staffer said, "Bob Kerrey was always hanging around wanting to use the telephone. He had long hair and seemed serious. I remember when I heard he was running for

Governor, I couldn't believe it, I thought, No way will that man be Governor."

Steve Fowler, who would be Kerrey's gubernatorial campaign architect, recalls meeting Kerrey in Lincoln at the Nebraska Club, where Senator Koch brought together some state legislators and members of the Ralston chamber of commerce. Kerrey was low-key and did not come across as politically ambitious, and in fact stood out in contrast to Koch, who by background was a coach and administrator and related to people in a gregarious, back-slapping manner. It was clear from that meeting that Koch had great admiration for Kerrey. And later, when Kerrey captured the governorship, though Koch did not claim credit, he was proud of the fact that somebody he had helped introduce to politics would do so well.

Six months after Koch made it into the legislature, on May 6, 1975 at 4:35 P.M. a tornado touched down in Omaha and cut a wide swath through the city. Three people were killed. Another one hundred forty-one were injured and more than five hundred residences and buildings were destroyed. Grandmother's Skillet was one of the razed structures. Omaha residents walked out of their homes late that afternoon to a jagged ribbon of destruction that cut from one end of the city to the other. Damage was estimated in the hundreds of millions of dollars. Kerrey still speaks about the tornado. In one of his earliest gubernatorial fund-raising letters, he wrote: "The Omaha tornado went through our neighborhood and destroyed the building. Completely. At the time, questions arose about the possibility and worth of rebuilding. We decided to go ahead and four months later were back in business."

Kerrey's first campaign brochure shows a picture of two men inspecting a demolished building at the top of a page, and the bottom picture shows a spanking new Grandmother's.

In August 1976, the Kerreys' second child, Lindsey, was born. In 1991, Kerrey would tell an interviewer that "watching Ben and Lindsey be born was the most powerful thing that ever happened to me. They made me want to live again." Shortly after her birth, the Kerreys were ready to return to Lincoln for new restaurant opportunities. Kerrey was anxious to see if a second Grandmother's in his hometown would work, and he envisioned using his children's own grandmother, Elinor, more in the business. Since the beginning of the restaurant endeavors, Elinor Kerrey had advised her son and Rasmussen and had helped them with recipes and food practices. She confided in friends that she was grateful that her third son seemed to have found a career that excited him. Elinor was also thrilled to have new grandchildren and she was happy when the family moved back to Lincoln so she could see Ben and Lindsey more often.

Kerrey knew that his mother was close to retiring from the University of Nebraska–Lincoln, where she had been a home economics instructor for more than a decade. Kerrey and Rasmussen were planning to have her head up a demonstration kitchen for all Grandmother's restaurant workers. But before that idea could be executed, Elinor's health would decline.

By the time the Kerreys arrived back in Lincoln, the marriage also was seriously strained. Their problems were evident to family members, but the two attempted to put on a harmonious face, especially for Elinor. They knew she would be saddened by a divorce, so they decided to remain together for her sake. "The divorce didn't happen until after Mom's death," Nancy Kerrey Swarts said. "They stuck it out until Mom died." But Elinor sensed their troubles and confided in Marian Price: "I know something is wrong between Bev and Bob, and I wish they would tell me about it." Kerrey, especially, did not want to disappoint his mother, who, by 1977, was in declining health after an earlier diagnosis of Lou Gehrig's disease. She was confined to a wheelchair for nearly one year before she died on March 29, 1978, after refusing all artificial life-support.

For her funeral, Kerrey composed a tribute that he delivered, typed, and presented to friends and family in attendance. It read:

> *She was sweet, our mother. Like a dew covered flower or freshly ripened fruit.*
>
> *She was tender and loving like a selfless saint. She was vulnerable and open like a fawn in the forest or a new born calf.*

She was fresh and clean like the woods after a spring rain or the unexpected smell of pine.

She was mysterious and complex like the deep and dark oceans, or the infinite heavens.

She was steady and dependable like gravity. She pulled hard on us without trying and without us knowing.

She was strong and able bodied and seemed tireless and efficient like clockworks.

She was fine like silk and wholesome like cotton.

She was the rarest and most exquisite gift we ever had.

We assumed we would have her forever; She became an indispensable possession. And when the maker and rightful owner of this gift came and took her away, we suffered.

But her gifts to us have a permanence that only spirit can. She gave herself to us. Her sweetness, her tenderness and her love, her freshness and her support, her knowledge and her mystery: All these she gave to us.

In the face of mounting evidence that the world was deceitful and cruel and corrupt, she was there to calm our anger and to take away our doubt. She enabled us to trust in mankind and to have faith in our God.

Being with her gave us the same feeling you get watching a ballet dancer or a singer or any gifted individual perform. She made you happy to be human and alive. Watching her perform made us happy and made us want to live.

She died like the saint she was; smiling at us to calm our fears, caring more about our disappointment and anxiety than her own, and peacefully and cheerfully enduring her fate.

We remember her fondly and excitedly like a picture of our past, and hope that we can be worthy of her praise.

To truly understand Bob Kerrey, an examination of his relationship with his mother is crucial. She played a paramount role in shaping his character. As a child, she had to give him special attention because of his asthma, and their bond would remain strong until her death. It was his mother who guided him closely through his formative years. It was Elinor who monitored his homework and coordinated his sports activities. It was Elinor who gave him words of comfort immediately after his surgery at the Philadelphia Naval Hospital. It was Elinor who encouraged him and supported him in the restaurant business. It was Elinor who developed his sensitive side. And it was Elinor's life that inspired him.

Described by her children as a modern-day saint, Elinor Kerrey was, by accounts of everyone familiar with her, a selfless, compassionate, unassuming woman whose tireless devotion to her family was an example for all who witnessed it. She was, quite simply, an exemplary mother. In her March 1991 Mother's Day tribute, Jessie Rasmussen wrote: "She acted her beliefs. . . . She assumed she had a rightful place in the community and in the working world and she took it. She did not march in protest of social inequities but rather she opened her home to those friends of her children who were abused and neglected and had no place safe to be."

Kerrey, when asked to describe her, said: "She was beautiful, not physically, but she was beautiful." Nancy Kerrey Swarts said: "I remember when Dad would be in a bad mood. He'd come home after a real tense day and the worst my mom ever said was 'Gads, he's owly today.' That was all the complaining you would ever hear out of her." Dave Littrell, a friend of Kerrey's since their college days together, said: "She was an extremely intelligent woman and he loved her very much."

After her death, the Kerrey clan would congregate at their father's home in Capitol Beach. Bev would often show up with her kids and no husband. When asked where Bob was, she'd respond that she didn't know. The family was aware that a breakup was imminent. Four months after his mother's death, Bev and Bob Kerrey were divorced. He filed.

The period of the breakup proved difficult for Kerrey. Although his restaurants were thriving by this time, his personal life was less than stable. His mother's death heightened his nebulous feeling that he was not living his life precisely the way he wanted. The divorce was so fraught with tension that Kerrey considered pushing for custody of his two children. There were parking lot encounters, episodes of jealousy, anger, bitterness, resentment, charges and counter-charges. Communication between the couple became nonexistent for a while. Nancy Kerrey Swarts said: "When things were really troubling Bob, it used to be hard for him to open up and so I think that communication was probably the biggest problem in their marriage." With time, the two would reestablish a friendship—the wounds of the marriage war would be healed. By the time of his 1988 Senate race, the former Mrs. Kerrey would speak nostalgically about their four short years together. In September 1991, before Kerrey's presidential announcement, Mrs. Higby told a reporter for the *Chicago Tribune*: "I wish he could be elected today. We are great friends and, as a citizen, I believe he can make positive changes in the country."

Nancy Kerrey Swarts recalls that another Kerrey sister speculated that "the reasons my brothers haven't had a very good track record in their marriages and the gals have is probably because my mother was so tolerant of the way my dad behaved. When he'd get calls, Dad would just get up and leave. He'd call my mother at suppertime, maybe later, and say, 'I'm not going to be home tonight, honey, I'm in Colorado.' And when he first did that to his second wife, Lois, she just had a cow, but he did it with my mother all their married life. . . . And Mom would just keep his dinner warm in the oven."

Elinor Kerrey possessed a quiet strength that allowed her to keep the Kerrey clan together. According to Marian Price, after her death the family fell apart for a while. "She was the strong, magnetic one and when Elinor died, the family just went like this, *pppffft*. They would always draw together in times of crisis, but otherwise they'd just kind of go their separate ways."

During the four years between 1978 and his 1982 run for Governor, Bob Kerrey worked hard at managing his business, branching out into fitness centers and even a bowling alley. But being in business did not satisfy him completely the way it had

his father. He continued to look for new challenges. He cultivated friendships and he began to sharpen his interest in politics
and public policy. He closely watched the 1978 gubernatorial
election of Republican Charley Thone and he flirted with the
idea of possibly someday running for office.

It was in this period that Bob Kerrey forged and cemented
friendships that, with the exception of his childhood chums and
his SEAL buddies, probably remain the strongest today. It was
during this time that Kerrey met a young transplanted Iowan,
Donna Karnes, who became one of his most trusted friends until
her death of cancer on December 23, 1989. Donna Karnes was
an olive-skinned, small-framed woman with expressive eyes and
hands. She was strong willed and exceptionally bright.

The two began dating in the late seventies, and their relationship quickly evolved into a deep friendship. Jim Crounse,
who worked in the Kerrey administration and who dated Karnes
after Kerrey, said, "They were simpatico. They were definitely
soulmates. They understood each other in a way that few others
understood them."

Karnes played a vital role in Kerrey's political evolution.
She was different from the women Kerrey had been close to before. Extremely savvy, Karnes helped cultivate and hone Kerrey's interests in more than politics, as she was an avid lover of
the arts, especially film. Karnes was one of the founding members of the Friends of the Sheldon Theater, a film theater located
on the University of Nebraska campus. She introduced Kerrey
to many in Lincoln's large arts community. In 1981, Kerrey,
through the recruiting efforts of Karnes, was asked to join the
board, where he would serve until he quit to run for Governor.

It was to Donna Karnes that Kerrey expressed his feelings
that Governor Charley Thone could have run the state more ef-
ficiently. They discussed politics, the women's movement, business, and movies, continuing to keep in touch long after their
romance cooled.

Karnes had moved to Nebraska from Iowa and carved out
a niche for herself in Lincoln's business, political, and artistic
community. A 1976 graduate of the University of Nebraska–
Lincoln law school, Karnes was the first female general counsel

in the insurance industry and later would serve as a member of Governor Kerrey's cabinet. In 1991, UN-L announced a Donna Karnes scholarship program to honor the "committed feminist who was always willing to be on the front line." Many of Kerrey's first supporters for his gubernatorial run were culled from Karnes's network of friends and associates. For many politicos in Lincoln, their first recollection of Kerrey was being introduced to him by Donna Karnes.

When Kerrey moved on to the Senate in January 1989, Karnes acted as an adviser. Later, when she learned of her terminal illness, she said, "Now I won't get to see Bob in the White House."

Chapter 5

KERREY WHO?

Before there was Bob Kerrey, there was John J. Cavanaugh. In 1976, the thirty-one-year-old Cavanaugh surprised Nebraska by becoming the first Democrat to capture Omaha's second-district congressional seat in twenty-eight years. Before Bob Kerrey, if talk centered on a bright, young, charismatic, Irish-monikered rising political star from Nebraska, political cognoscenti would have instinctively assumed that the conversation was about Cavanaugh. Before Kerrey, Nebraska Democrats viewed Cavanaugh as the state's most appealing politico and the man most likely to succeed at the national level.

No one in the congressional class of 1976 received as much press as Cavanaugh (although Tipper and Al Gore together came in a close second), and many of his House colleagues at the time tabbed him as a future contender. So it was a shock to them when, after just two relatively uneventful terms in Congress, Cavanaugh announced that he was quitting politics.

Democratic Party elders were devastated. They had seen Cavanaugh as a favored son who would one day segue to the Senate and eventually make a run for the White House. But he had quickly tired of the incessant fund-raising, the schmoozing, and a House routine that kept him shuttling between Washington and Nebraska. Cavanaugh was eager to return to his roots, spend time with his family, and make money. Bob Kerrey,

meanwhile, was burned out making money, and the restless restaurateur was entering political orbit.

In the fall of 1981, Bob Kerrey was ready to run for Governor. He had been approached by two prominent Nebraska Democrats, Gerald Whelan of Hastings, former lieutenant governor
under Exon and the 1978 Democratic gubernatorial candidate,
and Norm Otto, Exon's longtime chief assistant. Whelan, a jocular, well-liked politician, had observed Kerrey in the business
world. He thought that Kerrey's entrepreneurial background,
coupled with his war hero status and agreeable personality,
would make him an attractive candidate. Whelan's father, W. M.
Whelan, had been an admirer and friend of Senator George Norris and as a child, Whelan spent time around Nebraska's courageous politician and creator of the unicameral legislature.

One of the first people Kerrey discussed the idea with was
Donna Karnes, who had believed from the start that he could
become a major political leader. She was thrilled and immediately reached out to Lincolnites she knew to be disenchanted
with politics after the first Reagan landslide. She expressed her
enthusiasm and began to introduce Kerrey to Nebraskans who
were in her circle and outside his. She called State Senator Steve
Fowler, a well-known liberal Democrat and social crusader, a
brilliant political tactician, and a policy wizard. At the age of
twenty-two in 1972, Fowler had become the youngest elected
member of Nebraska's legislature, a distinction he still holds today. Karnes had been Fowler's campaign chair during his 1980
race for the legislature and she had encouraged then-
businessman Kerrey to make a substantial donation to Fowler's
race. Kerrey and Fowler had fleetingly crossed paths since their
days as anti–Vietnam War activists.

Fowler was elated with Karnes's news. He and other Democrats had been through a setback ten days earlier when the candidate they had been supporting, State Senator Don Dworak,
had pulled out of the race because of fund-raising difficulties.
Fowler was one of a handful of progressive, young senators—Dave Newell, Chris Beutler, Don Dworak, and Bill Burrows (Kerrey's opponent in the 1982 Democratic primary)—who
had been hammering away at the Thone administration's mis-

takes in tax policy. Fowler said, "We watched how the Republicans kept beating up on the Democrats by repeating a negative theme over and over. We [the Democratic group of State Senators] started doing it and it worked." From the little he knew of Kerrey, Fowler felt that he had a good profile and was willing to get behind him. Fowler called Omahan John Green to see if Kerrey could attend a popular political bash that was coming up soon in Omaha. He wanted to make certain it was okay to bring Kerrey and he also needed someone in Omaha to make all the introductions, someone who would know all the players. That person was John Green.

Forty-two-year-old John Green and his family are prominent Omaha Democrats. Green's father, James, cochaired Robert Kennedy's 1968 Nebraska primary campaign and John, as a young man, accompanied Ethel and Bobby Kennedy on their legendary whistle-stop train trek through Nebraska's plains, a method of campaigning first perfected by William Jennings Bryan six decades earlier. In the late sixties, Green, another Omaha Democrat named Larry Primeau, and a few others began to host a Christmas party that evolved into a must-attend event for candidates during election years. The Field Club Christmas party was held during the second week of December and, although it was a casual get-together, invitations were required.

Fowler put in the call to Green and asked if Kerrey could come along with Karnes and Victoria Horton, a Lincoln lawyer and Democratic activist. Fowler explained that Kerrey wanted to run for Governor. To Green's surprise, Fowler rattled off Kerrey's qualifications, including the fact that he was a prosperous businessman—a boon in a state where small-business leaders are revered second only to farmers. He told Green that at thirty-seven, Kerrey was mature and had his heart in the right place on the issues. Green could be instrumental in Omaha and Kerrey, an outsider, would need lots of help. Fowler assumed the Omaha crowd would be cool to Kerrey in part because they were unfamiliar with him and also because he seemed so youthful. The record shows that Nebraskans have a long history of electing young Governors and those who had owned small businesses and were not traditional up-from-the-party politicians. Kerrey's background and age, while often portrayed as unusual, were completely within Nebraska tradition. Still, Fowler was dealing with perception, and he was aware that Kerrey would be considered shaky by the close-knit Celtic sons of the old crowd from the county courthouse. Green's support would be a good start, Fowler believed.

Kerrey had zero name recognition and little political experience save for his stint as chair of Jerry Koch's legislative campaign and another as a member of Lincoln's Human Rights Commission. "Just make sure that he meets everyone," Fowler said, knowing that the gathering drew rank-and-file Omaha Democrats as well as the party's pooh-bahs.

Green, then thirty, had recently returned from Washington, D.C., where he had worked as the chief legislative assistant for Democratic representative John J. Cavanaugh. He calls himself a crossover Democrat, one who feels as comfortable hanging out with the old-time pols as he does talking demographics, megabytes, and voting patterns with the new-age, high-tech, "Atari" Democrats. After hanging up, Green remembered that he had seen Kerrey a decade earlier on the steps of the Nebraska capitol during an anti–Vietnam War demonstration.

The night of the party, Fowler, Horton, Karnes, and Kerrey drove the hour trip to the Field Club at 38th and Woolworth Streets, a rambling county-owned golf and social club. Kerrey was briefed on the trip up, with the trio giving him background on the politicos he would meet. Fowler knew that the Omahans would be interested in meeting Kerrey because word had spread that an unknown restaurateur wanted to take on Thone. Upon arrival, Fowler immediately found Green and introduced Kerrey. Green greeted a pleasant fellow who looked different from the solemn, long-sideburned activist he had watched in 1972. The two men chatted a bit and Green asked Kerrey questions about his restaurant business. The reply was that Grandmother's had been around since 1972 and was doing well. Kerrey looked around awkwardly. There were repeated lulls. Green shifted the conversation to Charley Thone, the incumbent Governor. They agreed he was vulnerable, despite a large GOP majority in the state, because of Nebraska's ailing economy.

Fowler remembered noticing that Kerrey didn't know how to

work a crowd. For most of the evening, he stood in one spot, not a strategic place, and waited for people to come to him. People were curious but they were not milling around Kerrey the way they invariably would have had he already made a formal announcement. John Green periodically brought people to Kerrey, and he watched closely as the new face and the old crowd mingled.

The day after the party, Green called Fowler and said, "Whatever it takes to run for Governor, this guy ain't got it." Green expressed his and longtime party activist Primeau's feelings that Kerrey seemed uncomfortable pressing the flesh and somewhat reserved, not characteristics that make for effective campaigning. He did not appear especially confident, they argued. Green acknowledged that he liked Kerrey's business background and that he knew a Medal of Honor recipient would gain instant credibility. Still, Green argued, if he was awkward on the campaign trail, Kerrey couldn't pull it off. "Well, he's all we've got," Fowler responded, "so we're going to go with him." Green hung up his telephone in Omaha certain the Democrats were headed for defeat, but planning, as usual, to work hard to avoid it. Fowler got off the phone in Lincoln realizing the enormity of the task ahead.

One week later, right before Christmas, Kerrey was once again escorted to an Omaha party and shepherded around by longtime Democrat Norm Otto, a top political aide to Senator James Exon. After returning to Lincoln, Kerrey stopped by the house of Professor June Levine, who had invited him to a holiday gathering. Since the start of his restaurant ventures, Levine had only seen Kerrey sporadically. She always spoke with him after movies at the Sheldon Film Theater, and she ran into him occasionally at concerts. But Levine had remained friendly enough that she felt comfortable inviting him to her house for a big Christmas party. By this time, she knew he was running for Governor and she wanted to hear about the status of his campaign. Kerrey, dressed up, arrived after midnight, after most of her guests had left. They exchanged pleasantries and Kerrey ambled over to her living room couch and stretched out on it. She could see he was exhausted, and he told Levine he was discouraged by the event he had just attended in Omaha.

"I am not wanting to do this, June," Kerrey said, "if it means kissing people's asses." Levine recalls, "I looked at him as if he were a babe and I said, 'Bob, there's going to be a lot of that if you want to be Governor.' I was saying to him, 'Don't be silly, this is how it is!' But this was his first experience with the game and it was clear he didn't realize how it was going to play itself out."

At that point, there was a real difference between Kerrey's philosophy and Senator Exon's. Exon was and is a fundamentally conservative man—a much more conventional man than Kerrey. Their relationship has evolved to the point where they are close friends, and Kerrey considers Exon a mentor and an outstanding U.S. Senator. Back then, however, they were polarized politically and they did not truly know each other.

Levine said, "I knew Bob well enough at that point to know that whatever loosely formed political picture he had, his gut instincts were certainly not as conservative as those of Jim Exon or Bernice Labedz [Nebraska's leading pro-life legislator] and all the other people whom he would have had to be seeing in Omaha."

One of Kerrey's early speeches, at the Spaghetti Works restaurant in Lincoln, was an impassioned talk of a government responsive to human needs, rather than a budget-driven one. State Senator Don Wesely, who represents the Bethany neighborhood where Kerrey was raised, recalls it as a moving speech but not one to win an election in Nebraska, where the voters "like their chief executives to be cheap and tight with the budget." Still, Wesely was impressed—he had last heard Kerrey as an angry attendee at a Democratic dinner where New Orleans Mayor Moon Landrieu had addressed Lincoln's business community.

On that occasion, Kerrey, one of the businessmen, had assaulted the Democratic panel with belligerent questions, rejecting the answers. Wesely recalls him as fairly disruptive. After the Spaghetti Works speech, however, Wesely offered to work for Kerrey and would change his assessment.

"I found him to be a real joy, a dynamic and thoughtful individual. Evidently, taking that anger that was so evident at the Moon Landrieu meeting and constructively channeling it into the race for the governorship did something to him." Later, Ker-

rey would tell several Nebraskans that it was the night of the
Landrieu dinner that he had decided for certain that he was going to run for Governor. He became convinced that night that
he shouldn't simply complain but should get involved himself.

After Kerrey's maiden speech, several other Democratic
politicians also approached Kerrey to offer strategy that would
be more acceptable to Nebraskans. They praised his talk but
pointed out the need to mention balancing the budget and containing the cost of government. Kerrey adjusted the content of
his speeches quickly and soon espoused more standard policies.

Meanwhile, Kerrey told Levine that he was hurt by people's
doubts about his qualifications. "You know what really makes
me angry is that people don't understand what my qualifications
are to even run for Governor," Kerrey said. "Well, Bob, why
does that surprise you? I think it's a perfectly legitimate question," Levine replied. "And he looked at me, wounded and
hurt, because here was his friend, June, and she was expressing
the same sentiment. I was amazed too, because Bob had not
been very involved in politics."

Another prominent Democrat who expressed reservations
was former Representative John J. Cavanaugh of Omaha. Kerrey
later reported, "I went to John Cavanaugh and I told him of my
plans, and he told me, 'Bob, you're incredibly naive and you can't
possibly do it.' And I got very angry and said, 'Of all the things I
am, John, I am not naive.' What I was speaking about was based
on my military and business experience. I had seen enough of the
world that I didn't like to have anybody tell me that I was naive.
But politically, I was terribly naive and green, and I had no business assuming that I could be Governor."

Kerrey decided to press on and gradually he stopped worrying about whether people felt he was qualified. In an interview
as Governor, Kerrey said, "I always thought I would win."

Beginning in January 1982, Kerrey, Karnes, and Fowler began organizing strategy sessions that were usually held at Kerrey's house in the near south neighborhood not far from the
Nebraska capitol. They each invited Lincolnites whom they
wanted to enlist in the campaign. One of the earliest meetings
included Jim Pribyl, who would become Kerrey's campaign man-

ager around Labor Day, as well as Horton, Fowler, and a handful of state senators. Also present was Renee Wessels, a gifted young woman who had just graduated from the University of Nebraska–Lincoln, where she had been president of the student body. She recalled being impressed with Kerrey from their first meeting. "I could tell this was a rare person," Wessels said.

Kerrey's issues research team was culled from a network of existing and former legislative staffers, including Wessels, Don Norden, Horton, Rod Armstrong, Barbara Richardson, Sonny Foster, David Howard, Jim Crounse, and Deb Thomas. They briefed Kerrey and provided research materials that he used in speeches, press releases, and television commercials.

Fowler also used research compiled by Fran White, a longtime assistant to Senator Exon, who had daily gathered newspaper clippings on Thone even when it was not clear the Democrats would field a candidate against him. White's clippings became the documentation for many of Kerrey's attacks on Thone.

Democrats became convinced that this campaign could go all the way when Kerrey announced that he would be willing to take some risks financially and borrow money to get the campaign started. Democrats held back from writing checks because they weren't convinced that there was a Democrat strong enough to go against Thone. Thone had been an exceedingly popular four-term member of the House of Representatives before he became Governor in 1978, and Nebraskans were fond of him and his intelligent, outspoken, and liberal wife, Ruth, an accomplished writer who once rode side-saddle in a pair of jeans down the gubernatorial bannister, and his three daughters. Because of this reluctance, it was imperative that Kerrey have an independent base and feel confident enough to take a major risk. Kerrey stated that he would secure a line of credit to help underwrite the start of the campaign. Fowler recalled, "I think he was willing to go up to one hundred thousand dollars for the primary, which, in Nebraska, was a considerable sum." That news made listeners feel that this was going to be a real race. Kerrey did not see his actions as risky; he felt certain that Charley Thone was beatable and he knew that he had quality credentials.

Since Kerrey at this point was the neophyte, he listened.

Ideas, strategy, logistics, mechanics—all were tossed around, with Kerrey taking in what was needed. Pribyl and Fowler drafted a comprehensive strategy for victory, discussed it in detail with Kerrey, and began to execute it.

Fowler and Pribyl planned to draw on the base of then-Lincoln Mayor Helen Boosalis, whose election in the late seventies broke the political power of the "O Street Gang," the good old boys who ran community politics for years. Fowler said, "He's very task oriented so that it was easy to describe what needed to be done, to introduce him to people who could help him."

But what Fowler and other party people would learn immediately is that Bob Kerrey's modus operandi was not in the traditional kitchen cabinet mold. The coterie of Democratic activists, so instrumental in his first success, would never make up the core of Kerrey's closest circle; several key aides remained only through the first two years of his administration. From the outset, Kerrey relied on a broad range of advisers culled from the different scenes in which he had been involved, however briefly, including some members of the Sheldon Theater group.

Kerrey, as he had done with his restaurant business, spent much of his time in the early months of 1982 reestablishing ties with old friends and acquaintances to tell them of his plans and ask for their support. He didn't usually ask directly for money on the first go-around. He would just pop in, talk for a few minutes, announce his plans, and leave. One of the first people he informed of his decision was Rod Bates, a confidant since the middle seventies. Long before he decided to run he had tossed around the idea with close friends like Bates. Bates tried to discourage him, talking about the power of incumbency and the risk of taking time away from a successful business. "I told him he was crazy," Bates said, "but he went ahead and did it. Bob has a history of listening to the advice I give and going out and doing the exact opposite."

"Four or five of us would be in a discussion with him and then he would call someone like Larry Price," Fowler said. Price recalled the first time Kerrey told him of his plans. Kerrey laid out his spiel, they discussed the difficulties of beating an incumbent, and then Kerrey left. "After he walked out the door," Price said, "I realized that I didn't have any idea whether he was running as a Democrat or a Republican. I thought probably Republican, but I really didn't have any idea."

State Senator David Landis, the Renaissance man of the legislature and an astute observer of the Nebraska political scene, recalled the time Kerrey approached him about running. "I was sitting in my office on the eighth floor of the legislature and he walked in and said, 'I'm Bob Kerrey and I'm thinking of running for the governorship. What do you think? Do you think I should?' I said I thought it would be a very, very sound thing. One of the things you have going for you is being a businessman and being able to establish credibility on that score. I was encouraging. I asked him what issues he cared about passionately and I recall that his answer was somewhat amorphous, vaguely the sense of empowerment of people. He was well dressed. he looked young and yes, I did know about the Medal of Honor."

Marian Price, Kerrey's longtime neighbor and friend, a Price sister-in-law, found out through the Bethany grapevine that Kerrey was going to run and brought it up with James Kerrey before Bob had a chance to bring Marian officially into the campaign (she acted as his treasurer). "I said to Jim, 'I hear Bob is going to run for governor. Goodness, he's never held a local office, never been on the city council, never held an ofice at all' and Jim responded, 'You don't think he can do it?' and I said, 'I know he can do it but he's running against someone who is experienced and you have the power of incumbency. Then again, we know all of Charley Thone's warts.'"

Bringing in people from his old Bethany neighborhood and others like them around the state, who normally would not participate in political campaigns, was typical of Bob Kerrey's first gubernatorial drive. These were not disaffected individuals, recently disenchanted with politicians and campaigning; rather, he drew in people who would never have become politically active were it not for his candidacy. Marian Price was representative. She had never toiled for a politician, and if she had ever considered doing it, she most certainly would have signed on with a Republican. Price would become so enamored of the political world that she would go on to run and be elected to the board of the Lincoln public schools. Many others like Marian Price would get their first whiff of politics on the Kerrey campaign.

Kerrey's eagerness to connect again with people from the past caused him to make a few political faux pas in the name of campaigning, missteps that the seasoned Kerrey of the 1988 Senate would not make. One oldtime Bethany resident recalled the time Kerrey returned to Bethany Christian Church early in the campaign. "Bob Kerrey came to church one Sunday and then came up to fellowship hour and pumped hands like it was old home week. He hadn't been there in years [when he moved to south Lincoln, Kerrey joined the First Plymouth Congregational Church and became a Congregationalist] and I had more people say, 'That was not in good taste.' It was just like a political rally after church and people in Bethany believe the church is the church and you don't hold political rallies up there like you had a captive audience." But Marian Price countered, "He is a product of Bethany and northeast Lincoln. The people of this community have seen this boy be born here, and grow up here, and we don't always agree with him on every issue but he's our guy."

One aspect of Kerrey's personality that began to emerge at these meetings was noticed by brainstormers—his ability to absorb information rapidly. Kandra Hahn said: "He was exceptionally quick, you could tell that instantly." State Senator Don Wesely, who represents Kerrey's old Bethany neighborhood and who advised Kerrey on issues after his election, said that briefing Kerrey was a complete joy. Weseley added, "I'd say, 'Governor, this is where we are at' and I would start in on something and he'd say, 'Now, that's good but what are we going to do about this, I'm thinking' and Kerrey would go right to where I was going and in some cases, beyond that, he'd just leap over all the preliminaries. He would have already considered where I thought we needed to go and brought up something else as well." Norm Otto, a longtime aide to Senator James Exon and one of the grand old men of the Democratic Party, called Kerrey a "boy wonder." Early on, Otto sat down with Kerrey and outlined all the issues he would be called upon to discuss. He described Kerrey as a sponge and said he was the most rapid learner he had ever met.

Another Democrat Kerrey enlisted was Lincolnite Hess Dyas, who had chaired the party in the late sixties and early seventies. Dyas is roundly credited with keeping cohesion within the party during the tense antiwar years. Although he lost several bids for the Congress, his campaign's grass-roots operations, designed by skilled campaign manager Dick Kurtenbach, built a political field infrastructure that laid the foundation for a new generation of Democrats at the local level in the 1970s and the state level in the 1980s. He also introduced Rothstein and Buckley, Washington, D.C.–based media consultants, to Kerrey and other Democrats in the state.

During this time Kerrey began to work on his announcement speech. Observers remember discussing it with him and helping him crystallize some ideas, but it was Kerrey who labored over it and who spent days fine-tuning his remarks. He had a couple of briefings and discussions with policy people about specific points on which to attack the Thone administration. Fowler urged Kerrey to discuss specific issues; instead, Kerrey crafted a speech about life-defining experiences and personal motivation. Because Kerrey did not bring the conventional Democratic activist perspective to his race, he addressed the issues in a much broader and more appealing fashion. Fowler said, "It was good that he could talk about things that would appeal to business people and he could talk about things that would interest nonpolitical folks like you would meet in Bethany. He understood things from his restaurant employees. Sometimes as an adviser, you would be surprised. As someone who had nine years in the Nebraska legislature, I would have talked state issues, state issues, state issues, and he wanted to talk about 'why.' He felt that was the question his peer group would ask—'Why, Bob, if you're doing so well with your businesses would you dare gamble to do something like this?'"

Campaign workers spent weeks organizing the announcement across the state and finally, on February 15, 1982, again at the steps of the capitol, Kerrey announced his run for Governor of Nebraska. Old pal Dan Ladely, in his trademark hair-to-the-waist ponytail, remembered a joke Kerrey made to him right before he headed to the podium. "Do you want to come up here and stand by me?" Kerrey quipped. "Yeah, do you want to make sure you don't get elected?" Ladely responded.

By the time of Kerrey's announcement, the Nebraska media were out in full force. He began: "My decision to offer myself as a candidate, to ask Nebraska people to trust me, this difficult decision to leave private life, is based upon many personal things which I need to share with you now." After reviewing his SEAL history, his war experience, and the evolution of his love-hate attitude toward government, Kerrey discussed his entrepreneurial success and his reasons for running. Finally, he focused on the failings of the Thone administration and what he would do to address the twin problems of moribund leadership and fiscal mismanagement. Perhaps the most revealing line of Kerrey's speech came in the last minutes: "Nebraska needs a Governor who can develop new markets like a businessman, not like a bureaucrat, a Governor who knows his way into and out of a business deal." That line reflected a pragmatism that would be a hallmark throughout the Kerrey administration.

Later, one of the major accomplishments of the Kerrey administration would be the creation of the Research and Development Authority, an entity that put Nebraska, for the first time, in a position to invest, in the form of venture capital, in high-tech and research facilities. Kerrey's "new markets" line was a reference to his interest in bringing food-processing plants and telecommunications and information services to the state, an interest later stymied by a deep recession but one that has proved, in the words of Steve Fowler, "amazingly visionary." Fowler recalled that the first time they met to discuss issues, Kerrey talked about Nebraska and telecommunications being a perfect match; Kerrey was the only politician Fowler knew of at that point hammering away at the necessity of shifting Omaha's base from industry to communications.

Kerrey's ideas were prophetic. A journalist in a July 20, 1991, article in *The New York Times* wrote: "Omaha has shown that state-of-the-art telecommunications can be a 20th-century advantage comparable to sitting aside a railroad line in the 19th century. The city best known for its slaughterhouses now has well over 10,000 jobs in telecommunications—more than double the number of meatpackers—and an unemployment rate below 3 percent." The next day a staff writer for the real-estate section of the *Times* wrote: "Indeed, so many catalogue companies, credit-card servicing centers, and hotel reservation services are consolidating their 800-number operations in Omaha that the city—whose geometric towers rise from the pancake-flat surrounding prairie like the fabled city of Oz—might easily qualify as the toll-free capital of America."

But before Kerrey could take on the GOP, he had to win the May Democratic primary. Running against him was a State Senator from Gage County, Bill Burrows, a longtime party activist who had run for Congress in 1970 when no other Democrats would come forward. Burrows had worked long and hard in the legislature, challenging the Thone administration consistently, and to some degree he and other Democratic Party regulars felt he deserved the nomination.

Nebraska has two Democratic traditions—one is southern-based, which was symbolized by pioneer J. Sterling Morton, and the other is the populist tradition of William Jennings Bryan. According to Nebraska political scientists and authors James F. Pedersen and Kenneth D. Wald, the divisions in the Democratic Party, at least through the Vietnam era, were along those lines. Kerrey does not come from either tradition although he carries elements of both.

Burrows, on the other hand, comes from a long line of populists. His grandfather had been a turn-of-the-century populist, and he has carried on that tradition in his rhetoric and ideology. He believed that he had a message to deliver about economic justice and tax policy, and he saw Kerrey as a businessman, not a true keeper of the Democratic populist tradition. DiAnna Schimek, head of the Nebraska Democratic Party at the time, remembered the friction between the two camps. The Burrows campaign believed that the state party was, in subtle and not-so-subtle ways, supporting Kerrey's efforts. Fowler remembered admiring Burrows but feeling that he would never raise enough money for media to get his message across. Kerrey turned out to be a skillful fund-raiser. He had a large network of successful people to approach and he had sharpened his social skills for presentation to potential contributors.

Then thirty-eight, Kerrey was blessed with an appealing face, soulful Irish eyes, and a large forehead. (Donna Karnes routinely encouraged him to comb his hair forward in a way that she thought minimized its expansiveness: "Your forehead is too big," she would joke with him.) Of average frame and weight, Kerrey comports himself in a straight-back, serious, and intense way that belies his capacity for effortless one-liners, barbed comebacks, hilarious rejoinders, and when the mood strikes him, salty repartee.

Nebraskans began writing checks, and gradually, the campaign began to get on solid financial ground. By this time Kerrey had raised enough money to hire a professional pollster, the firm of Hamilton and Staff, with Harrison Hickman as his personal pollster, and the media team of Rothstein and Buckley. Both had done commercials for Democrats in Nebraska before, including for Lincolnite Hess Dyas in his own unsuccessful bid for the U.S. Senate. Both were recommended by Pribyl, who had worked with them in previous campaigns. So, although Hamilton and Staff was a Washington polling firm, it had a reputation for doing superb "Morning in America" style commercials. Once Kerrey's commercials started running in the primary, he overwhelmed the Burrows camp, and it quickly became evident to Nebraska Republicans that Bob Kerrey would be a far more formidable foe than they had ever imagined. Kerrey the candidate came across compellingly on television, and GOP insiders soon began to hope that his campaign organization would not be as good as his media.

At that time, it wasn't. Bill Kerrey and his wife, Terry, moved from Hawaii back to Nebraska to help run the campaign. Bill, who had served in the Peace Corps in Peru, had signed on with an international agricultural research and training project in Hawaii but was willing to leave it to come home and help his brother. Bill Kerrey, a blonder, slighter version of Bob, acted as the campaign organizer until it became clear that the top job was outside his realm of experience. He had never run a campaign before, and this was a race that the Democratic National Campaign Committee felt could be won. Some staffers began to lobby Bob to hire someone more politically astute. While they felt that Bill was a capable person, he didn't exhibit a sense of urgency, and they became convinced he wasn't aware of the rigorous timetable a campaign engenders. Your brother is not calendar-driven enough, they would tell Kerrey.

In March, Kerrey hired Jim Humlicek, a South Dakotan known in Nebraska for his work for Senator George McGovern. A campaign professional, Humlicek had been heading up various Democratic races since the late sixties. He knew how to rev up a traditional campaign and this one definitely needed a jumpstart. Progress was being made, but strategy was not being executed with precision. Humlicek began to put the pieces together. During the weekend of March 26–27, 1982, Kerrey won the official endorsement of the Nebraska State Education Association (NSEA) and spoke to the delegates at the assembly. He received a rousing response as he spoke of his commitment to public education and as he stressed that it was time Nebraska had a Governor who saw education as an investment as well as an expenditure. In an April 22, 1982, letter that Kerrey wrote to the members of the NSEA, Kerrey said: "It is time we had elected officials who will speak for our schools, our colleges, and our university, not against them."

Kerrey's endorsement by the education association was engineered by Herb Schimeck, its political director, who after a decade of intense building had politicized the teachers, trained them in campaign techniques, and raised their political action fund to unprecedented levels. With registered Republicans making up much of their membership, their endorsement was crucial to Kerrey's later success at the polls.

Later, Kerrey would find himself in the uneasy but ultimately correct position of speaking against the University of Nebraska and its top-heavy bureaucracy. While many Nebraskans familiar with the institution agreed completely with Kerrey, most politicians had generally treated university administrators with kid gloves. Kerrey donned boxing gloves and repeatedly sparred with university heads. The usual man in the ring with him was then UN president Ronald Roskens, now the head of the Agency for International Development, a Bush Administration appointee. Kerrey and Roskens, in the words of one professor, got along "like two cats in a paper bag." Roskens and other University of Nebraska administrators were traditional Republican contributors, and some speculated that the friction began with Kerrey's knowledge of that practice. Most of the university's high-paid administrators gave money to Charley Thone in 1982.

By April 9 of that year, Rothstein and Buckley had created three thirty-second television spots entitled "Rich State," "Jobs," and "Endorsement" and one sixty-second commercial called "Biography." Democrats who watched the commercials could barely contain their glee that they had a bona fide telegenic candidate whose résumé quieted the usual Republican rantings about Democratic liberalism. Fowler recalled, "My recollection is that once TV hit, fund-raising took off. Until then, his image was not defined even to people who knew him."

On Saturday, April 3, 1982, when Bob Kerrey stepped up to the mike at the Democrats' annual Jefferson-Jackson Day dinner, many among the party faithful began to sense, some for the first time, that this new politician from Lincoln was a striking, albeit unknown, man who might actually be able to win in November. That realization came at different times for different people, but without question, there was a surging sense that someone special had just stepped into the Nebraska political scene. As he had with his announcement, Kerrey drafted the speech himself, with Fowler and a few others hunting fitting quotes from Franklin Delano Roosevelt, Thomas Jefferson, and Andrew Jackson. He declared: "It angers me today to hear it said that Roosevelt was the beginning of a period of forty years of Democratic mismanagement. And it saddens me when I see that even many Democrats are embarrassed and apologetic about the issues and concerns he asked our government to address. Let me say here tonight, we should not be embarrassed. We cannot apologize."

Again he spoke of his time at the Philadelphia Naval Hospital and his subsequent reentry into private life in Lincoln. "The care and concern provided me and thousands of other veterans was not provided to us because it was cost-effective—it was provided because it was fair, because it was right, and because it was good."

In this speech, his first major address to his Democratic

compatriots, Kerrey described his motivation for running as one of restlessness with the plodding progress of the Republican administration: "And this is the response from our statehouse: that we must wait for our interest rates to come down; that we must wait for the economy to recover; that we must wait for some federal program to help us; that we must wait; that we can only react; that we cannot control our own destinies."

This passage illustrates Kerrey's aversion to inaction. Almost a decade later, Kerrey would describe his run for the presidency as a "restless, fearless journey," a theme that is not a rhetorical flourish but one that genuinely reflects the life he lives. Instinctively, as Kerrey worked on the speech, he wrote about what he knew, and what he knew was action.

Kerrey, who had practiced delivering the speech, felt he could have been more forceful, but overall he was pleased with his performance and the reaction it ignited. What had also buoyed his spirits was the news he received a few weeks earlier from his pollster at Hamilton and Staff. The summary declared: "Charles Thone is clearly vulnerable to defeat in his bid for re-election. Voters are dissatisfied with his performance. . . . Voters are very responsive to Bob Kerrey when they hear about him. In our professional judgment, Bob Kerrey has an excellent opportunity to defeat Charles Thone . . . provided [Kerrey] has the financial support required to take his campaign to the voters."

Kerrey felt supremely confident about fund-raising. He knew he could count on monetary help from Lincolnites like Price; Jim Stuart, a prominent and well-off Lincoln banker and Vietnam vet who tried to talk Kerrey into running as a Republican, and Bill Wright, also wealthy, who would remain a close friend and adviser until a controversial real-estate partnership rendered contact difficult. He knew that his sister Jessie and her husband, Dean Rasmussen, would be energetic and effective fund-raisers.

In an interview with the *Lincoln Journal*, Jessie Rasmussen described their early fund-raising efforts: "At first it was just a few friends tossing out ideas. We were all political novices." But the Rasmussens would not remain novices for long. Eight years later, Jessie Rasmussen would run for the Nebraska legislature and win. After one year there, she would be labeled one of the most effective legislators and today is still considered a rising star in Nebraska Democratic politics.

The state Democrats also organized fund-raisers and found that Kerrey excited volunteers as no candidate had in recent memory. Women and men were eager to volunteer their time and money for Kerrey. To no one's surprise, on May 11, 1982, Bob Kerrey won the Democratic primary, easily beating Bill Burrows. The next day he held a powwow to discuss general election strategy. He continued poring over briefing papers, economic analyses, and agriculture statistics, and made appointments with policy people for briefings on agriculture, probably the area about which he knew the least at the time. Fowler recalled from their initial policy sessions that Kerrey had definite ideas for improving agriculture but that later, as Governor, he would admit he promised to do too much in an area over which a state chief executive can do little. Various Republican and Democratic agriculture experts, farmers, and ranchers came forward and offered their advice because many were put off by the Thone administration's policies, which could do little but reflect federal farm policy.

After the primary, Kerrey lost a key worker. Press person Renee Wessels, who had been wooed by corporate recruiters, accepted a job in telecommunications. Kerrey hired Lincolnite Kandra Hahn to replace her. Eight years earlier, Hahn, in an astounding upset, had become the youngest clerk ever elected to the district court. A year before Kerrey's announcement, she had been encouraged to go out to Grandmother's Skillet because the owner had "political aspirations."

Hahn recalled, "I met him at a table and he made no impression on me at all. I didn't think he was going anywhere, but he looked like another guy who *thinks* he's going somewhere in politics. In those days, people would tell wannabes, 'She got elected against the odds, you have to talk to Kandra.' Another time, Donna [Karnes] introduced me, still no impression." Then, according to Hahn, "He walked into my office in May and said, 'I want you to be my field coordinator' and I thought, 'That's not what I do in politics.' He didn't know what that was, he didn't care; what he wanted me to do was get on the campaign. He loves to talk people into jobs. That's his thing. If someone says they don't want to take it, if someone says, 'No, Bob, I don't think it's right,' he says, 'Oh yes, it is, you have to come.'"

For Kerrey's die-hard workers, the summer of 1982 could be summarized as the good news–bad news days. The good news was the astonishing ascendancy of candidate Kerrey and the emergence of his personal magnetism. Maxine Moul, elected Lieutenant Governor in 1990, recalled meeting Kerrey at an early summer event and noticing that Kerrey, though still not surefooted on the campaign trail, had unhoned charisma. She had agreed to meet him in a small Nebraska town and help him work a parade. Kerrey pulled up in a red convertible with his young son Ben. He casually hopped out of the car, sauntered over with his boy in tow, and said, "Okay, Maxine, what do we do?" "That's when I realized that he didn't have it all down yet. But all I had to do was point him in the right direction and make some suggestions, and that was it. He picked up the process incredibly quickly. And I watched that day and saw how people reacted to him. He came across as genuine, and people sensed it."

Those who were close to Kerrey in the beginning agree that he was not a natural politician. He was a businessman who could, when he wanted to, be outgoing, but he was not a salesman. In any profession, there are certain rituals that go with the territory. At the Field Club, Kerrey had not yet figured out what the political rituals were. As a restaurateur, he had played the role of manager many times; a role that required him to take his position behind the restaurant podium, dispensing information about reservations and so forth. Candidates, on the other hand, are expected to intrude on people's space, to interrupt and join their conversations. Most people expect politicians to approach them, rarely feel irritated when they do, and, in fact, consider it a treat when a candidate makes personal contact with them.

Once Kerrey figured out the rituals, as he had with other subjects, he mastered the art of campaigning quickly—so quickly that most Nebraskans do not remember a time when Bob Kerrey was not a polished campaigner. Kerrey's political performance improved so dramatically by Labor Day of 1982 that Omahan John Green could not believe he ever had considered Bob Kerrey an ungainly candidate. Nor could he believe that he had once considered him shy; he was now a self-confident, scrappy, and engaging individual. So much for first impressions, many Field Club observers thought.

Another factor that improved Kerrey's performance on the campaign trail was the effectiveness of his commercials, from the primary on, introducing him to Nebraskans. By the summer of 1982, Nebraskans recognized him and rushed forward to meet him. As anyone who has campaigned can attest, it is far easier to work crowds when your name and face are known than when you're pounding the pavement in anonymity.

Fowler recalled the effect of Kerrey's advertising as his first experience of the power of television to define a candidate. "And Kerrey has a visual story—it's a great story for television; it's got action and drama. The power of television was so overwhelming that once Kerrey's commercials came on, everybody wanted to get to know him."

Kerrey's quality TV ads and his compelling and telegenic appearance in the segments did not go unnoticed by Nebraska Republicans. Several advisers to Thone decided they wanted to improve Thone's image. One drafted a memo called "Image." Toward the end of the first page of the memo, the drafter wrote: "It would seem that Thone and Kerrey are quite opposite in the image that each can display to best advantage. . . . The right slogan or slogans will come in time, but only after we really brainstorm this business of image. Without delving into a copy of Roget's, here are some adjectives and phrases that might be used to describe Charley Thone:

PRO	*CON*
Honest	*Overtaken by events somtimes*
Sincere	*Indecisive*
Dependable	*Reclusive*
Caring	*Colorless*
Steady	*Negative*
Conservative	*Enigmatic*

Hard Working	Reserved
Proven	Not a polished speaker before audiences (but
Experienced	growing in this ability)

Let's look at Kerrey:

PRO	CON
Handsome	Slick
Smooth	Glib
Charismatic	Inexperienced
Caring	Unproven
MH winner	Does poorly in Q and A sessions
Handicapped	Has low flash point
	Easily angered

In sum, Charley Thone and his values are the quintessence of Nebraska. Bob Kerrey seems too polished in his appearance and his values are those of the knee-jerk liberal who pays little or no attention to how government will pay for its bill."

With friends like the memo drafter, Charley Thone didn't need enemies; he was ill served enough by his own party advisers. The fact that "handicapped" was listed as a "pro" suggests a cynicism rarely articulated in American politics. More than anyone, Kerrey was aware of the sensitive nature of his injury.

Kerrey, in fact, grappled from the beginning with how to use the Medal of Honor. Fowler recalled rummaging through Kerrey's memorabilia that might be useful for media and campaign literature and finding the Medal of Honor tucked away in the middle of it. Fowler was surprised that he didn't store it in some special place. It wasn't until the end of the campaign that Kerrey agreed to allow the medal to be photographed. Fowler said, "It was really only toward the end of the election when the attacks had gotten really strong, that he agreed to let us use it in photographs. In the primary he was really reticent." He did approve of a logo that was designed to simulate the medal with red, white, and blue colors, which they used for bumper stickers and other lapel paste-ons.

Watching Kerrey's astounding progress buoyed even the

most pessimistic spirits; and then, the rumors started. There were three main rumors. One was the "Kerrey burned the flag" rumor. Another was "Kerrey threw his Medal of Honor in a fire or a garbage can." The third was one about his sexual orientation. Supporters in small towns in Nebraska began calling Kerrey headquarters asking about the truth of the statements. "There never was any proof that Republicans were starting these rumors, but they seemed to show up far too often to be accidental," Fowler said.

When Kerrey was told about the rumors, he ordered everyone to simply ignore them. Fowler said, "We felt that Kerrey would be attacked on lack of experience or some things like that so we were prepared to deal with that but we weren't prepared to answer fictitious charges." Aide Kandra Hahn was amazed at Kerrey's equanimity. Finally, campaign workers, including Fowler and Hahn, and family members began to urge Kerrey to answer the charges. He refused. Kerrey argued that since the charges were untrue, he would give them credence by denying them. He was puzzled and infuriated by the phony charges and resisted responding. According to Fowler, "It was difficult explaining to him, to any candidate, why they have to say that something isn't true when it should be obvious it isn't true. 'Not one of these rumors is true,' Kerrey declared, 'so why should I have to say it never happened?' We told him, 'When a rumor gets a certain currency across the state, we must deal with it.'" Finally, the press started making inquiries and Kerrey agreed to answer the flag- and medal-burning charges in an *Omaha World-Herald* interview where he, in effect, said he had never, ever burned a flag or thrown his medals in a garbage can or fire. It turned out that a Vietnam veteran had thrown a medal into a makeshift coffin during a protest at the state capitol building in 1972, a rally that Bob Kerrey had attended.

After Kerrey's vehement denials, the rumors died down. It helped that the *Lincoln Star* wrote a scathing editorial about the rumors: "The recent circulation of a letter among potential contributors to Governor Charley Thone's campaign for reelection continues the disgraceful attempt to denigrate the patriotism of Bob Kerrey. The letter . . . tries to capitalize on statements about the draft and the Vietnam War attributed to Kerrey and over which there appears to be some confusion." That reference is to a 1970 interview with Kerrey in which he told a reporter that he would not go to Vietnam if he had it to do over. Later, Kerrey said his statements were those of an embittered man with a bloody leg, fresh from Vietnam, who was asked if he would volunteer again. The editorial goes on to print verbatim Kerrey's Medal of Honor citation and ends with "Enough said."

By his 1988 Senate race, Kerrey was able to joke about the medal-in-the-garbage rumor. Nebraska journalist and statehouse reporter Kathleen Rutledge wrote that Kerrey regaled a group of National Guard members with the story of how one of his SEAL buddies, who was campaigning for him in western Nebraska, handled a question about Kerrey tossing his Medal of Honor in the Potomac River. Rutledge wrote: "'That was sort of a new wrinkle on an old myth,' Kerrey remarked. Kerrey said Gray [former SEAL campaigner Gary Gray] angrily stood up and said, 'That's not true. That's a lie. I know Bob Kerrey and he would never do such a thing. Besides, I've seen that Medal of Honor.' Kerrey said Gray paused, then added, 'Of course, you know, it was a little muddy.'"

The final rumor, however, was not as easy to dispel and lingered throughout the campaign. Nebraskans were wise enough to dismiss it for what it was—a scurrilous, outrageous, and untrue attack intended to derail a candidate who was picking up steam. In discussing how to respond to the rumor, Kerrey made the final decision to ignore it. Still, the period of the rumors was a dark and difficult time for the Kerrey campaign. Di-Anna Schimek, then Nebraska Democratic chairwoman and now a State Senator, said, "There were some real down times when the charges were being flung and the underground rumors that were taking place really made a question as to whether he could pull it off. I think the rumors were specifically planted by Republicans. Those kinds of things don't just start by themselves. I mean how do those rumors start and spread statewide?"

Democrats believed that the rumors were spread over the summer because polls taken by both parties showed Kerrey overtaking his opponent. Later, a last-minute Thone commercial alluded to one of the rumors but, fittingly, it backfired. People were catching on to the desperation in the Republican campaign, and the last-ditch efforts came across as mean-spirited, immoral, and pathetic. Then *Lincoln Journal* statehouse reporter Thomas A. Fogarty wrote, "Kerrey's response included commercials asking the question why Thone would be spending $1 million 'to spread lies' about him. The commercial suggested the Thone record was too weak to run on."

During the last week of July 1982, a random telephone survey conducted by Lincoln's KLIN radio showed Kerrey leading Thone 51 percent to 27 percent. While the survey was not scientific, it received so much coverage that a July 25, 1982, *Grand Island Daily Independent* (a paper that covered Hall County in Nebraska's generally Republican third congressional district) headlined an Associated Press story: POLL SHOWS BOB KERREY WOULD WIN GOV'S RACE. In late August 1982, Harrison Hickman at Hamilton and Staff wrote, "Thone is very vulnerable. Kerrey is close at present with room to grow, and the trend lines are clearly in his favor."

Both sides awaited the traditional Nebraska state fair debate, a forum in political years for lesser-known candidates to prove themselves, especially on agriculture issues. Though uplifted by the results of their poll findings, the Kerrey camp knew a strong performance was critical, and their candidate provided it. Kerrey supporters were jubilant because this was his first serious, comprehensive debate. He had projected strength and vigor, and most important, had come across as someone thoroughly well versed on the issues. Afterward, Thone still declared himself the winner, acknowledging, however, that Kerrey had handled himself adeptly.

In an interview with Fogarty, Thone said Kerrey "was obviously well coached." Earlier Thone had derided Kerrey's lack of knowledge about agriculture issues with the barb that Lincolnite Kerrey didn't know an ear of corn from a ukulele. Fogarty concluded an August 1982 interview with Kerrey: "While in Pender, he [Kerrey] told his driver to take him to the implement dealership. He was supposed to look up a local man to say hello. Kerrey emerged from the implement store. Wrong place. He told the driver to go to the local feed store instead. 'There is a difference between implements and feed, Bob,' the driver said. 'Hey, you're talking to a guy who doesn't know an ear of corn from a ukulele,' Kerrey responded."

The summer of 1982 was the time Nebraskans learned that Bob Kerrey had true wit and, as Senator James Exon would later say about him, "true grit."

Chapter 6

GOVERNOR KERREY

James Kerrey was driving down O Street one stunning summer day in 1982, his car plastered with KERREY FOR GOVERNOR stickers. Beside him was the former Lois Flaherty, whom he married in 1980, two years after his first wife, Elinor, died of Lou Gehrig's disease. At a stoplight, the young driver of the next car surveyed the political paraphernalia and yelled, "He doesn't have a prayer!" then drove away.

In fact, few Nebraskans actually believed Bob Kerrey could win in November, despite polls that showed him surging. Boyhood buddy Frosty Chapman, for example, recalls phoning Kerrey to express his support and Kerrey responded that he wanted to come over and talk about it. "I can remember before he got there I thought I had this figured out," says Chapman. "When he arrived at my house, I said, 'Bob, you're just doing this to get your name out there, right? You can't beat Charley Thone; he's an incumbent Republican, nobody knows you. I'm your buddy, you can tell me—you're really doing this to get your name out there, and it's great. Then you'll run again, *really* run in four years.' He looked me dead in the eye and said, 'Absolutely not. I'm running to win, and I'm going to beat him.' And at that point, I knew that he probably would, that he could win."

Like Chapman, most Democrats assumed that Kerrey was only running to establish a name for himself—a strategy that would leave him well positioned in 1986, when Thone would have been ineligible for office by the two-term limitation on gubernatorial seats.

Despite the naysayers, the candidate remained confident, his optimism stoked by the impact he sensed he was making throughout the state. During the primary, Kerrey crisscrossed Nebraska in a van that for months doubled as both his office and home, his road time expanded by reading clippings and reports while he waited for calls to connect. Often, after a full day of campaigning, he would stay up long past midnight reading and reworking speeches, his energy and drive soon trickling down to campaign aides who joyously struggled to keep pace.

Critics watching this behavior described Kerrey's enthusiasm as a lust for votes. In truth, however, Kerrey's overtime was in large measure fueled by a desire to write his own speeches—or as much of them as he possibly could. In a process he would repeat as Governor, Kerrey would blend material from briefing sheets with his own personal narrative, his constant lament being that he didn't have sufficient time to polish his text. As Governor, he would become so fanatical about writing his own speeches—even though he didn't have time to do so—that he regularly began speaking extemporaneously.

It has long been common knowledge in Nebraska political circles that hometown boy Ted Sorensen crafted most of President John Kennedy's loftiest and most powerful writing. Sorensen never said so publicly (his loyalty to the former President remains to this day), but Nebraskans with knowledge of his brilliance and his close working relationship with Kennedy put one and one together long before biographers revealed it as fact. Thomas C. Reeves, in his biography of Kennedy, *A Question of Character*, writes: "Prior to Sorensen's employment, one searches Kennedy's writings and speeches in vain for the beautifully flowing sentences, rich historical allusions, and often brilliant wit seen and heard afterward." Of Kennedy's inaugural address, Reeves writes: "Kennedy undoubtedly made contributions, but Sorensen was clearly the principal architect. (As always, he loyally denied it.)" Of Kennedy's Pulitzer Prize–winning book, *Profiles in Courage*, Reeves writes: "Sorensen was responsible for the book's lucid and compelling style."

Kerrey knew enough of the Sorensen-Kennedy relationship to know he didn't want to get in the habit of relying on others to fashion his thoughts. Even if he could have found another Ted Sorensen during his gubernatorial campaign, Kerrey wouldn't have wanted to turn over his speech writing to that person. He has always felt strongly that both minor and major addresses should, if at all possible, be written by the person who gives them. As a result, during his run for the governorship he worked exceedingly hard at honing his writing skills.

So while summer prognosticators maintained that Republican Charley Thone would keep his job, Democrats flirted with the thought that they just might regain the office. Thone was elected in 1978, succeeding James Exon, a two-term Governor who in 1990 ran successfully for his third term as U.S. Senator. The popular Exon, whose grandfather founded the Democratic Party in South Dakota, gave the Kerrey campaign a major boost when he agreed to appear in a televised commercial endorsing the charismatic newcomer. In fact, Kerrey's pollster at the time believes that airing the Exon commercial in the closing days of the campaign may have made the difference.

Mike Boyle was one politician who thought Kerrey would win in November. The Mayor of Omaha embraced Kerrey from the beginning and was instrumental in fostering his acceptance in the state's most populous city, where Democratic voting patterns in certain precincts have changed little since the turn of the century. As Fowler and Pribyl had indicated in their comprehensive strategy, it was imperative for Kerrey to do well in Omaha. Kerrey's pollster discovered that Thone would get a larger percentage of votes from Democrats than Kerrey would get from Republicans, and he urged the candidate to concentrate most of his time in the Omaha area, where Thone's lead was perceived as very soft. In particular, Kerrey was counseled, he needed to woo older, blue-collar Democrats.

Traditionally, Democratic candidates must ring up high numbers in Nebraska's two largest cities to offset rural Republican returns. Nebraska has three congressional districts: The first encompasses Lincoln, the second includes Omaha, and the third covers the rest of the state. The area west of Lincoln, which runs approximately three-quarters of the state's width, is routinely referred to by natives as "outstate Nebraska"—a phrase that has come to include all but Lincoln and Omaha, which sits on the Iowa border.

Boyle broke with tradition by endorsing Kerrey in the Democratic primary, and he worked tirelessly to introduce him to connections he had spent a lifetime making. By 1982, Boyle and his politically savvy chief of staff, Larry Primeau, had built an expansive base by bridging traditionally Democratic south Omaha with Omaha's corporate community; included in the coalition were yuppies from the sprawling western suburbs, some of whom were raised in ethnic Omaha. At the time, the Irish-American Boyle was in his thirties, but the breadth of his experience made him considerably more mature. Reared in Omaha's Cathedral area, Boyle was married to the former Ann Howell, a potent politician in her own right and daughter of one of Omaha's pioneering Democrats, Sam Howell, who continues to dominate the city's old courthouse crowd.

Mike and Ann Boyle represented Omaha's new-breed Democrats, who had been introduced to politics the old-fashioned Irish way—by living it. Bob Kerrey needed the support of this crowd to win, and he got it. Mike Boyle escorted Kerrey to Omaha events, he hosted fund-raisers, he imparted strategical advice. Kerrey learned much from the Omaha gang, including how to lighten up on the campaign trail. Suddenly, the once reserved gubernatorial candidate was dancing the polka, eating sausage, and schmoozing with the elderly at a party at the Polish Home in south Omaha. A few years later, after a bitter falling-out, Boyle would insist that Kerrey never would have been Governor if not for his help in Omaha.

One wet weekend in August, Rothstein and Buckley shot two Kerrey commercials that began airing in mid-September. One showed a professional Kerrey talking about good government against the backdrop of his business office, while the other was a personal account of Kerrey given by his father, James. Kerrey was pleased with his media thrust but unhappy with the direction of his overall campaign, which had been crafted by South Dakotan Jim Humlicek. Kerrey had never completely warmed up to Humlicek.

Their personal styles clashed, and as Election Day neared, Kerrey felt their fall strategy had not sufficiently crystallized. In August, Kerrey dismissed Humlichek from his post.

As a restaurant owner, Kerrey had hired and fired many people, and although he did not relish the task, it did not make him uncomfortable. In a July 13, 1983, interview, Kerrey said, "I'm an arbitrary and judgmental person. I feel remorse about some things." But letting people go, suggesting alternative employment for campaign workers, and eschewing traditional patronage were not among them. He then hired Jim Pribyl, who, along with Fowler, had been serving as an adviser; he also brought in State Senator Steve Wiitala to manage the final stretch, with the two men dividing campaign responsibilities.

Kerrey had toured the entire state over the summer, and by Labor Day the campaign was moving into high gear. One Hastings resident recalls urging her husband, a retired railroad employee, to go with her to hear Kerrey speak in the hopes of hearing firsthand what all the hoopla was about. But her spouse sat in his overstuffed La-Z-Boy recliner watching television and, without looking up, said: "He's got the Medal of Honor—that's good enough for me."

Once ordinary Nebraskans learned of his Medal of Honor, Kerrey's stature was solidified. Many voters—most particularly World War II veterans—wanted to meet a Medal of Honor recipient as much as they wanted to meet a candidate for public office. Many voters who normally would have supported Charley Thone, an officer in World War II, leaned toward Kerrey and awarded him instant respect. He may have been an unknown, but because he had proven his leadership in another vital arena, they felt comfortable putting their faith in him.

Over the summer and throughout the fall, Kerrey fundraisers headlined with such politicians as Vice President Walter Mondale, Governor John Y. Brown of Kentucky, Senator Gary Hart, and Governor Charles Robb of Virginia. Democratic Committeeman Charles Manatt also campaigned for Kerrey. By October 3, an *Omaha World-Herald* poll showed Kerrey with a 42-to-38-percent lead, the first time the challenger had outpolled the incumbent Thone. Seven months earlier, Kerrey had trailed by 46 percent to 21 percent.

Nebraska Democrats smelled victory and worked wildly to keep up the momentum. Thousands of volunteer hours were spent preparing a massive get-out-the-vote campaign. Kerrey confided to Kandra Hahn and other aides that he felt certain he would be elected. On October 22, he learned that he was positioned to win a narrow victory, although his climb had leveled off. Kerrey was heartened by the news, but at the same time concerned about his pollsters finding that Nebraska voters were holding him to a higher standard than might voters from other states. "In most states," his pollsters noted, "aggressive challengers can usually win if they convincingly demonstrate the failings of only moderately popular incumbents and prove that they [the challengers] are OK. It is as if they are saying that not only must we point out Charlie's failures, but also *prove* that you will be better than he has been."

As expected, the *Omaha World-Herald* (often derided by citizens exasperated with its right-leaning philosophy as the "Weird Herald") endorsed Charley Thone. The paper would also decide against endorsing Kerrey six years later in his bid for the U.S. Senate. After Kerrey announced his intentions to run for the presidency in the fall of 1991, a writer for the *World-Herald* interviewed publisher John Gottschalk and asked if the paper would endorse Kerrey if he were the Democratic nominee, given its dogmatic ties to the Republican Party. Some Nebraskans viewed Gottschalk's potential dilemma jadedly and advised the paper's editorial board not to anguish over a Kerrey endorsement. In keeping with the *World Herald*'s past lack of vision, it should simply not endorse him again and "make it three out of three," as one Lincoln resident said. Lincoln's liberal morning paper, the *Lincoln Star*, endorsed Kerrey; surprisingly, the *Lincoln Journal*, the city's widely read evening paper, endorsed neither candidate: "Kerrey has too many unknowns to win from the newspaper the margin of comfort he ought to have to permit a counsel that citizens vote for him. The *Journal* has an institutional preference for leadership, but in this particular race, it is constrained by two uncertainties. The first is whether Kerrey's performance can be as good as his words. The second is whether in a time of general public and private retrenchment, the state will accept strong leadership. Not willing to recommend Thone a second time, and faced with these concerns about Kerrey, the *Journal* endorses neither." The *Journal*'s decision hurt Thone more than it hurt Kerrey, creating extra doubt about the incumbent.

On Election Day, Kerrey campaign workers awoke to a cloudy, Cornhusker-crisp morning. The get-out-the-vote effort began at dawn and would continue until 8:00 P.M., when the polls closed. Kerrey was serene and collected, as though the reality of the day's import had finally registered with him. He had often thought about a victory speech, but had not written one; as the campaign went on he became increasingly comfortable speaking off the cuff, and he figured he would let the audience move him.

The Kerrey family fanned out across Lincoln and Omaha. Brother Bill campaigned for Kerrey on Lincoln street corners, and motorists who thought they were seeing the candidate himself honked, waved, and screamed their support. The Rasmussens were busy in Omaha getting out the vote. Fowler and Kandra Hahn and others were holed up in Kerrey's business office at Lincoln's National Bank of Commerce tracking returns and delegating duties to volunteer workers.

Forty minutes before the polls' 8:00 P.M. closing, Fowler received word from Omaha campaign headquarters that exit polls indicated the race was extremely close and there was concern that every vote be cast in the Lincoln stronghold. Rumor had it that the lines were staggeringly long in some northeast Lincoln polling places, a bastion of Democratic voters and the area that included Kerrey's hometown suburb of Bethany. Fowler, like others aware of Nebraska's weak tradition of poll watching, feared that voters might decide they couldn't make it to vote by eight and leave in frustration. Supporters streaming into the NBC Center for an Election Night celebration were frantically redirected to northeast Lincoln to tell voters they could vote if they were in line by eight. Recalls Fowler, "People walked in to party and we'd send them right back out to a polling place with the command, 'Now you just make *sure* that nobody walks away from that place.'"

After voting, Kerrey spent the day in Omaha; that evening he joined the rally at the city's Old Mill Inn, where he was joined by his family, John Cavanaugh, and hundreds of joyful supporters. Kerrey gave a brief, extemporaneous talk and said he was ready to begin work immediately. He then headed for Lincoln, where campaign workers were not so gleeful.

A computer foul-up had caused a vote-counting snafu and prevented the returns from Lancaster County, which encompasses Lincoln, from being reported. As hand-counted Republican returns came in from western Nebraska, it appeared briefly that Kerrey was losing his lead. But Thone did not receive the strong support in western Nebraska that a Republican needs to offset Omaha and Lincoln. More than 73 percent of Lancaster County voters went to the polls—in part to show support for their hometown boy, but also because of the unprecedented work by teachers and disgruntled state employees, who had been angered by a gratuitous remark Thone made after nixing a pay raise. Final results show that nearly 30 percent more Lancaster County residents voted in 1982 than did in Thone's 1978 race.

Kerrey's victory was assured by midnight, and he spoke briefly, again extemporaneously, to cheering supporters at NBC. He also spoke at the Lincoln Hilton, where he was introduced by James Exon, and sometime after 1:00 A.M. Thone finally conceded. Kerrey's day of reckoning had arrived, and he had made it in spite of an exceedingly difficult final ten-day period—one that had President Reagan in the state campaigning for a desperate Thone. Toward the end of the campaign, the state's most expensive gubernatorial race ever (Thone spent more than $1 million and Kerrey spent $700,000), Nebraska voters were subjected to the sort of down-and-dirty politics they had not seen before. It was the memory of untrue and outrageous rumors leveled against Kerrey that brought from him a dash of election-night prophecy: "I'm going to be the most heterosexual Governor this state has ever seen."

The morning after the election, Kerrey appeared on network news shows and was interviewed by national publications. Political analysts were intrigued by the news that a Democratic political neophyte in territory perceived as rock-ribbed Republican had upset an incumbent Governor for whom the President of the United States had campaigned. Kandra Hahn, who had skipped the election party to get a good night's sleep, arrived at Kerrey's Lincoln campaign headquarters Wednesday morning to find the place deserted. "Nobody knew where Bob was, and the phones were ringing off the walls. Everyone wanted a picture, so I started putting packets together. I was the only one in the whole campaign who had had governmental experience. I had been a county officer and I knew what had to be done."

Nebraska Democrats were predictably elated. They now had two Democratic Senators (Exon and Edward Zorinsky) and two high-profile Democratic Mayors in Boyle and Lincoln Mayor Helen Boosalis, an ardent Kerrey backer who, along with Republican Kay Orr, would make history in 1986 by being candidates in the nation's first all-female gubernatorial race. And now a Democrat had won the Governor's office. Tuesday night's celebrations spilled into Wednesday morning, as Kerrey's restaurant treated campaign workers to a free breakfast. Fowler recalls: "The feeling was exuberant. People saw it as a breaking of an old guard. It wasn't a partisan mood as much as it was one generation to another and new ideas and an aggressive Governor versus a passive Governor."

Summing up the election later, Fowler said, "Kerrey drew upon Boosalis's good government network in south Lincoln; he added to them the progressive activists and liberal Democratic legislators and created his own base built upon his northeast roots and business contacts. That combination of forces enabled Kerrey to gain a commanding lead in Lincoln, which is what he needed to do to win."

Kerrey spent the rest of November and December working on the transition and preparing his inaugural address. As he had on the campaign, he often stayed up until early morning writing and studying state issues, about which he had become fairly well versed. He was deluged with Nebraskans offering advice, support, and suggestions for every conceivable issue and subject. He scheduled meetings with business leaders and members of the Nebraska legislature, who were anxious for one-on-one time with their new Governor. One of the first people he spoke with about a specific job was Candy Exon, the youngest child of Nebraska's senior Senator, who had spent her teenage years—1970 to 1978—in the Governor's mansion. Kerrey offered her a job, and after ruminating awhile, she realized what role she'd like in the administration: As a bachelor, Kerrey would need a person to run the mansion, to take over the duties normally carried out by the Governor's unpaid spouse. Having watched her mother for eight years, Candy knew the position was a full-time job that entailed entertaining, hostessing, coordinating and overseeing tours, and managing the mansion budget. Kerrey said he'd consider Exon's idea, and it suddenly dawned on her that the Governor-elect was thoroughly unfamiliar with his new quarters. "I don't think he'd ever been in the mansion," says Exon. "He wasn't even familiar with what the setup was, that there were private living quarters and public viewing areas." By contrast, when Candy Exon's father was first elected Governor in 1970, he was a close enough friend of the previous occupant, Democrat Frank Morrison, to have been a regular fixture in the mansion and the Governor's office. Kerrey eventually opened the mansion to philanthropic organizations and allowed state agency staff to meet there, but unlike previous Governors, he nixed the use of the publicly funded residence for political fund-raisers.

Bill Wright, a member of Kerrey's inner circle throughout the campaign, served as point man for the transition team, aided by Fowler, Karnes, Hahn, and others. Within weeks, Kerrey had wooed Nebraskan Bill Hoppner away from Senator Exon's Washington staff to oversee the transition. For two months, from an office in the capitol, the trasition team hired staff, Hoppner himself eventually agreeing to serve as chief of staff. Speculating about whom Kerrey would hire became exciting political sport. As he had done in the campaign, Kerrey sought advice from a wide assortment of Nebraskans. And again, he rejected the traditional political mind-set to assembling a staff—an approach that automatically rewarded campaign workers with a job. Among those offered positions were Fowler, Karnes, Hahn, and Wessels, but only because Kerrey had faith in their capabilities; as campaign aides quickly learned, he eschewed traditional patronage. In fact, his business background had so permeated his psyche that he seemed unable to reward individuals simply for campaign support. "He didn't just automatically take the people that designed his campaign and let them run his campaign, nor did he automatically take the people who ran his campaign and then let them run the government," says Fowler. "He'd say, because you know how to be a campaign manager doesn't necessarily mean that you know how to be chief of staff. That was probably a wise move." When all was said and done, Kerrey hired the youngest and most diverse staff in Nebraska gubernatorial history. In an interview with writer Pat Higgins, Kerrey said, "I'm from a different generation from my predecessor. There is a tendency to identify with people in your own age group. I've tried to hire committed people."

While Kerrey deliberated over his inaugural speech and the selection of his staff, others organized inaugural-week activities. James Exon's wife and Omahan Kathleen Kelley acted as ball chairpersons. Kelley and her husband Mike, a prominent Omaha attorney, had been active in Democratic politics since before former U.S. Representative John Cavanaugh's 1976 election. They kept in close touch with Kerrey, who had definite ideas about the tone he wanted to set for the celebration. One mandate he issued from the start was that his SEAL buddies participate. Those who did were given carte blanche to attend any and all inaugural weekend functions. It was Kerrey's SEAL buddies who later provided Nebraska's most memorable gubernatorial inauguration.

On January 6, 1983, Bob Kerrey, a political princeling who one year earlier had a name recognition factor of about 1 percent, was sworn in as Nebraska's thirty-fifth chief executive.

Kerrey's sense of the dramatic was evident on the morning of his inauguration. It was a calm, clear winter day, with bystanders filling the sidewalks surrounding the capitol and the Governor's mansion. Word had it there would be something to see, and state employees and curious citizens looked up and waited.

Suddenly, a dark green twin-engine plane appeared from the south, circled east, turned south again, and leveled off at about twenty-five hundred feet. As the crowd watched in anticipation, a man stepped from the plane and fell briefly until a bright, multicolored parachute opened above him. Then, in quick succession, another appeared, and another, until six para-chutists—all members of the SEAL jump team—were guiding their descent directly toward the capitol tower.

As the team leader reached a point almost level with the statue of the sower on the capitol dome, the crowd gasped, fearing a collision might tangle the shrouds of the chute. But the chutist deftly maneuvered a turn and swept downward toward the mansion, across the street from the capitol. A large canvas target with a bull's-eye had been placed on the front lawn, and the first jumper landed on it, then gracefully walked away. At ten-to-fifteen-second intervals, the others landed in the center of the target.

Kerrey had given a preview of his propensity for surprises, and the commander of the SEALS could chalk up another accomplished maneuver for his prized jump team, the Leapfrogs.

Later that morning, the George Norris Legislative Chamber was packed with members of the Kerrey clan, Nebraska politicians and their families, SEALS, and other friends as Kerrey was administered the oath of office by Nebraska Supreme Court Justice Norman Krivosha. For some observers in the serene west legislative chamber, the day had special significance—the passing of the torch to a new generation. Bob Kerrey, the state's youngest chief executive since 1918, exuded that day the same quiet intensity that had drawn thousands of Nebraskans to him. In one short year, the Bethany boy wonder had achieved a connection with Nebraskans that transcended ordinary political bonds, a connection that would continue to strengthen as the days unfolded.

In his inaugural address, Kerrey presented the concerns he had spoken of so often in his campaign—economic development, education, agriculture, and the state's grave financial woes, a problem he described as serious in nature, although painfully simple. In fact, the man accustomed to having his orders carried out would find in dealing with the independent and strong-willed Nebraska legislature that actions indeed would be painful but, regrettably, not so simple. Also, in what some listeners saw as a portent of his future role on the national stage, Kerrey devoted part of his speech to federal issues: "While none of us want to permit the erosion of vital defense programs, we can no longer afford to short-change those strategies that are essential to our economic recovery. Billions of dollars in the defense budget can be cut without harming our national security. Indeed, prudent reductions will improve our posture. As Governor, I intend to insist that our national leaders get tough and pay for only those things we genuinely need for a lean, modern, and professional defense. This country is in economic trouble, and getting tough is the only way we can get out." Earlier in the speech, Kerrey had expressed outrage at the burgeoning federal deficit, which he saw as devouring private investment, keeping interest rates high, and depressing farm prices. And he concluded with this: "As technological and political changes have swept over us, I have also witnessed a disturbing trend. People in this state and in our nation feel an increasing sense of helplessness. They do not feel a part of their government. They wonder what difference one person and one vote can make. But I tell you that one person can, with facts, with force, and with conviction, have a tremendous impact upon the course of events. As it is chiseled into the granite on the north face of the Capitol as a reminder to all of us, 'The salvation of the state is watchfulness in the citizen.'"

That evening's inaugural ball, the largest gala in gubernatorial history, was held at Lincoln's Pershing Auditorium. (The building was named for General John Pershing, who considered Lincoln his home.) For ten dollars apiece, thousands of Nebraskans gathered in the cavernous civic building to watch their thirty-nine-year-old bachelor Governor walk down the long auditorium aisle. More than two hundred and fifty dignitaries formed reception lines down the length of the room, and when Kerrey finally stepped on stage, he was flanked by his eight-year-old son and six-year-old daughter, who had moved with their mother to Texas in 1980. A roar of *hoo yeah* went up from his SEAL buddies, who later explained that the huzzah was a vocal slap on the back for a job well done. One of those chosen to make the march before the final announcement of Kerrey and his children was Bethany boyhood friend Frosty Chapman, the Governor's first outside appointment, who had signed on as state personnel director. "There was a lot of hilarity about it, a lot of yelling," says Chapman. "It was a very informal time. But seeing Bob with his kids—I almost get tears in my eyes now thinking of him walking out onstage with Ben and Lindsey." Chapman and Kerrey didn't have to say anything that night for each to realize just how far they'd come. It had only been a decade earlier that the two unfocused Vietnam vets, for lack of better projects, spent their time at Duffy's Tavern swigging beers, swapping stories, and chasing women.

Kerrey originally wanted only a rock band at the inaugural (some Nebraskans maintain the nickname Rockin' Bob originated that week and had nothing to do with his Debra Winger days), but in the end he settled for tradition with a twist—a conventional band (the Bobby Lane Orchestra) played upstairs, and a driving rock band (the Rumbles) played down. Dateless for his own ball, between acknowledging guests and caring for his kids Kerrey said that it was just as well: After all, he had no time to spend with a partner, and in fact he only danced that evening with his stepmother, Lois Flaherty, who later recalled it as one of the most precious nights of her life.

The next day, Kerrey began settling into both the mansion and the Governor's splendid baroque office, decorated in fifteenth-century Italian Renaissance style. Kerrey told friends he thought the mansion was not particularly appealing or comfortable. Built in the fifties, Nebraska's gubernatorial residence is often mistaken by out-of-state visitors for a funeral home or motel. A Lincoln newspaper editorial claimed that Kerrey found the mansion so tacky he tried to convince the state patrol to let him live in his own Near South home. But move in Kerrey did, and within six months his frequent house guest, Debra Winger, would give new prominence to the residence of Nebraska's bachelor Governor.

With his living quarters settled, Kerrey turned his attention to appointments. Nebraska Governors choose department heads and their deputies for more than twenty agencies and Kerrey, like his predecessors, brought in his own team. Donna Karnes was asked to run the Department of Revenue and Kandra Hahn to run the Energy Office. Steve Fowler was appointed policy research director after finishing the 1983 legislative session, his last as state senator, and Rod Bates eventually became Kerrey's telecommunications deputy. Renee Wessels was asked to return from Minnesota to become press secretary, and she accepted. Kerrey looked for committed, talented people, and nearly everyone he approached accepted.

There was an enthralled air between Election Day and Kerrey's staff being finalized—a time that coincided with the holidays and a classic Cornhusker winter. Kerrey huddled with state budget experts during that period, and ultimately spent hundreds of hours drafting his first budget address. Along with Donna Karnes and other confidantes, he examined every agency budget in a process he called "learning, searching, and realistically evaluating." He referred to the labor-intensive work in his budget message: "We began this difficult and strenuous task immediately after the election. And, although we certainly approached the job with gusto, we did not, as the saying goes, 'only go around once.' We went around at my office at the Department of Administrative Services, and at the Governor's mansion. We met during the morning, afternoon, evenings, and weekends."

Bob Kerrey assumed office raring to go. He had always been a task-oriented person, and now it was time for him to undertake his most difficult task yet—managing Nebraska during one of its worst recessions. In the budget message he presented to the Nebraska legislature on February 1, 1983, Kerrey let it be known that he indeed was a fiscal conservative, in keeping with the historical pattern of Nebraska Democratic chief executives. In essence, Kerrey responded to the state's basic fiscal conservatism in the same way that Governor James Exon might have—mirroring that conservatism.

In his first budget, Kerrey requested of the legislature a half-cent sales tax increase, with an automatic expiration date, to resolve the shortfall. Although he was urged by some advisers to raise the Nebraska income tax rate, Kerrey refused, reiterating, as he had done in his budget speech, that it was unwise for the state government to try and tax its way out of its fiscal problem. Again, Kerrey approached the issue from a business perspective. In a letter sent during his primary campaign to State Senator Cal Carsten, chairman of the Revenue Committee, Kerrey wrote: "As a businessman, I've had to collect the state's sales tax from my customers and the state's income tax from my employees. I've had to pay the corporate tax and numerous licensing costs and fees levied by the state. I know how precipitous changes in tax rates can affect personal and business planning. . . . Our revenue projection system has failed to match our need for stable tax rates. . . . Our state found itself this summer taping its fiscal structure together with interfund transfers due, in part, to overly optimistic revenue projections." Later, Kerrey would also present optimistic revenue projections in his first budget in the hopes that the economy would pick up. But at the same time he warned his constituents to be prepared for further economic deterioration.

At the end of the first legislative session (the Nebraska legislature convenes in January for a few months, and special summer or fall sessions are often called to deal with revenue shortfalls), lawmakers refused to enact Kerrey's cuts. As a result, he did not have the necessary revenue to initiate his programs. But Kerrey still would not raise taxes, so the Governor and the legislature found themselves in a stalemate: He wasn't interested in raising taxes and they weren't interested in cutting programs.

Fowler, who served as policy research director, recalls: "As Governor, he proposed a series of cuts and argued, 'Here are things that aren't really working.' He wanted to apply that revenue to new programs, but the political reality was that to the legislature, many of the things he proposed to cut were programs that had been recently passed or recently funded. Their egos were on the line, and they didn't want to hear a newcomer come in and say, 'Those programs aren't working, let's cut those and fund mine.'" State Senator David Landis, an articulate liberal spokesman, recalls one disagreement in particular—an unrelenting attack by the Kerrey administration on the Foster Care Review Board, which Landis took to be one of the better programs the legislature had created for children in recent years.

Variations of that conflict existed throughout the four years Kerrey served as chief executive. Still, legislators held great respect and trust for Kerrey, and several of Kerrey's goals were accomplished during the first legislative session. In a 1985 interview, Kerrey pointed with pride to a repeal of the sales tax on food. In an interview with writer Pat Higgins, Kerrey admitted he wasn't happy with the implications for the city of Omaha, which stood to lose some $30 million as a result of the new law. But he also noted that all but two of that city's state senators supported the measure.

But if the legislators were acquiescent, Omaha Mayor Mike Boyle was not. In fact, he felt thoroughly betrayed by a man he had helped put in office. As Boyle and others would discover, however, Kerrey was indeed a true paradox when problem solving and personalities were involved. On the one hand, he showed strong personal loyalty to trusted friends whose abilities he has faith in, and he acted accordingly; the flip side was that he was just as likely to embrace his enemy and disappoint or punish his friends.

Based on his first year's performance, some Democratic Party regulars began to believe that a conflict existed between the values Kerrey expressed and the traditional list of liberal solutions, most notably his fiscal policies. Kerrey agreed with that assessment. He had never subscribed to a traditional list of anything, let alone solutions to governmental problems, and he had never presented himself as a liberal or populist. Throughout his campaign, in fact, he pitched himself as a businessman who understood the bottom line but who nonetheless felt that government had an important role to play in the enhancement of individual lives. Thomas A. Fogarty, then a *Lincoln Evening Journal* political reporter, wrote: "In an ironic twist for a Democrat challenging a Republican, Kerrey could present himself as someone who knew from experience the difficulty of meeting a payroll. He sold himself in Main Street businesses outstate and in the corporate board rooms of Lincoln and Omaha." Since his days at Philadelphia Naval Hospital, Kerrey had developed a love-hate relationship with government that precluded him from viewing it one-dimensionally, as he believed many doctrinaire Democrats did. He seemed to believe that much of Democratic ideology was just plain, old-fashioned, "they-ought-to-know-by-now bullshit," and he didn't have any patience for it.

Senator Landis thinks the problem was not with Kerrey but with individuals who had read too much into Kerrey's candidacy. "He was a relatively ambiguous novice with tremendous physical and rhetorical appeal, and into this vessel everyone poured their own hopes and wishes—assuming, I think, that Kerrey shared their own personal agendas." They learned about Kerrey that they couldn't dislike him personally—even when they found themselves outraged at his actions. "People have great affection for Bob Kerrey," says policy researcher Bill Lock, "even in the face of great disagreement."

Kerrey's first year was the quintessential political honeymoon period. Average citizens were eager to know more about their new chief, and they rushed him at state functions. State legislators appreciated Kerrey's candor and willingness to work hard to solve problems. Journalists enjoyed covering him as much for his own enigmatic ways as for his differences from the more reserved Charley Thone. Kerrey so enjoyed his weekly press conferences that he often casually discussed policy at them—a habit that once forced seasoned aide Hoppner to literally yank his boss out of a particularly revealing, stream-of-consciousness session.

But Kerrey continued to be an open, lively, straightforward interviewee and reporters looked forward to one-on-one sessions. Ed Howard, bureau chief of the Associated Press, sums up the first year this way: "Charlie Thone was oatmeal, Bob Kerrey was pizza. The trouble was, nobody knew what kind of pizza."

One characteristic that emerged clearly from Kerrey's first encounter with the legislature was his inability to toe the conventional line. State Senators and other political observers learned early they could not use conventional orthodox measurements on him; he simply would not, or perhaps could not, abide by tradition. Those few confidants already acquainted with Kerrey's mercurial ways often cautioned legislators and journalists not to pigeonhole their man, because it was gross simplification.

Compared to many other state constitutions, Nebraska's grants wide authority to its chief executive. However, according to *Nebraska Government and Politics*, a comprehensive analysis of state government written and edited by political scientists at the University of Nebraska–Lincoln, in practice Nebraska Governors historically have acted as caretakers who "have been content to let the legislature define much of its own agenda, stepping in to veto whenever budgets are felt to be too high."

Of course, Kerrey had no intention of being a caretaker. From the first, he exhibited an active, critical, managerial style of governing. During his campaign Kerrey often used restaurant metaphors, declaring, for example, that the taxpayers and voters of Nebraska were the customers. If what you're doing is not to the liking of your customers, the restaurant fails, Kerrey would explain. If the menu isn't working, you throw it out and serve up something the customer wants. For Kerrey, the menu paralleled policy: The voters were customers and the Governor was the restaurant owner who could only succeed by listening to the customers. What Kerrey encountered, however, was a situation less like a restaurant and more like a potluck supper, with forty-nine state senators serving up their individual dishes.

Kerrey stopped using the analogy after a time. He discovered that working with members of the Unicameral to streamline state government—as he had pledged to do in his inaugural address—was more frustrating than he had envisioned it would be. Kerrey approached governing like an athlete training for a triathlon. He came charging in on many fronts, and he expected to succeed quickly on all of them. As he learned, the political process is often plodding and slow, but he was still satisfied with his maiden outing.

Kerrey spent the summer of 1983 entertaining his children. He and his former wife, Beverly Higby, had divorced four years earlier, but their relationship would improve dramatically during the gubernatorial years.

The summer would be a memorable one for Kerrey, for that's when he solidified his relationship with Debra Winger. He was in great demand not just throughout his home state (charitable organizations clamored for him to appear at fund-raisers, attend events, or read public service announcements), but he was also beginning to be in demand nationally.

On August 17, 1983, ten days before his fortieth birthday, Kerrey stood before thirty-five hundred delegates of the Veterans of Foreign Wars national convention at the New Orleans Hilton and accepted a citizenship award and a gold medal for his Navy service in Vietnam. Kerrey, who only a year earlier had been a struggling, rumor-dodging gubernatorial nominee, delivered to his fellow veterans an eloquent and impassioned speech about war and peace, patriotism and freedom, courage and country. In the speech, later described by University of Nebraska–Kearney professor Larry D. Theye as "a model of how to disagree," Kerrey challenged the VFW on seven specific issues close to veterans' hearts. Kerrey managed to walk away to thunderous applause, which may have shocked the media and other politicians, but not the Governor; after all, he knew veterans, he was one of them. In fact, Kerrey told aides from the outset that he believed his speech would be well received.

Kerrey drafted the address himself with help from speech writer Kate Joeckel, who left in the middle of Kerrey's tenure to become a professor of communications at a small college near Des Moines, Iowa. A brilliant writer, Joeckel was trained in the techniques of rhetoric and understood the rhythm of language. All the concepts and ideas were Kerrey's, and Joeckel would fine-tune drafts he sent her; they worked back and forth, with Kerrey eventually completing the final draft on the plane.

Kerrey carved out time from his schedule to tinker with the speech, writing longhand on a yellow legal pad. Not everyone who knew of his plans approved, but Kerrey was adamant—he had been mulling the speech over in his mind for a long time, and he was eager to give it. Later, he found himself elated with the response, confirming for him that he needed to follow his instincts. Kerrey knew it was a risky proposition, but he felt confident that he could earn the appreciation of the veterans. Says Theye: "Consummate skill was required to stand before a national convention to challenge that organization's ideals and walk away to a standing ovation."

Slated to precede Kerrey at the podium were President Ronald Reagan, Secretary of Defense Caspar Weinberger, and the Chairman of the Joint Chiefs of Staff, General John Vessey. Unlike these men, Kerrey chose the VFW forum to outline positions contrary to those long held by the members. The *Omaha World-Herald* reported, "Even though the delegates have adopted resolutions supporting positions opposed to those presented by Kerrey, delegates rose to their feet and gave him a thunderous ovation as he left the rostrum in the New Orleans Hilton Hotel."

Nebraskans reacted proudly to Kerrey's first foray into the national arena, and his actions were widely hailed and discussed in taverns from Omaha to Ogallala. Kerrey, in essence, was expressing his faith in the veterans and their ability to view his nonconformism correctly. Kerrey was an honest critic of some dearly held tenets of the VFW, and yet its members recognized that disagreement did not preclude mutual admiration. They knew the firebrand before them was as loyal a patriot as any one of them.

Kerrey's speech before the VFW confirmed for a few Nebraskans their impression that their young Governor wanted to be a player on a bigger stage. Kerrey had been in office for eight months, presiding over only one session of the Nebraska legislature. As a result, many political observers were still assessing him. To some, the VFW speech was an indicator that the governorship was a stepping-stone, and since he was motivated more by national and international issues, Nebraskans should not count on him to try to make a profound difference within state government.

Others disagreed, arguing that both state and national issues touched Kerrey; regrettably, they added, the nature of the economy blunted all of his initiatives on education, economic development, and the environment, and he was haunted by the fact that he couldn't do more.

Nebraska State Senator Don Wesely, who represents Kerrey's old legislative district, says: "Kerrey was deeply saddened by the dire economy. He came in all excited and wanted very badly to effect change, and he simply couldn't. It was tragic, and I think he felt totally disheartened. I mean, here was a man who was so idealistic when he first started in the primary; he had so many ideas and dreams, but the economy was so bad he just couldn't do anything. I think that's why he didn't want to run again—he was so depressed by how little he could accomplish. He didn't want to go through it again."

Kerrey spent much of September and October preparing for the new legislative session that would begin in January. He discovered that he truly enjoyed his job, and his confidence was at an all-time high. He was receiving thumbs-up reviews, and he knew he was considered a good Governor. Within two months, his resoluteness would be severely tested by the collapse of a major state industrial savings and loan company. But in the meantime, Nebraskans found that they enjoyed having Kerrey as Governor.

Of course, even in the best of times Kerrey's missions would have been difficult; what he encountered was in fact the worst of times, a paralyzing recession that did not abate throughout his four years as Governor. In addition, President Reagan's new federalism meant that tax rates needed to be raised just to compensate for shrinking federal dollars. Kerrey made it clear from the start that he would not raise taxes, and he didn't. History shows that Nebraska Governors who raise taxes don't win reelection. But even if Kerrey wasn't concerned about future political office—and he always maintained he wasn't—the idea of raising taxes was repulsive to him. Norbert Tiemann, a Republican who served from 1967 to 1971, was not reelected despite his record as one of the state's most outstanding Governors. His sin: repeatedly restructuring the state's tax base, even though he did so to improve higher education, introduce state aid to local school districts, and push economic development.

Fifteen years later, Governor Kerrey was concerned about most of those same issues; yet, unlike Tiemann, Kerrey refused to raise taxes to accomplish his goals. Kerrey felt strongly that existing revenue could be more effectively reallocated; he also maintained that there was government waste, and as manager of the state, raising taxes was the last resort for Kerrey.

Journalists and political observers typically refer to Kerrey's four years in office as a whole, but those who worked closely with his administration perceived things differently. For them, there were the two years when Nebraskan Bill Hoppner served as chief of staff and the two years where native Floridian Don Nelson held that title. The years with Hoppner are characterized as a time when people participated in the executive and legislative arenas with optimism, vigor, and enthusiasm. His tenure dovetailed with the first honeymoon year most new chief executives are accorded. The second half of Kerrey's term is remembered less for accomplishments and more for the disappointment and resentment that pervaded the atmosphere—an atmosphere clouded by the actions of Nelson, characterized by one Nebraskan as "a man who makes John Sununu look like Mother Teresa."

On January 6, 1984, Kerrey presented his second budget to the members of the Nebraska Unicameral, a state of the state address titled "The Promise of the Prairie." Again, Kerrey spent days drafting the address, which received polishing help from speech writer Kate Joeckel. Kerrey had made it clear he wanted the speech to be more than a morass of numbers, that he wanted to inject literary allusions, and together he and Joeckel settled on the character of Alexandra Bergson from *O Pioneers!*, Willa Cather's famous novel set in the Great Plains. While parts of "The Promise of the Prairie" are Kerrey's thoughts reshaped by Joeckel, much of the language is Kerrey's and all of the themes are unquestionably his.

"The Promise of the Prairie," perhaps more than any other speech, reveals how Kerrey views the role of government and his faith in the ability of Americans to accomplish the loftiest of goals if provided with opportunity. In this address, Kerrey spoke of individual perseverance and the pursuit of dreams—themes that continue to reverberate in his speeches today. And although "The Promise of the Prairie" did not touch on Kerrey's Vietnam experience per se, it nonetheless managed to again draw on the lesson of that war; it is just as personally revealing, because he digs deep into his heart when he expresses faith in the individual to overcome adversity. In large measure, Kerrey was speaking of himself when he talked about interfacing determination and governmental assistance. It was, after all, government that nurtured him in Philadelphia, it was government that gave him small-business assistance loans to start his restaurant, it was government that provided insurance after a tornado demolished his business. But it was Bob Kerrey who in each instance seized the opportunity. In "The Promise of the Prairie," Kerrey seemed almost to be urging his fellow Nebraskans to go for it: "And I tell you now with unshakable faith that no boundary has been set—no boundary will ever be set—to constrain what the individual Nebraskan can accomplish when they discover opportunity."

Vietnam nearly sprung Kerrey from his mortal coil, and when he spoke of "unshakable faith," he was speaking as someone who had watched his own flesh burned and knows that the rest is relative. From Vietnam forward, Bob Kerrey, the man, cannot be shaken. In "The Promise of the Prairie," Kerrey not only provided an innovative and creative budget, he provided a window into his feelings about the role of government to provide opportunity for its citizenry. He began:

> *In her finest moments, Willa Cather wrote of what she knew and loved best: the Nebraska frontier and the men and women who settled it. When Cather set out to write* O Pioneers!, *she succeeded in creating a character—Alexandra Bergson—who captures the essence of those men and women, past and present, who have seen the infinite possibilities in Nebraska and have been willing to devote their lives to realizing them. . . . With unshakable faith in the land, in herself, and in the promise of the future, she succeeds. Where others saw certain failure, she saw opportunity. And so, Cather writes, "For the first time, perhaps, since that land emerged from the waters of geologic ages, a human face was set toward it with love and yearning. It seemed beautiful to her, rich and strong and glorious. Her eyes drank in the breadth of it, until her tears blinded her. Then the Genius of the Divide, the great, free spirit which breathes across it, must have bent lower than it ever bent to a human will before."*

Nearly six months to the day after Kerrey delivered this speech, New York Governor Mario Cuomo captivated a nation in a speech about the family that is America. In one of the most stirring passages, Cuomo said:

> *The Republicans believe the wagon train will not make it to the frontier unless some of our old, some of our young, and some of our weak are left behind by the side of the trail. The strong will inherit the land! We Democrats believe that we can make it all the way with the whole family*

> *intact. We have. More than once. Ever since Franklin Roo-*
> *sevelt lifted himself from his wheelchair to lift this nation*
> *from its knees. Wagon train after wagon train. To new*
> *frontiers of education, housing, peace. The whole family*
> *aboard. Constantly reaching out to enlarge that family.*
> *Lifting them up into the wagon on the way. . . . Some of*
> *us are in this room today only because this nation had that*
> *confidence. It would be wrong to forget that.*

Bob Kerrey and Mario Cuomo befriended each other during their gubernatorial days, and while Cuomo electrified the delegates at the 1984 Democratic National Convention introducing Walter Mondale, Kerrey introduced presidential contender Gary Hart in an address to veterans in which he began with a reference to Cuomo:

> *Let me tell you from the start that I am one of the people*
> *Mario Cuomo referred to as having greater wealth and*
> *greater income than most. In the years that separate my*
> *return from Vietnam and my start in politics I have been*
> *working to build a successful business in Nebraska.*

The two men call each other frequently, and down the line would enjoy pundit discussion of a Cuomo-Kerrey Democratic ticket as a "dream scenario."

Neither of Kerrey's speeches at the convention made an impact the way his New Orleans VFW speech had. The audience for his veterans speech was inattentive and talkative. His introductory speech for Hart did give him national exposure (he gave it in prime time), and it was well crafted and personal. Kerrey did a credible job, but he clearly had not yet honed his speechmaking skills.

The speech is barely a page and a half, and in keeping with his propensity to approach events through the prism of his personal experience, Kerrey said: "When I was young, we had it all. I was strong and educated, self-confident and self-reliant. There was nothing I could not do. There was no limit to the potential of this nation. And then in one explosive moment in Vietnam the physical strength of my youth was blown away. The spirit and virtue of this nation was also shattered and torn—like the bodies of the young men sent to fight in that sad and confused war.''

Following the convention, Kerrey returned to Nebraska to prepare for the upcoming legislative session. His 1984 budget was widely hailed as innovative and judicious, the most creative proposal being a plan to earmark $25 million for raising teachers' salaries. He said: "I am today challenging Nebraskans to set a goal of recruiting and paying a teaching force in the upper ten percent in the nation. This is, I believe, a reasonable, aggressive goal given our own high individual aspirations. . . . But if we are to pay our teachers in the top ten percent, we should expect that we have the top ten percent of the teaching talent. In return for truly competitive salaries, teachers must be willing to sacrifice some of the protection they have traditionally enjoyed." That trade-off was vintage Kerrey—an approach to issues that characterized the Kerrey administration throughout. Kerrey's approach resulted in a *Lincoln Evening Journal* editorial that said: "The second Kerrey budget is a more adroit document than his first. It affirms executive policy priorities and preferences. Nebraska going somewhere and taking selective risks, rather than desperately holding the line against changing times, is the core. That direction is to be applauded."

As the year unfolded, however, bright tax revenue projections dimmed and the Kerrey budget basically was left unfunded. In fact, Kerrey's bold teacher salary proposal was not funded while he was in office (it was gradually implemented under Kerrey's successor, Republican Kay Orr). But it was Kerrey who first framed the issue, who set the challenge, so that even after leaving office, the legislature and the new Governor saw fit to make the proposal law.

Despite legislative defeats, 1984 was a wild and wonderful year for Kerrey. On the one hand, his relationship with Debra Winger was sailing smoothly along (at least as smoothly as the volatile duo could sail). He enjoyed her increasingly frequent visits, her stays giving him a respite and a reason to stop working. When Winger wasn't around—and she was away a great deal of the year—Kerrey did nothing but work. When she came, she cooked for him, she made his favorite snack (chocolate chip cookies and milk), and she made the mansion seem homier. It was that same year, however, that Kerrey and company realized the recession was deepening dramatically.

In an interview, Kerrey once discussed the recession and Nebraskans' response to the worst agricultural climate in decades. "What I find so remarkable is how evenly people in the state have reacted to this crisis," he said. "If the price of real estate had declined elsewhere as a result of the decision of the Federal Reserve Board to control inflation by keeping the supply of money tight, people would be close to jumping off buildings. The atypical scene here is someone at wit's end, someone acting frantically. It's typical of Nebraskans to say, 'We've suffered through many things in the past and we will suffer through this.'"

Kerrey had participated in one complete round with the Nebraska legislature and he felt more seasoned, more politically astute, heading into his sophomore year. His relations with the legislature were still good, although that would change by the end of his term.

But the beginning of 1984 still saw Kerrey energized and enthusiastic about what he could accomplish as Governor. He was a fountain of ideas, and he was continually pushing his people to be creative in their approach and their thinking.

For the first year and a half of his administration, Kerrey's chief of staff was Bill Hoppner. A poised political pro, Hoppner had worked as the administrative assistant to Senator Exon since 1978. Hoppner was anxious to return to his native Nebraska, so when Kerrey offered him a job in 1982, he eagerly accepted.

Hoppner was born and reared in Pender, an agricultural community of thirteen hundred people in Thurston County (known widely as the home of Native American reservations). Introduced to politics as a youngster by his father, an activist in state party campaigns and Exon's races, Hoppner was well versed in the art of politics. He graduated from the University of Nebraska–Lincoln in 1972 with a business degree and went on to earn his law degree. Hoppner was later hired as Governor Exon's legal counsel, a position he kept until 1978, when he moved to Washington as Senator Exon's top aide.

Hoppner stayed with Kerrey for two legislative sessions, then quit to team up with a friend who had started a small trucking business. (He would later return to chair Kerrey's 1988 Senate campaign, then, in 1991, join Kerrey's presidential campaign.) Kerrey's staff viewed Hoppner as tough but fair, and were sad to see him leave. The news that Don Nelson was coming on board made some aides nervous because he had a reputation as an arrogant and difficult man. Both Hoppner and Nelson had reputations as talented, intelligent, and capable executives who were hard-working and exceedingly well versed in the machinations of government.

Nelson arrived on the job at a time when Nebraska was experiencing its worst recession in fifty years. As a result, there would be a great deal of naysaying by the Governor, and Nelson bore the anger directed at his boss. Tall, fair, and handsome, Nelson quickly earned a reputation as a rude man who enjoyed curtailing access to Kerrey. Longtime friends of Kerrey's felt that Nelson relished his role as gatekeeper to the Governor, and that he enjoyed being the bad guy far too much for him to be effective. Down the line, Nelson lost much effectiveness because people began circumventing him and going directly to Kerrey.

Nelson's arrival in Lincoln heralded a change in the Kerrey administration. Before Nelson, despite the gloomy economic picture, those in Kerrey's administration felt upbeat and eager to push his agenda. With the arrival of Nelson, however, many people who had had close and frequent contact with Kerrey began to feel shut out. One was Donna Karnes. As head of the Revenue Department, she met with Kerrey often, both in professional and personal settings. Periodically, after a grueling week of work, Kerrey would invite a group of agency heads and other staff members and head over to the Zoo Bar to unwind.

Kerrey's treks to the Zoo Bar did not go over well with everyone in Lincoln. Most people thought it was refreshing that an openly acknowledged workaholic got out occasionally to take a break; others didn't approve of the setting, a college bar.

Nelson enjoyed traveling with Kerrey, and the two often showed up in out-of-the-way places, occasionally with Debra Winger in tow, and they always appeared to be having a grand time. When the Governor's limousine ferried Kerrey and Nelson to the Zoo Bar, the first thing they often did was call female staff members and invite them to drop by for drinks and dancing. This tendency to flaunt their good times irritated some Nebraskans. It also contributed to the series of rumors about Kerrey that began with his annual Halloween parties and his romance with Debra Winger. In fact, the treks to the Zoo Bar and elsewhere were merely harmless diversions by a group of obsessive workers.

Ed Howard, Lincoln bureau chief of the Associated Press, says: "Stories just flew about Kerrey. And because of the nature of his personality, his capacity for being flippant, he lived the same realities that perhaps a popular kid in high school lives. People said outrageous things about him—that he did this, that he did that, that he's never in his office, that he's in his office until four o'clock in the morning. All the things that were said about him could not possibly have been true, and Bob is the kind of person who didn't give a damn about what people said."

Before her death of cancer in 1990, Karnes told friends that she felt Don Nelson's time as chief of staff was an unproductive period for Kerrey. In her opinion, Nelson drew out a dark side of Kerrey that was a sort of "macho boys club" mentality, and she believed Kerrey should have distanced himself from Nelson. As the head of Kerrey's Revenue Department, Karnes was in a position to watch the dynamics up close, and she became discouraged during Nelson's tenure.

State Senator Don Wesely agrees. "The last two years of Kerrey's administration changed to more of a personality conflict and a kind of macho two years," says Wesely. "There was fighting for fighting's sake. I tend to blame Don Nelson—Don has changed since that time to the point where I really like the guy now, but through those last two years, it seemed that Nelson and Kerrey fed off of each other and produced a negative environment."

Nelson was once described as "the Elliot Richardson of the Rocky Mountains/Great Plains" because of his long history of agency work and staff assignments to Governors. Before Kerrey he worked for the Governor of Wyoming, and he acknowledges that working for Kerrey was decidedly more invigorating. Kerrey was enthusiastic and focused and eager to make his mark on the state. In addition, Kerrey was dating a celebrated actress, and Nelson began to be quoted in national magazines. In November 1986, *Newsweek* quoted Nelson as saying, "We [our generation] realize that dancing may be more important than another heavy political discussion. We're more likely to put everything in perspective."

At the time, Nelson and Kerrey both had the same take on life—a cavalier attitude about the prescribed roles of government officials and a determination not to be forced into hypocrisy.

The way Steve Fowler saw it: "Sometimes he's enthusiastic about being in the public eye and then sometimes he's a reluctant public figure—he's tired or uncomfortable being a public person so he goes off and insists on doing things that any other person forty years old could and nobody would think anything of it."

Nebraska residents outside the cocoon of state government did not notice a change in the Kerrey administration; only those closely aligned with government began to notice the difference in the way things were being dealt with under Nelson. Word spreads quickly in Lincoln, and every time Nelson insulted someone, others heard about it.

People gradually started bypassing Nelson, and many began to develop an animosity toward him that rendered him ineffective. Some aides told Kerrey unflattering stories about his chief of staff, but Kerrey supported Nelson and believed that people's feelings about him were irrelevant. Kerrey and Nelson enjoyed each other's company so much that the two went into business together after Kerrey stepped down as Governor.

Kerrey wanted a chief of staff who was brilliant and tough, and that's what he had in Nelson. Kerrey is a realist, however, and during his 1988 Senate race he made it clear to Donna Karnes that, despite his friendship with Nelson, he viewed him as a political liability. Among Nelson's supporters was Kerrey energy czar Kandra Hahn, who believed that Nelson was the only person who could have handled dispensing the word from the Governor's office during the horrific economic downturn. She believed that Nelson acted as Governor during the last year and a half—a time when Kerrey became so disenchanted with the legislature that he didn't want to deal with members personally. Bob Kerrey was looking elsewhere.

Chapter 7

ONE TERM OF ENDEARMENT

T he Paramount Pictures movie trailer was parked in front of Saint Mary's Catholic Church, directly across the street from Lincoln's state capitol building. With tinted window-shades drawn, the truck displayed a large sign that read: PLEASE DO NOT KNOCK ON WINDOWS OR DOORS, THE ACTRESS IS ON A BREAK AND NEEDS QUIET. At 12:30 P.M. the streets were crowded with Lincolnites eager to watch the filming of *Terms of Endearment*. By 1:00 P.M. actress Debra Winger was running from her costar, Jeff Daniels, and the cameras were rolling. Back and forth she would run in her flowered, mid-knee-length dress and flat shoes. Time after time they repeated the scene until, finally, a man just slightly taller than the small-framed star stepped out of the sidelines and embraced her, patting her on the back: "Great job, great, great, great!"

For James Brooks, the screenplay writer and director, shooting was over. The crowd clapped and watched as Brooks walked away with Winger. People rushed at her, eager for an autograph, but Brooks implored: "No, she's exhausted; later, please." Shoulders were shrugged and autograph seekers acquiesced, missing what they were certain was their last chance to see the celebrated star. Only later would that day's onlookers realize that there would be many opportunities to meet Miss

Winger. Only later, during the March Academy Awards ceremony, would that day's witnesses learn that they had observed
the filming of the year's best picture.

No one observing the filming that airy April day could guess
that their Governor, holed up in his private office, and the young
actress across the street would forge a lasting friendship. No Lincolnite had a clue that day that their chief executive, a former
naval officer and a sometime gentleman, and an urban cowgirl
christened Mary Debra Winger would fall wildly, passionately in
love. Within weeks, however, Winger indeed was the Governor's
girlfriend. Within months, she would return to Lincoln and live
in the Governor's mansion.

In retrospect, their meeting seems preordained, for despite
all their obvious dissimilarities, the two had much in common.
Like Kerrey, Winger was raised in a middle-class household with
a businessman father and a working mother. He volunteered for
extrahazardous duty with the Navy SEALS; she endured several
months of military training upon applying for Israeli citizenship
after early graduation from high school. He faced death at
twenty-six in Vietnam and recovered from war wounds for nine
months in a naval hospital; she stared down death at eighteen
after being thrown from a moving truck, and recuperated in a
California hospital, where she nearly died from a cerebral hem-
orrhage. He emerged from war with a physical challenge—a
right leg amputated below the knee; she suffers from a punc-
tured eardrum that prevents her from flying. He used the near-
death experience as a springboard to jump-start his life; she
called her close encounter with death a "huge hunk of grace"
and thereafter stretched life to what some observers suspected
was almost a breaking point. He showed leadership tendencies
and a thirst for adventure even before his brush with death; she
exhibited rebellious tendencies and a lust for life long before her
accident. He is roundly hailed for his intelligence and drive; she
is praised for her intellect and dedication to her art.

That the couple would meet in Lincoln while she was filming
the story of a young mother who battles cancer in Lincoln could
not have been a more endearing and intense introduction had it
been arranged by a *shadchan*. Later, in a *Vanity Fair* interview,

Winger would say: "I told Bob when I met him and we had fun together, I said, 'Wait. You don't really know me. You think you know me, but this isn't really me.'" She went on to describe how the person Kerrey was enchanted with was being filtered through the fictional woman in the movie.

Winger, by her account, almost passed up her chance to go out with Kerrey. He had barely finished his first hundred days in office when Brooks and company arrived in Lincoln to shoot the movie version of Larry McMurtry's book. Residents had been awaiting the arrival of the stars and crew with great anticipation, as a Paramount movie scout had earlier prepared folks for a "three-ring circus." Nebraska's State Film Office accommodated Paramount throughout their month-long stay, happy that Lincoln's local economy would be boosted by more than $1 million.

Paramount Pictures, in conjunction with the city, organized a press conference to kick off the project, and a near-festive atmosphere reigned. Reporters, politicos, and members of Lincoln's business cognoscenti assembled at the Villager, a large motel-restaurant complex at the east edge of town. It was this reception that provided the inevitable meeting between the thirty-nine-year-old divorced Governor and the twenty-seven-year-old unattached actress (she later celebrated her twenty-eighth birthday at the Villager's Sadie's Saloon).

When Kerrey entered the basement room that April afternoon, Brooks, Winger, producer Martin Jurow, and others were seated behind cables at a table with a standing podium. Jack Nicholson and Shirley MacLaine did not attend, so Winger was served up as the only star. Kerrey approached the group, shook hands all around, and then gave a short, extemporaneous speech in which he welcomed the entire entourage to Lincoln. He presented Winger with an admiralship in the Nebraska Navy, a farcical certificate that plays on Nebraska being one of the nation's most landlocked states, a proclamation routinely awarded to dignitaries or, more precisely, to anyone who really wants one. Kerrey then described himself as "a naval officer and a sometime gentleman." He concluded, "Have fun in Nebraska," to which Winger responded in her trademark low voice, "You, too!"

A young Bob Kerrey in his Bethany days.

*James and Elinor Kerrey posing before the
Headdress Ball in 1966.*

Kerry (bottom row, third from the right) with his fifth-grade classmates.

Kerrey (top row, seventh from left), pictured here with the Northeast Elks Midgets, played football from grade school to high school.

Kerrey's high school yearbook photo.

Kerrey with his sister, Jesse Rasmussen, as they appeared in the Northeast High School yearbook. The other politician in the Kerrey family, Jesse was elected to the Nebraska legislature in 1990.

Standing top middle, Kerrey poses for an official photo of the University of Nebraska-Lincoln Innocents Honor Society.

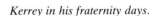

Kerrey in his fraternity days.

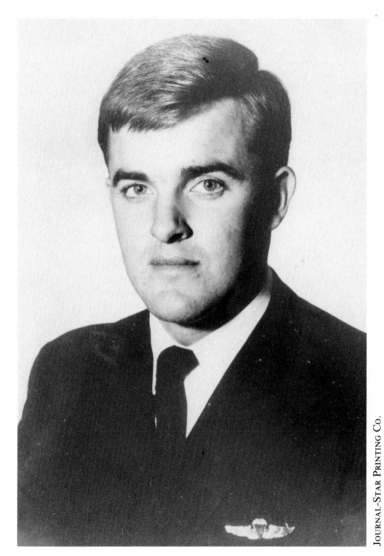

Kerrey's official Navy photograph, taken before he was wounded in Vietnam.

Because of his objections to the Vietnam War, Kerrey was reluctant to accept the Medal of Honor from President Nixon on May 14, 1970, but was persuaded by his Navy SEALS comrades and accepted it on their behalf.

Bob Kerrey being sworn in as Nebraska's thirty-fifth Governor in 1983.

Kerrey and Debra Winger share a moment at the Governor's mansion during a party for the cast and crew of Terms of Endearment. *Steve Fowler, Kerrey's adviser, stands to the left.*

Kerrey in front of the Nebraska State Capitol Building.

Cornhusker Camelot: Kerrey with longtime girlfriend Debra Winger.

Kerrey spends an afternoon with Debra Winger's son, Noah Hutton.

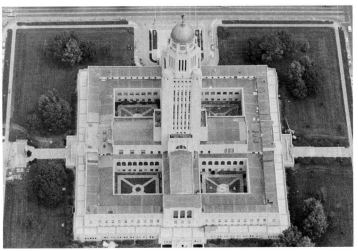

The architecturally renowned Nebraska State Capitol building towers four hundred feet above the plains.

TOM PLAMBECK PHOTO

Kerrey with financier Warren Buffett, a longtime supporter.

BILL BATSON/OMAHA WORLD-HERALD

*Senator-elect Kerrey and fellow Navy
SEAL Gary Parrott listen to taps at
Omaha's Memorial Park on Veterans Day.*

Kerrey's powerful orations are liked to William Jennings Bryant.

Kerrey gets a kiss from his daughter, Lindsey, twelve, during a break from his 1988 Senate campaigning.

Kerrey posing as "the thinker."

Kerry in the Senate.

Interstate 80 and the Oregon Trail. The road that leads into Nebraska also leads out of Nebraska.

At the Vietnam Memorial in Washington, D.C., Kerrey traces the name of a lost friend.

Kerrey announces his candidacy for President in September 1991.

After his announcement, Kerrey onstage with his children.

Renee Wessels, Kerrey's press secretary, recalls the exchange as pro forma, and says that no one gave their first encounter much thought. "It seemed very standard to me," she says. "It was out of the ordinary because you don't deal with the Hollywood element every day at the Nebraska Governor's office. I did think he was intrigued by her, but initially he was reluctant to go at all to the Villager."

So was Winger. In a 1986 *Esquire* interview, Winger recalled strongly resisting attending the press conference until forced by her agent. Said Winger, "I knew I had to because she had backed herself into something and it was her ass. But I was so pissed." Later, at the state capitol, when asked by a colleague what he thought of Debra Winger, Kerrey responded: "She wasn't wearing a bra."

Later that same afternoon, Kerrey summoned Wessels and asked her to find Winger's telephone number. Winger was staying at the Lincoln Hilton, and Wessels called the unit publicist to request Winger's number for the Governor. Wessels gave it to Kerrey and he telephoned soon after. The first time he called and asked her out, Winger declined. Kerrey called again, and again she passed. Eventually, director Brooks overheard Winger turning Kerrey down and chided her. He rattled off Kerrey's war-hero background and told her not to be so arrogant, that she might learn something from Kerrey. The next time he called, she accepted. Winger told *Esquire*: "Brooks totally intimidated me. So I said yes. And after Bob and I walked for five hours over the town of Lincoln, we decided we had things to talk about." That Winger went out with Kerrey only after being briefed on him by Brooks makes somewhat dubious her 1991 claim in *Vanity Fair* that she knew instantly that Kerrey, like herself, had faced death.

Ten days after their introduction, on Saturday, April 30, Winger and Kerrey had their first formal date. They spent part of the evening walking the streets of Lincoln and part of the night at Lincoln's Zoo Bar, a dimly lit, smoky hangout for rockabilly and blues aficionados. The Zoo Bar is frequented by University of Nebraska–Lincoln students, politicos, and lobbyists. Patrons were not surprised to see Kerrey, as he had been to the bar before. They were stunned to see Winger in tow, however, and news of the duo's date spread so quickly that by Monday morning it was literally the talk of the town. Soon it was the talk of the state, and by early June their romance was chronicled by *People* magazine. A TORNADO NAMED DEBRA WINGER HAS A WHIRL WITH NEBRASKA'S GOVERNOR ROCKIN' BOB KERREY, read the headline.

The Wednesday after their Saturday-night date—which had not yet been mentioned in any Nebraska newspaper—Kerrey held his weekly morning press conference. As she always did, Wessels wrote a briefing sheet for Kerrey on issues she thought might come up. This time there were a dozen subjects, the last being Debra Winger. The entire press corps knew the two had been at the Zoo Bar, but by the end of the press conference no one had asked about it. Wessels recalls: "All the reporters were giggling about it and looking at each other sheepishly as if to say, 'Who is going to ask it?' But no one did. It was very jocular."

When Kerrey finished the press conference, he headed for the exit, the assembled reporters aware that they were losing their last opportunity. Just as Kerrey approached the door, a reporter, perhaps prompted by him, asked, "Governor, there is one more thing. How was your date with Debra Winger?" Kerrey turned and, without missing a beat, quipped: "Fluff up your pillow and dream about it."

"The room went wild," Wessels says. "The reporters ate it up." With an ending of such levity, Wessels assumed Kerrey had been pleased with the denouement. But back in his office, a furious Kerrey called Wessels in and expressed displeasure that she had focused on this outing. Says Wessels, "He made it very clear to me that he didn't want me *ever* raising to him items about his personal life, that I should not have even put it on the sheet. He said it was inappropriate. He said, 'Don't ever worry about it again, it is not your concern. This is my personal life, it has nothing to do with my public life.' He was very stern." Wessels insisted she was simply doing her job, and Kerrey stressed again that his personal life was off-limits.

But Kerrey would quickly learn that while he could control what emanated from his office, he had no mastery over the routine sensationalism that his affair with Winger would engender. Within days, *People* writers were placing calls to the Governor's office. Wessels was told by Kerrey never to take the calls, that she was to refer them to him. "When the *People* magazine stuff broke, it was a mess," she says. "My instruction was that if they had questions about his personal life, they should direct them to him." Kerrey did not return *People*'s calls, but the magazine ran a two-page story anyway. What's more, national society reporters were out hiding in the bushes of the Governor's mansion. "It was a real miniature paparazzi situation because they wanted to see the two of them together," Wessels said. As Kerrey's press person, she was silent; she had, after all, been instructed to stonewall. Kerrey felt he had been burned by *People*, but he later agreed to talk with celebrity reporters a bit more about the romance.

"From the beginning," Wessels adds, "Bill Hoppner and Bob made it very clear to the staff that it was his own private business, and if reporters called, no one was to talk with them. He regarded it as his private personal affair."

Kerrey's "fluff up your pillow" quote marked the beginning of his ascension into "Entertainment Tonight" territory. It also catapulted him into the ranks of that elite handful of Governors whose names are recognized even by apolitical Americans. Over the next two years, as the relationship evolved, the Kerrey-Winger romance was tracked by gossip columnists and included in serious profiles of his governorship. From the outset, Kerrey professed lack of interest in the resulting attention. Unlike other ink-hungry politicians, Kerrey was not eager for press coverage. After just a few months in office—and before he ever stepped out on the town with Winger—Kerrey had received laudatory profiles in *The New York Times* and the *Wall Street Journal*; he was also featured on network news and talk shows. One close friend says, however, "Kerrey read the magazines, he knew what the effect was. It was a heady time." And there were some who believed that Kerrey fueled the focus by such flippant remarks as the pillow quote. Others ventured that Kerrey was just being Kerrey, and that he didn't prepare the pillow remark; he's just quick-witted, they argued, and the one-liner was the perfect zinger for an inappropriate question.

Kerrey's verbal nimbleness is legendary. State Senator David Landis recalls asking Kerrey after his primary fight with Bill Burrows how relations were between the two men, and Kerrey quickly responded: "We're not car-pooling."

Sunday, May 8, Governor Kerrey hosted a cocktail reception–wrap party for the cast and crew of *Terms of Endearment.* Rod Bates, a longtime Kerrey friend and later a telecommunications player in his administration, suggested that the state throw the party to thank the film company for choosing Nebraska as the state. Invitations were prized, and the Nebraskans who did attend enjoyed mingling with Danny DeVito, Jeff Daniels, and other cast and crew members. Shirley MacLaine, dressed in a flowery chiffon gown, was offended because she couldn't get a strawberry daiquiri. An animated Winger flitted around asking guests movie trivia questions. (Jack Nicholson, who was supposed to attend the party, instead jetted to Los Angeles for a Lakers game and flew back to Nebraska the next day for filming.) Kerrey and Winger talked with each other at the reception, but did not appear especially chummy; instead, she spent much of that afternoon playing anagrams with hometown boy Dick Cavett, who was in Lincoln for a visit.

During filming, Winger was friendly with the media and coverage of her was upbeat and complimentary; in fact, her press was so high-profile that her costars were more or less neglected. Early on, MacLaine and Nicholson tried to maintain some anonymity by wearing weird headgear and sunglasses—she cavorting in turbans and he wearing red in hopes of blending in with Nebraska Big Red fans. But as Winger's coverage elevated, Nicholson and MacLaine seemed to become more receptive to attention; later, at the end of a day's shooting, both could be seen chatting with a line of fans and willingly signing autographs. Filming of *Terms* ended on May 20, and the crew moved on to New York for final shooting. Before that, Kerrey visited Winger occasionally on her movie sets and saw her socially a few times. Winger left town by train—the same way she had arrived—aware that she wanted to know more about the Governor than her month in Lincoln had allowed.

Most observers assumed that once Winger left Lincoln, she

and Kerrey would drift apart. But the two kept in touch by telephone, and it soon became obvious to close friends that the relationship would endure. And after the final segments of *Terms of Endearment* were completed, she returned to Lincoln.

That fall the two would be spotted dining out and attending sports events, and it gradually became public knowledge that she was staying at the governor's mansion as Kerrey's guest. Kerrey maintained—as he had from the start—that the glare of publicity was disconcerting, and his personal life should be kept out of the spotlight. In general, the Nebraska media agreed. When Winger accompanied Kerrey to an event, journalists noted it but did not dwell on it. Marian Price, Kerrey's childhood friend, says: "I saw them together at an Omaha Jefferson-Jackson Day dinner. She was right there with him, but yet when it came time to talk with the press to interview him, she stepped aside and stayed with his bodyguards. She was seated with him at the head table, but when the press approached, it was not the Winger-Kerrey interview. It was the Kerrey interview, and she was very quick to pull away." A photo of the couple would occasionally appear in Nebraska newspapers, but it wasn't as though photo hounds were casing the governor's mansion waiting to record their every outing. *Lincoln Evening Journal* reporter Thomas A. Fogarty, now with the *Des Moines Register*, coined the tongue-in-cheek phrase "Wingi sightings." A handful of Nebraskans became obsessive "Winger watchers," but in keeping with their penchant for respecting the privacy of others, most residents left them alone.

The mood in Lincoln was merry. Autumn brought football, and Debra Winger could be seen playing Frisbee in running shorts on the mansion grounds. The Nebraska Cornhuskers played to their usual seventy-six thousand die-hard fans—Kerrey and Winger among them—making the coliseum on Saturdays the state's third-largest city. Many mornings, she could be seen leaving the mansion with her massive light-brown German shepherd, Pete. (Word in Lincoln had it that she had so named her beloved dog because "all he does is pee and eat.") She would walk or run several blocks, with the Governor's bodyguards staying behind at a distance. Winger was affable, and would stop to talk with Lincolnites who greeted her. When it became apparent that Winger was staying for extended periods at the mansion, the news was readily accepted by most Nebraskans.

That Nebraskans would accept the living arrangements surprised many, and national writers routinely expressed shock that in "staid Nebraska" Kerrey's live-in affair with Winger did not draw fire. Those intimate with Nebraska, however, know that the state has a strong legacy of unorthodoxy in its culture, manners, and institutions. University of Nebraska–Lincoln Distinguished Professor of History Frederick C. Luebke writes: "Nebraska did not inherit a comparable cadre of politicians whose Yankee moralism and commitment to commonwealth principles led to the enactment of prohibition and other forms of state regulation of personal behavior in the post–Civil War decades. Kansas thereby acquired an early reputation for political moralism that attracted pietists of all kinds, including Swedes and Germans of such tendencies. But this identity also deflected to Nebraska more numerous immigrants who preferred a place where there was less interference with European traditions, customs, and manners."

The idea of a bachelor Governor entertaining his actress girlfriend did not arouse the ire of most Nebraskans. Kerrey's personal popularity undoubtedly was a factor; in addition, the majority of Nebraskans are not the raging conservatives they are often portrayed to be, and they chose not to hold their Governor to a standard not met by themselves. By the time Winger became a part of the landscape the voters knew they had a workaholic Governor, and they chose not to force Kerrey into hypocrisy. Says one Nebraska native: "People were charmed by it. I think everyone saw that they were in love and it rekindled that feeling you get when you watch two people truly in love. You're happy for them. People figure the man had been through a lot, and he deserved a love affair."

The fact that the two met on his home turf—Kerrey was not hobnobbing in Hollywood or dining in Paris when they met—did not escape Nebraskans; he was simply doing his duty as Governor, and a romance started. Columnist and political pundit Mark Shields later wrote of the liaison passing the respectability test precisely for that reason. Shields argued that Kerrey did not seek out a star; rather, Winger lived in Lincoln for a month during a shoot and they fell for each other in the center of the nation. And it was Winger who returned to Lincoln; Kerrey did not slip off to New York or start spending long weekends at her Malibu home or New Mexico retreat.

The filming of *Terms of Endearment* was the first major feature shot in Nebraska in decades, so there was considerable attention paid to the stars. The national press, however, mistakenly alluded to the fact that the redneck rubes in Cornhusker country went plum crazy over the sight of their Governor with a real-life movie star. In truth, while Lincolnites eagerly participated in the production (hundreds applied for calls for extras), they responded to the event and the stars with typical respectful reserve. Nebraskans are familiar with celebrity. After all, this is a state to which Johnny Carson, Marlon Brando, and Ted Sorensen have often returned.

Says Fowler: "What I think she liked in Nebraska was that people respected her privacy. I mean, they might point her out across the restaurant with 'There's Debra Winger,' but people wouldn't stream forward and ask for autographs."

Still, some Nebraskans were bewildered that the arrangement was accepted with such equanimity. Natives know better than anyone that Lincoln is the headquarters of the "Back to the Bible" program, internationally known for its messages of love and faith beamed around the world. Lincoln has one of the nation's largest unaffiliated parishes. The Reverend Gil Rugh, a charismatic spellbinder, preaches each Sunday to more than four thousand dedicated servants who until recently allowed their names to be published in the church bulletin when their behavior was deemed unacceptable by Rugh and his staff.

The city is also the domicile of the bishop of the Lincoln diocese, considered even by ardent Catholics to be more conservative than the pope. In Lincoln, Catholic women still lobby for the right to partake in some of the minor church chores and rituals handled exclusively by men. (The same rituals are performed regularly by Catholic women in the Omaha diocese.)

Nonetheless, many of the city's elderly matrons—both Prot-

estant and Catholic—explained away Winger's visit with variations on the sentiment: What else can he do? A governor has to
be hospitable, and there are plenty of extra rooms in the mansion. Says one old-timer: "That nice Irish Catholic boy from
Northeast wouldn't do anything unbecoming." It was acknowledged during his gubernatorial campaign that Kerrey had a political advantage: Most Catholics thought he was one of them
because of his Irish name (Omaha is an Irish-American Democratic stronghold), and all the Protestants knew he wasn't.

Although their arrangement was generally accepted, Kerrey
and Winger nonetheless created a cottage industry in conversation. From the first, their romance was a topic of discussion
among Nebraskans. Politicos debated the prudence of it all. Cyn-
ics and critics made jokes. Reporters and lobbyists buzzed about
it. Students cheered Kerrey on. Video stores stocked up on
Winger's previous hits, including *Urban Cowboy*. When she first
became known in Nebraska, her movie reputation was in large
part based on her role as Richard Gere's hot young girlfriend in
An Officer and a Gentleman. Friends of friends who saw Kerrey
on infrequent occasions wondered whether Debra had been present. Groups touring the Nebraska mansion looked more closely
up the stairs to the second floor. By 1984 Nebraskans realized
this one was for real. Their young chief executive, still relatively
new to the electorate, was now known throughout the country
as Debra Winger's governor lover. The idea of a Mrs. Bob Kerrey or a Mr. Debra Winger began to be bandied about.

Friends and politicians worried that Kerrey's liaison with
Winger would forever eclipse and overshadow his own accomplishments. But those close to Kerrey knew that raising such a
possibility would not have been appreciated by him. If he wanted
to be near Winger—and he did—then banish the thought that
he might distance himself from her because somebody didn't approve. He had fallen in love, and as his ex-wife later would tell
the *Omaha World-Herald*, Kerrey did not fall in love easily. Kerrey's incredible confidence was exemplified by his decision to
allow Winger to stay at the mansion. Later, when longtime
friend Jim Nelson chided Kerrey and warned that letting Debra
Winger stay at the mansion was not politically wise, Kerrey

agreed. In an interview with the *World-Herald*, Nelson recounted the conversation: "My God, Kerrey, what were you doing?" Nelson said he asked. "'I know, it was the dumbest thing I could have done,'" Nelson said Kerrey replied. "'Well, I just wanted to be with her.'"

Kerrey loved her, and Winger loved him. They were, however, at different stages in their careers and personal lives when they fell for each other. She was in her late twenties and at the height of a promising movie career; Kerrey, then forty, was at the beginning of a new political career that would keep him in Lincoln at least four years. Winger was tearing around, Kerrey couldn't move; Winger was in midair, Kerrey was on the ground.

Later, Winger said she wanted to begin thinking of a family and pressed for some kind of commitment. But Kerrey already had two young children from his first marriage, and what little time he had for family was committed to them. Winger was said to be considering buying a home in Lincoln, but Kerrey was not receptive to the idea.

The two began dating in May 1983 and continued their romance through the fall of 1985. Intimates knew a breakup was coming, because in the last few months of the relationship their time together had been curtailed and their squabbles escalated.

In a 1986 interview with *Esquire,* Winger said, "I was the one who made the decision to break it off, although we both came out of it better human beings. And I think he definitely knows that now, but at first he was having a hard time. Plus, he's in the public eye. I had to call him, and he had to have a press conference about it. It's horseshit, but I knew it would happen that way."

The couple had a grand time during those two and a half years together. Even before Winger, Kerrey's governorship was exciting. He was young and handsome. He didn't let the office dictate a role for him. He would drive the state car himself, stop and pick up treats at a bakery, and pop in at a friend's house to eat cookies and milk. He left offbeat, clever messages on people's answering machines. He would wander out of the capitol on a sunny day and play a pickup game of basketball.

Nebraskans witnessed in Winger a woman who adored their

Governor and made him happy. Their time together dovetailed with the grimmest period in Nebraska economic history since the depression, so most natives were thrilled to have a diversion. The couple created a Cornhusker Camelot. A spirit of adventure reigned. It was a time when Nebraskans felt enthused and energized.

Many Nebraskans were able to meet Winger, and a few still maintain a friendship with her. In both the social and political sense, Nebraska is a small pond; you don't have to be a pooh-bah to come in contact with politicians and their confidants. Nebraska's political system is an accessible one. It's a small system with few gates or doors or walls to people wanting to interact with decision makers. As a result, hundreds of Nebraskans had contact with Winger, however brief.

One facet of her personality that emerged early was her penchant for swearing—an ongoing subject of discussion, the general consensus being that she was an otherwise charming person. Don Nelson, Kerrey's chief of staff for the last two years of his governorship, says, "When someone talked to Ben Bradlee, the [former] editor-in-chief of the *Washington Post*, about Jack Kennedy's swearing, Ben's rejoinder to that was, 'Jack Kennedy was profane, but not'—and he used the perfect word—'obscene.' I would say that about Debra Winger, that she was profane, but not obscene."

Not everyone agreed that Winger was the right companion for Kerrey. Former Representative John J. Cavanaugh told Kerrey once, "She's too wild. She's trouble." Kerrey's former wife, Bev Higby, told him on a number of occasions that he would be crazy to marry Winger.

Later, Winger was ticketed for driving seventy miles an hour in a residential zone near Pius X High School, Lincoln's only Catholic secondary school. Winger was alone in the Governor's car, and her ticket made headlines. Kerrey announced that she would no longer drive the state-supported car, and Winger promised to slow down. In an interview with a Nebraska paper, Winger later said that she'd never been in love with a Governor before and didn't know all the rules that went along with the territory of dating a chief executive. Few Nebraskans pointed out that she had broken the rule of law and not the rules of etiquette associated with dating a public figure.

Says Kerrey friend and banker Jack Moors: "It was great the day she got a ticket driving Bob's state car. People were upset, but everybody just kind of laughed it off. Bob handles those kind of things just great. He just said, 'She's got a heavy foot. The trooper will have to drive from now on.'"

Nebraskans were divided on two issues regarding Kerrey and Winger—whether she was an asset or a liability, and whether his decision to allow her to live in Nebraska throughout their liaison was a wise one. Many Nebraskans thought Winger was an asset, and that even if she wasn't, their bond was nobody's business. But others believed that politicians' private lives are fair game for examination, even if the politician in question is a bachelor, and especially if the object of his affection is an unpredictable actress who moved into a state-supported building for extended periods. Kerrey vacillated between feeling irritated that his private life was conversation material and feeling that it was part of the sacrifice public figures must endure. But given their respective roles in life, he was aware that he and Winger would be fodder for celebrity-fixated Americans.

Winger was and is the quintessential American artist. She introduced Kerrey to new music and poetry, and he introduced her to Nebraska poets she had never before read. One was Ted Koozer, a businessman by day and a poet by night. Often, Kerrey would visit Koozer in his Garland, Nebraska, home when he needed inspiration for something he was writing. Both Winger and Kerrey write poetry, although she has not made hers public. Kerrey's Christmas cards contain poetry, mostly his own, but he occasionally includes the writing of others. On a 1991 Thanksgiving card, Kerrey included an original poem:

> *There is cause*
> *In the course of experience*
> *To relinquish all hope for mankind*
>
> *There is cause*
> *At home today*
>   *(on the eve of Thanksgiving)*

with the doors of life
  wide open

to love
to ride on the edge of existence,
to give the reins of hope
  the freedom required of all

  laughing courage.

  November 21, 1990

Steve Fowler recalled some people joking about Kerrey's cards, but most Nebraskans were touched that he would have the confidence to share his own poetry. "I mean, when you look at ninety-nine percent of most political holiday greetings, they are reduced to one white-bread line so as not to offend anyone, and they're meaningless. Kerrey's have some power," says Fowler.

In a 1991 Christmas message that pictured Kerrey and his children at his Senate victory party, Kerrey he an original poem:

Fear visits me just before dawn:
  In the window I have seen my face.

Beside me he awakens;
His voice is gone but still
He greets me with a hand
That holds warm and big.

Beside me he awakens;
His mask is gone and chill
Greets me from child eyes
That hold deep and direct

Beside me his hand points;
I follow but do not leave,
In silence a message is passed
"Trust," he says, "and prepare always."

His reflection guides me now,
And the day begins anew.

> Bob Kerrey
> December 8, 1988

During his years as Governor, Kerrey's Christmas cards always included original poetry. Nebraskans receiving his greetings often debated the meaning of his messages. Says one friend: "His cards got stranger every year, but I enjoyed them. I wouldn't want to not be on his mailing list." Others on his mailing list looked forward to receiving his greetings, and the type of poem he would include in the upcoming holiday's card became a source of speculation. Kerrey once commissioned a wooden dresser with poetry inscribed in the drawers, then gave it to Winger as a present.

Visitors always knew when Debra was at the mansion, because her dog, Pete, would be roaming the place. Also, Winger wore a special perfume, the smell of which lingered long after she had exited a room. Men found it alluring, and when a visitor asked her about it, she said it was made from the stamen of a Chinese flower, and it was concocted specially for her at a little Beverly Hills apothecary.

As Governor, Kerrey intiated a tradition of Halloween parties that soon became the most sought-after invitation of his administration. The most notable of these "Scary Kerrey" parties took place when Winger was supposedly out of town. In fact, she had arranged to sneak into Lincoln that afternoon and dress in costume, then surprise Kerrey at the party. Hundreds of Nebraskans were roaming the mansion, when someone in an exotic black cat costume nuzzling up to the Governor got the crowd buzzing. To the delight of the partygoers, Kerrey seemed truly uncomfortable—at least until he figured out that the person cozying up to him was Winger, who wanted her return to be a surprise.

Kerrey's annual Halloween parties were more than a source of good times during his administration: The parties also gave rise to rumors of sex, drugs, and rock and roll in the Governor's house. Because there was dancing and drinking and carousing at the packed parties, people began spreading rumors about Kerrey and others in his administration. Winger admitted to drug use during this period, and some argued that if she had a substance-abuse problem, that somehow meant she carried the problem with her to the mansion. Winger says she has been completely clean since getting pregnant in April 1987.

Scores of interviews with close observers and participants in the Kerrey administration reveal that there is absolutely no truth to such rumors. Kerrey's close acquaintances know he has done some reckless deeds and said some outrageous things, but there is no evidence he has ever acted scandalously as a public official. Kerrey's association with Winger made him an easy target for rumors, but the gossipmongers were active even before her arrival. The reason, some contend, is jealousy. Ed Howard of the Associated Press says, "I have seen people envy that man to a degree that is just absolutely nauseating. I saw people who looked at Bob Kerrey and saw everything they ever wanted to be—a war hero, a successful businessman, someone who dated more women than the young Frank Sinatra. He succeeded at everything he ever did. Not only does he have this war wound—you get a leg blown off and the Medal of Honor—but he gets the perfect wound. He loses the leg below the knee so he can still walk and screw, and not limp. I mean, the guy—even when he has bad luck, he has good luck. The rumors are a result of outrageous envy and jealousy."

Most veterans would not agree that getting a leg blown off is a million-dollar wound, as that term has traditionally been reserved to describe a flesh wound or a hit that results in evacuation and removal from combat without a lifelong disability. Kerrey's success in dealing with his injury, however, encourages the perception that his war wound is less serious than, in fact, it is.

More than a decade before the rumors started, Kerrey was on his back in the Philadelphia Naval Hospital unable to move, a one-legged man who had to learn to walk a second time. Frederick Downs, in a *Washington Post* essay on wounded veterans, writes: "There is fear in becoming handicapped, a fear as old as human history. Imagine what happens to that fear when it becomes reality. First and foremost is the terror of the physical damage. Second is the mental anguish of trying to cope with this horrible thing that has happened to you. And third is the foreboding of what is to come. The unknown." For seven months, Bob Kerrey lay prone in a hospital bed and wondered about the unknown. Could he be agile again? How would women respond to him? Would he find work that interested him? He didn't have a clue what the unknown would bring, but he knew for certain that things didn't look good. Never could he have imagined that fourteen years later he would be Governor of his home state, a proud father of two handsome children, and that he would find true love with a gifted movie star. Never could he have dreamed that the unknown would be so fulfilling.

Kerrey always enjoyed introducing friends and journalists to essays, poetry, music, or anything that interested him at the moment. Like a good teacher, Kerrey is eager to share whatever artistic piece he has been moved by. Often, in response to questions, Kerrey tells a story, passes on an anecdote, reads from a poem, or quotes from a song or novel. After reading a book that fascinated him, Kerrey would often talk about it with any reporter who happened to be in the vicinity. He copied essays and urged writers to read them. One autumn during his gubernatorial days Kerrey had just finished reading Louise Erdrich's *The Beet Queen*, and by memory he quoted a line from the novel to a visitor. Another time, he passed on a story he had read about architect Frank Lloyd Wright: Wright was lecturing and a student asked what one has to do to become a brilliant architect. Kerrey told his visitor: "And Wright responded, 'You can't build a building any better than you are.'" Winger and Kerrey both thirst for knowledge. She loved acquainting him with novels she found inspiring, and he loved saving material for her that he thought she would enjoy reading. Winger and Kerrey had similar takes on life. They could attend formal functions and later laugh with each other about the standoffishness of it all.

As the relationship evolved, however, the two fought, occasionally in public. Both are strong-willed and independent, and there were times in Lincoln when, as one observer puts it, "they were attitudinal with each other." According to another Winger watcher, she knew Kerrey's buttons and "she hacked him off just to hack him off."

One advantage of their relationship was that her career kept her away from Lincoln most of the time. Kerrey and Winger's long-distance romance allowed the two to preserve a deep bond without the burden of daily compromises.

From the outset, Winger was wary of life in the political fishbowl, and she often lamented the superficiality it engendered. In a 1990 interview with *Vanity Fair*, Winger said: "If I wanted an aquarium, I would've bought one and lived in it. . . . I cannot be clear about the whole political thing—I've never been clear about it. When he was Governor, I'd get some distance from him and I'd say, 'I'm never going back. I hate that life. Why don't they leave me alone?' Then I'd see him and turn into mush. It's not a thing you can deal with logically when you love someone."

She found going through political motions tedious, and she started acting up a bit in Lincoln. One popular story had Kerrey introducing Winger to an elderly prominent Republican woman. Winger shook her hand vigorously and said, "Nice as shit to meet you, honey!" One observer notes that she made it clear she detested the schmoozing required of political partners. Winger was not mean-spirited about it, but as one journalist says, "When she was being called on to do shtick, it was very clear that 'I am being called on to do shtick, here is my shtick. Okay, thank you.'" She viewed much of politics as artificial and phony; she ridiculed much of the pomp and circumstance surrounding it, and some Nebraskans viewed her honesty as refreshing.

By all accounts, Winger fit in nicely with the Kerrey family and was treated the same as Kerrey's other dates. Nancy Kerrey Swarts says, "She's just a person. She's a good actress, like Bob's a good Senator, like I'm a good farmer. I don't think anyone should think she would benefit him or hurt him. Last Thanksgiving she prepared the whole family dinner. She's a good cook, she organized it all and I appreciate her for that."

Overall, Nebraskans thoroughly enjoyed Winger, although

she lost much of the goodwill that she had accrued in the last year of Kerrey's term after he announced that he would not seek reelection. At a well-attended good-bye party for Kerrey held at Lincoln's Pla-Mor Ballroom, organizers showed a videotape of a Winger message to Nebraskans. In what some observed as a cheeky, patronizing voice, Winger announced that Nebraska doesn't have trees, oceans, or mountains, that it doesn't have much of anything, but the state does have one valuable natural resource—Bob Kerrey. "Lucky you," Winger told the Nebraskans in her sign-off.

Many in the audience felt stung by her tribute and suggested it was in poor taste. "It had the same effect on most people," Bill Lock said. "It sounded like a condescending statement on the order of Nicholas von Hoffman's infamous remarks in *Esquire* magazine that Nebraska women lavish the kind of attention on Kerrey that outsiders thought they only reserved for their hogs." Nobody has ever determined whether Winger wrote her words or was given them to read by a Nebraskan who will not admit to it.

Debra Winger was in her prime during those years she spent in Lincoln. Her picture graced the cover of *People* magazine; she had a two-page spread in *Life*, with a photograph of her partially nude kissing her dog; her performances were widely praised, and after *Terms of Endearment* she was selected star of the year by members of Hollywood's motion picture establishment. But in the late 1980s Winger's career nosedived. She acted in a series of flops, and her performances were not singled out as they had been before. After she broke off with Kerrey, Winger married actor Timothy Hutton, had a baby named Noah, divorced Hutton, and took up again with Kerrey after he had served one year in the U.S. Senate. As Winger's career fizzled, Kerrey's political fortunes sizzled.

Chapter 8

THE INSOLENCE
OF OFFICE

ob Kerrey's mettle was severely tested not quite one year into his governorship. In November 1983, the state's largest industrial savings and loan was closed by Nebraska's banking commission. Devastated depositors, many of whom swore they were led by the state to believe their money was safe, lost $67 million. They learned too late that their money wasn't covered by Nebraska or federal agencies.

The Commonwealth Company, a family-owned savings and loan, was chartered by the state but was not subject to the regulations that governed other S&Ls. Since the 1930s, the company had been owned and operated by the Copples, a prominent Lincoln family. Always regarded as stable, Commonwealth provided loans to thousands of middle-income people in the Lincoln area. In the 1960s, the Copples' reputation was assured when they completed the development of Capitol Beach, which transformed a salt swamp west of Lincoln into a lake surrounded by hundreds of nice homes. (Bob Kerrey's parents moved there in the early seventies.)

In 1983, at age eighty-six, E. J. Copple, the chairman of the board, was still active in the business. He and his son Marvin, then in his late fifties, had pursued an aggressive marketing campaign for more deposits. Their approach was theoretically sound, given the continued appreciation of real estate in Nebraska since the 1940s. The Copples advertised that they would pay interest one-half to one point above the local market rate. Depositors flocked to their windows, and in ten years Commonwealth deposits had increased from $7 million to $67 million. Uninhibited by regulations, the Copples started making high-risk loans on land that might turn into residential developments or shopping centers. But a statewide drop in real-estate prices ensued, and before long Commonwealth's actual worth was about one-tenth of the book value—the value being presented to depositors and state investigators. During the same period, Marvin Copple began loaning money to a brother and a brother-in-law who operated another financial institution in Nebraska.

Until the three Copples and the brother-in-law were sent to the Nebraska state penitentiary, they enjoyed a life-style that was foreign to Lincoln's families of quiet wealth. Marvin had a home in Phoenix and was a Las Vegas regular. Newt, a youger brother, was not directly involved in the Commonwealth organization, but operated on the periphery, using the Copple name as a credit card to the trappings and activities of the affluent. A onetime 145-pound state wrestling champion, Newt Copple grappled competitively through his forties and later became a national officer of the Amateur Athletic Union. Operating out of a suite of offices in Lincoln, he employed secretaries and assistants who were available to fly to Buffalo or San Diego to monitor matches. Newt's spontaneity was a positive morale factor in his office, illustrated by 3:00 P.M. Friday decisions to fly to Chicago for dinner with selected employees.

Prior to 1983, many Lincolnites possessed a certain awe, if not reluctant appreciation, of the Copples and their free-spending ways. One of them was Nebraska Attorney General Paul Douglas, who had been elected easily to a second term in 1982, the year Bob Kerrey was elected Governor. Douglas was undoubtedly the state's most popular Republican, and the consensus at the time was that he eventually would be Governor or a U.S. Senator. A barrel-chested, Greek-American bachelor with a wide smile and an engaging personality, Douglas began doing business with the Copples in the late seventies after socializing with them for a while. Douglas and a partner borrowed money from the Copples for investment in a residential development; later, on several occasions, he took title briefly to residential lots as a straw man and then transferred them to someone in the Copple organization, the result being inflated property values and profit to Douglas. Although these transactions had little real effect on the fall of Commonwealth, the press and public perceived Paul Douglas as a principal player. Douglas, who had long nourished an image of worldliness and shrewdness, was called before a legislative committee to testify. Embarrassed by the fact that he had been seduced into the Copples' scheme, and that he had exhibited major lapses of judgment (he was, after all, the state's attorney general while making deals with the Copples), Douglas hedged to the committee. In January 1985, Douglas was convicted of perjury. Although his conviction was ultimately reversed by the Nebraska Supreme Court, state law required that he resign. In Nebraska, when a constitutional official has to leave office, the Governor must choose a replacement to complete the term.

Kerrey's response to this duty was an indicator that he was not a traditional politician—that he was either a maverick or a potential statesman or both. He appointed a prominent Omaha Republican, attorney Robert Spire. Spire had never been involved in politics, and only agreed to serve at Kerrey's request.

When Spire was summoned to the Governor's office, he assumed Kerrey wanted his opinion on some of the leading contenders since he was familiar with most of the state's legal community. Not long into the interview, however, Kerrey informed Spire that he wanted him as attorney general. A shocked Spire replied that he was a Republican, to which Kerrey repeated his offer. "I don't care," Kerrey said. "I want you." Spire considered it for several days, then accepted.

Many Nebraska Democrats were furious. Republicans had had a lock on the office of attorney general for fifty years; now, because of a completely unexpected turn of events, the office opens up, and yet another Republican gets the nod. Kerrey was told it would be political suicide for a neophyte Governor to make such a major appointment outside the party. Republicans were baffled—but naturally pleased—and many Democrats were in fact impressed; still, doctrinaire Democrats wondered, Who the hell does this guy think he is? DiAnna Schimek had recently been appointed Democratic state party chairman, and along with State Senator David Newell and activist Charles ("Chuck") Pallisen, called for a meeting with Kerrey to discuss the Spire appointment. "Dave Newell and I both flew into a rage," recalls Schimek, who met with the Governor at the state party headquarters in Lincoln. "We had a real good thrashing out of the whole issue. Dave and I both made public statements criticizing the decision. For me, at last, it wasn't anything against Bob Spire. I felt that when you worked your heart out for somebody of your party to become Governor, then it seemed to me that you ought to expect at least some appointments, some major ones, if they came up."

No one questioned Spire's sterling qualifications and character; they simply believed that party loyalty required Kerrey to choose an exceptional Democrat. In a city of nearly four hundred thousand, the Omaha die-hards protested, Kerrey could find *one* outstanding lawyer from his own party to fill the post.

But Kerrey insisted on Spire. Some Democrats seethed; they villified the Governor in off-the-record conversations, they pleaded with Kerrey to abandon the idea, they threatened to withhold future help, they screamed, swore, and hung up telephones, they pouted, and, finally, they acquiesced. But not before alienating more than a few Democrats who believed that, despite Spire's accomplished record, Kerrey was thumbing his nose at fellow party members. One Nebraska writer recalls being in Kerrey's office when a group was discussing the appointment. Someone said, "Bob, you know the institutional Democrats, the machine Democrats, will really be pissed off," and Kerrey replied, "Okay." "Okay, you'll appoint a Democrat?" he asked the Governor with a hint of hope. And Kerrey said, "No, it's okay if they're pissed off. Tell them I said, 'Be pissed off.'"

Kerrey was not going to be steamrollered into appointing a Democrat for something as elusive as party loyalty. He had been a Republican himself a few years earlier, and he had been elected with the help of Republicans, including his brother-in-law, Dean Rasmussen, and other family members. Republicans were not bogeymen to him.

In addition to having the nation's only one-house legislature, Nebraska is the only state with a nonpartisan legislature—the legacy of Senator George Norris, who convinced voters in 1934 to abolish the party system. According to *Nebraska Government and Politics,* a 1984 political science text, the state's responsibilities were in no sense partisan, and such a blueprint would enable the legislature to function more like a business corporation. Legislative candidates in Nebraska run in nonpartisan elections without party labels, although they are often encouraged and financed by members of their respective parties, and almost everyone understands he is voting for a Republican or Democrat. For a time, however, Kerrey's appointment of Bob Spire as attorney general convinced some Democrats that he was really a Republican in Democratic clothing.

Choosing Bob Spire was a brilliant and farsighted decision. Kerrey wanted someone with superior intellect and integrity. He believed that stability and trust had to be restored quickly to the attorney general's office. He knew that nobody in Nebraska would be as instantly effective in doing that as Spire. A high-profile Omaha lawyer, Spire was revered in the legal community for his intellectual prowess. In both public and private persona he was a gentlemanly scholar. A World War II Pacific combat veteran who had studied at the Juilliard School of Music and Harvard Law School, Spire brought to the office a broad base of experience and study.

When it became apparent that Spire's character was not only faultless but his legal opinions would be congruous with traditional Democratic ideology, the mea culpas came rolling in from previously disgruntled Democrats. Later, Schimek raved about the Spire choice. "I love Bob Spire," she says. "He is a wonderful man, one of the real genuine people in the world. I have told Bob this, that he couldn't have appointed anybody better. Kerrey needed someone who could inspire and who would give people confidence in the system again. Bob Spire certainly did that. I've since come to realize you have to be aware of the total picture when you make appointments."

During his tenure, Spire showed a compelling interest in the welfare of minorities, the disabled, and the poor, and his office displayed an aggressive commitment to affirmative action. Following Kerrey's lead, Spire appointed more blacks, Hispanics, and Asians to his staff than any other public official in the state's history. In fact, the great irony of Spire's tenure was that he endeared himself to Democrats and became something of an enigma, if not an irritant, to fellow Republicans.

As attorney general, Spire delighted colleagues and staffers with memos quoting everyone from Muddy Waters to Justice Oliver Wendell Holmes to Professor Roscoe Pound, a Nebraskan who was dean of Harvard Law School from 1916 to 1936.

The Spire story is noteworthy not only because of his distinguished work, but because his appointment was the first example of Kerrey's political courage. Spire is so roundly appreciated (he later became chief of staff in Kerrey's Washington office), it's easy to forget that Kerrey took considerable heat for choosing him in the first place.

Spire brought renewed faith to the attorney general's office. The Commonwealth situation, which triggered his selection, became the major thorn of the Kerrey administration. The unraveling of Commonwealth also precipitated the decline of two other state-chartered thrifts, one of which, State Securities Savings Company, was directed by Kerrey confidant and personal adviser Bill Wright. Before the failure of State Security Savings, Kerrey had been a coinvestor with Wright and was involved in a partnership with him that included an investment in a Lincoln commercial property called Shoppers Fair. Later, state investigators concluded that improprieties on Wright's part led to the thrift's demise—that Wright "milked and drained" the institution. Eight months after the collapse of Commonwealth, State Security Savings filed for bankruptcy and was later reorganized. After exhaustive legislative investigations Kerrey was cleared of any wrongdoing; however, coming as it did on the heels of Commonwealth, some Nebraskans believed that, at the very least, Kerrey exhibited poor judgment in conducting business with Wright. Kerrey later agreed and curtailed his friendship with Wright, who slipped out of Lincoln one night and headed for California.

In a 1986 interview with the *Lincoln Journal-Star,* Kerrey said that losing friends is one of the sacrifices that comes with being Governor, and Wright was one of those lost friends. "I just recently started talking to him again," Kerrey told reporter Kathleen Rutledge. "I honestly told him, 'Bill, I cannot be associated with you. If I have contact with you, the perception will be that it's for devious reasons.'"

Kerrey had become close with Wright in the early seventies, a time when a number of young Lincoln businessmen were riding the agriculture-fueled boom in Nebraska. Economic opportunities were abundant; it was an era when people like Kerrey, a successful restaurateur, established themselves in Nebraska. The period of brain drain that former Democratic Governor Frank Morrison warned about during his service in the sixties resurfaced in the late seventies and early eighties. In 1984, Nebraskan Douglas Kruse completed a study on immigration patterns, discovering that the state's best educated were leaving during this time and recent arrivals were of lower educational achievement. As a result, there was a serious net loss of talent.

But in the early seventies, young Nebraskans stayed put. Many of the men Kerrey befriended were products of south Lincoln and east Lincoln, trust-fund babies whose fathers were among Lincoln's most preeminent businessmen. Many had become hardworking businessmen in their own right, and Kerrey, an outsider coming from the northeast part of town, enjoyed being part of the club. Kerrey got to know most of these men, and he no doubt was proud that a self-made northeast boy had made it to Lincoln's big leagues.

Kerrey later expressed regret about his dealings with Wright. Growing up, he had watched his father put together business deals, and it eventually became a way of life for him too. He still had a mind for business when he entered politics, and he admits that he should have shifted gears sooner. What's more, he realizes he was naive about the consequences of even the appearance of impropriety, and that some of his business ties should have been severed earlier.

Kerrey's willingness to examine his complex feelings about government and business was widely interpreted by his constituents in Nebraska as a sign of his maturity. Bill Lock, a public-policy expert during Kerrey's administration, said in 1990: "When people criticized him for the Shoppers Fair development deal, Kerrey was willing to be self-critical and say, 'I was new to politics and I would handle it differently today.' That gives me the impression he is deepening as a human being and as a political leader. So many leaders lose their self-critical perspective. Kerrey has not. I've worked with a lot of politicians and it is hard for them, once they've put themselves out someplace on an issue, to admit that they need to reposition themselves because they were wrong."

University of Nebraska–Lincoln political science professor Robert Sittig said in an interview that same year: "Kerrey's greatest vulnerability, and it looks as if he is dealing with it even more now than he did at the time, is saying that he made some mistakes in judgment about his personal friendships and acquaintances. He uses Bill Wright as an illustration. He says that he didn't use good judgment or he should have evaluated the advice he received better. Apparently, that's even a track to the White house. I assume that's what [White House spokesman Marlin] Fitzwater meant when he said that this person [Kerrey] who was hammering away on us on the savings and loans had problems of his own back in Nebraska."

Having to break ties with friends was difficult for Kerrey, because ever since childhood he had maintained strong bonds with a variety of people in nonintersecting circles. Kerrey feels strong personal loyalties, so when someone he believes asks to have something done, Kerrey is usually willing to comply. As Governor, Kerrey often made decisions based on what he believed about people, rather than what he believed might be right from a policy or political perspective.

One revealing incident occurred in 1984, when a member of the radical Posse Comitatus was gunned down in his farmhouse by the Nebraska State Patrol. The killing of Arthur Kirk, whose farm had been foreclosed on, ignited a great controversy among Nebraskans, the argument being that the state patrol had used excessive force. Kirk, who was believed to have mental problems, armed himself with semiautomatic weapons and barricaded himself in his Cairo farmhouse. The state patrol stormed the house, and in the confrontation Kirk was killed.

Kirk's death triggered an investigation and Kerrey appointed a respected former judge to conduct it. Much to the surprise of many Nebraskans, Kerrey expressed his full support for the members of the state patrol, insisting that officers were in a difficult situation being shot at by an apparently deranged person. To those who argued that the patrolmen should not have been in a situation which required such force, Kerrey disagreed and remained unequivocal in his support for the state patrol. Kerrey felt a loyalty to them based on shared experiences. After all, he once had to carry out the most violent of orders, and the memory of that experience would be the deciding factor for Kerrey, not what political advantage he might lose or gain from his position. Kerrey is the kind of politician who can belong to Nebraskans for Peace and the American Legion and feel strong loyalties to both organizations and their members.

Because Kerrey often made gubernatorial decisions based on personal loyalties, it was important to see who he had around him and what his top aides were like. Part of the reason Kerrey relied on personal loyalty during those days was that he was such a political neophyte with loosely formed ideas, and so much happened so quickly that he needed to be able to trust the people around him.

"Kerrey knew less about government than a pig knew about Sunday," says reporter Ed Howard. "He thought that being Governor, being chief executive, was going to be something like being the head of a chain of restaurants. He didn't realize the degree to which a Governor can be shit."

Kerrey himself admits to being green in the beginning, but he points out that he is roundly praised for learning quickly on the job. By his second year, Kerrey argued, he had figured out how to play the game.

Kerrey's relationship with the legislature deteriorated at the height of the Commonwealth crisis, and it remained strained for the last two sessions of his tenure. Accustomed as he was to dictating orders, Kerrey found it difficult dealing with the egos, wills, and demands of Nebraska's forty-nine independent Senators. And because Nebraska's legislators are nonpartisan, they bring a stronger sense of independence to their jobs than their counterparts in other states, where legislative-executive coalitions may be formed based on party ties. In *Nebraska Government and Politics*, UN-L political scientists state: "There is no group of party leaders in the legislature publicly bound in terms of party loyalty to carry the message of the Governor to the 'troops' in the legislature. Nonpartisanship denies to the Governor an institutional means of working through established party leadership in the legislature. Like any supplicant before the Unicameral, Governors must also strive to overcome the 'forty-nine generals' syndrome."

Kerrey fought hard and was frustrated with the legislature over Commonwealth, which he repeatedly cited as the most difficult issue he faced during his tenure.

The subject of Commonwealth resurfaced in Kerrey's 1988 Senate race, and Kerrey's chief of staff, Don Nelson, wrote in a letter to the editor:

> I read the relentless pounding that Bob Kerrey is taking from those who fell victim to the Commonwealth disaster. As a silent, but major participant in the events of 1984-1987, I believe it is time to remind readers of the facts: During Kerrey's governorship, more than half a dozen bills were introduced in an attempt to solve the Commonwealth fiasco. Kerrey is the only public official that has publicly acknowledged total and complete liability on the part of Nebraska. Unfortunately, the people and the many legislatures of Nebraska have (over time) established a Constitution and series of statutes that permit the state to duck (its moral and ethical responsibilities) behind an unintelligible tangle of legal doctrine. The fact of the matter is that under the separation of powers doctrine, no Governor can impose his will on the legislature. At Kerrey's direction, Roger Beverage and I spent more time on Commonwealth issues than any two souls should endure. We got no thanks from any depositor save one from Bee [Nebraska]. We did get angry phone calls (at work and at home) and a constant barrage of hateful criticism.

By his second year, Kerrey learned firsthand the maxim that the executive proposes and the legislative disposes. During his first two years in office, Kerrey worked well with the legislature. During the second half of his term, however, when he realized that much of what he wanted to accomplish was being thwarted by Nebraska's "forty-nine generals," he reacted angrily and sometimes bitterly. Eventually, he withdrew from the kind of hands-on approach that had been his style.

Northeast Lincoln State Senator David Landis said, "There was a difference in the first two years and the second two years in his relationship with the legislature in how active he was. He was very successful when he was personally active and the administration was less sucessful when he was working through intermediaries and pronouncements were set down and we wound up talking through the press. I think he found dealing with the legislature difficult. I'm not sure that he had all this many dreams and visions that were frustrated—he certainly had political agendas at different times which we frustrated, no doubt about it, but it was not like there was a grand agenda placed before us. I do know that early on he used to hang out with State Senator Gary Hannibal and some of the freshmen, and he would stop by and talk to people. When it came time, he would squeak by with twenty-five votes—some Republicans, mostly Democrats. Then, later on, he was not quite as effective in getting what he wanted."

Shouting matches between Kerrey and others became something of a regular occurrence during those difficult days. State Senator Don Wesely, who represented Kerrey's old Bethany neighborhood, recalled a scene at the Governor's mansion in which Wesely, Nelson, and Kerrey ended up in a brutal verbal battle in front of participants who were not prepared for what they witnessed.

Kerrey has a temper, which by all accounts he has moderated since joining the U.S. Senate. But during his gubernatorial days, a roused Kerrey would yell and swear in the heat of an argument. The flip side, however, is that Kerrey is known for not holding grudges, and for routinely apologizing to people he may have offended. Says Frosty Chapman, "Bob could get to yelling, but he could never stay mad. He would usually break out in a grin by the end of the fight or he would call you at home or at work the next day and say, 'Hey, I'm sorry,' and you had to forgive him because he was really genuine. Then he would give you that great laugh of his. Bob never could stay mad at people. It just wasn't in his nature. I think he always figured life was too short."

In fact, some Nebraskans' fondest memories of Kerrey—perhaps their most cherished personal recollections of him as Governor—are times that he either yelled or hung up the phone on them, because they always enjoyed his next-day apology.

Not everyone let Kerrey get away with what UN-L professor James McShane described as his adult temper tantrums. When Kerrey called him to discuss faculty salaries at UN-L, at one point he interrupted the conversation with a loud "bullshit." "I interrupted him and said, 'Governor, I do not approve of that language and I would ask that you refrain from speaking that way to me.'" Kerrey humbly agreed and apologized, and their conversation continued.

Many Nebraskans also had shouting matches with Don Nelson, chief of staff, and they found him altogether less forgivable than Kerrey. Chris Funk, a strong supporter of Nebraska's Commission on the Status of Women, which Kerrey essentially gutted, had a knock-down-drag-out screaming match with Nelson because Kerrey had personally promised her he would not cut funding for the commission. Even Funk, as furious as she was at the time, later found herself forgiving Kerrey.

Senator Landis recalls, "One morning he called me very early and yelled at me because we were making it easy for State Senator Howard Lamb. We weren't being tough on the budget; actually I think Kerrey wanted to outconservative Howard Lamb, and he wanted to enlist *me* to cut the budget more than Lamb would. Wrong! We have to remember here, Bob, I'm not a dyed-in-the-wool conservative. On occasion, though, Kerrey is."

Kerrey's fiscal conservatism depressed the state's liberals. Steve Fowler was director of policy research from June 1983 to December 1984, a time during which he urged Kerrey to raise taxes. "I felt to achieve the agenda it was going to require a tax increase, and he didn't want to do that because he felt it was too much of a burden. I tired of making these arguments, and they were falling on deaf ears. Also, I did not feel that Don Nelson and I had the relationship of trust and communication that existed with Bill Hoppner." When he realized Kerrey was adamantly opposed to raising taxes, Fowler resigned and moved to California, where he does political consulting. In looking back, Fowler says, "We brainstormed a far too ambitious agenda of ideas that wouldn't have been possible to do, but I didn't realize that at the time."

In the meantime, Kerrey kept in close touch with Nebraska's business community and advisers like Senator James Exon, all of whom advised him not to raise taxes. Kerrey's personal experience and his bottom-line approach in business made the idea of raising taxes anathema to him. Nebraskans expected Kerrey to hold the line on that, and he was hugely popular for it. In fact, when Kerrey ran for the U.S. Senate, one of his campaign themes was "I was Governor for four years and I did it without a tax increase." People loved him for it, but his successor, Republican Kay Orr, didn't learn from his success: She was booted out after one term, in large measure because she raised taxes.

Some liberals believed, however, that Kerrey could have raised taxes and still maintained his widespread popularity, and they were supremely disappointed that he chose not to. Because federal tax reform meant less revenues to the states, Nebraska's tax base was being diminished. But Kerrey was unwilling to raise tax rates to make up for the shortfall; rather, his approach was to cut items from the budget, and he repeatedly convened special sessions to propose dramatic reductions.

Kerrey picked the worst possible time to preside over Nebraska. In addition to the economic recession and the new federalism, he had to deal with the collapse of financial institutions. When the Commonwealth crisis erupted, the state coffers were empty. The land of hundreds of farmers was being foreclosed. Midway through his term, Kerrey began to fully understand the reality of the situation, and was anguished by it. It was painful for him to have come from speaking idealistically about the kind of budget he wanted to carefully craft for the state, only to end up slashing budgets. "Whatever his hopes, dreams, and wishes were of a policy nature, those had to take second place to dealing with the financial realities and fiscal realities of the time," says Professor Sittig. Kerrey was an idealistic, enthusiastic, take-charge kind of person who thought he would make a difference, and he was frustrated by not having the resources to do so. What bothered some Nebraskans, though, was that Kerrey took to cutting his budgets the way he took to everything else—with gusto and an enthusiastic determination. His budget-cutting zeal really rattled some of his supporters.

One institution that felt Kerrey's heavy hand was the University of Nebraska, headed at that time by Ronald Roskens, who would in 1991 become director of the Agency for International Development in the Bush Administration. Kerrey and Roskens disliked each other. Kerrey made it clear in his second budget that greater emphasis should be placed on elementary and secondary education, rather than higher education, which he believed benefited fewer people. Kerrey also believed passionately that universities—and the University of Nebraska–Lincoln, in particular—were overadministered, and he wanted to streamline them. He saw UN-L as a closed shop, and he did not have confidence in Roskens as an administrator.

Often, Kerrey equates a manager with an institution. In his view, Salomon Brothers becomes Warren Buffett. His trusted friend and adviser Donna Karnes was the head of the Revenue Department, and therefore the Revenue Department was Donna Karnes. Kerrey's instinctive tendency is to ignore an institution's long history; instead, he associates the total identity and character of the institution with the person at the top. He believed there was waste within the university, and that some programs were too small for a state like Nebraska to carry. At one point, Kerrey proposed cutting the very pharmacy school from which he had graduated. He told university officials that any improvements needed to be funded by internal reallocation and restructuring, which they resisted. Kerrey's budget director, Larry Bahr, agreed with him, but Steve Fowler, who was head of policy, disagreed. "I argued that there's a bureaucracy and a heritage in these departments. They have their own character and personality that no Governor or department head can completely change. They can influence, but there are institutional histories and forces bigger than the power of an individual." But Kerrey was adamantly opposed to taking a sociological view of institutions and structures. He viewed them through the same prism through which he viewed personal business relationships—you deal with so and so because he is honest, and you have to watch so and so because he is not.

The university traditionally presents to the legislature a budget that says, "I want to keep everything I have and I want you to give me another twenty percent." Kerrey responded with his own directives: Come in without lists of cuts, and I'm not going to work with you. I'm not going to give you what you want unless you start making hard decisions. He simply was not willing to pump money into higher education until he saw a sound administrative structure; this unwillingness did not endear him to the university faculty and administration. Others supported his approach, however. Dan Ladeley, curator of the Sheldon Film Theater, says, "He wasn't very popular with the university but he had great long-range influence. That was a hard fight to fight because the university is such a self-supporting, self-serving institution. I've always felt that the university had too many high-paid administrators, and that the administration was better in the past when there weren't so many layers and it wasn't so complicated. Kerrey generated interest in examining it, and now there is a lot of talk about changing the structure of the educational system." Like his proposal for state funding of teachers' salaries, Kerrey pushed the issue into the limelight. Once again, while it was not resolved in his own administration, the idea had enough merit to receive consideration after he left office.

In an interview during his last year in office, Kerrey admitted his disappointment over his relationship with the university, and he cited higher education as an area where he had not accomplished his goals. He mentioned his successful 1984 educational reform bill as a major accomplishment because it provided increased accountability to performance standards in the schools among students, teachers, and administrators. Kerrey's school reorganization plan passed the legislature in 1985 and was put before the voters in November 1986, but the proposal to reduce the number of Nebraska's school districts from 995 to 500 failed. "I was unsuccessful in convincing the people that they should not repeal it," Kerrey said. "But I did manage to get twenty-five votes and get that bill passed."

Kerrey succeeded in forging environmental legislation that satisfied both environmentalists and developers—no easy task, he says. Kerrey brought together a broad spectrum of people to try to work out compromises on two contentious issues: whether the state was going to invest public dollars in water projects and whether to try to protect the environment by establishing minimum stream flows and rivers. The interested parties Kerrey brought to the table negotiated a compromise solution that satisfied everyone.

In the area of economic development, Kerrey cited a multibank holding company bill. "We got limited branch banking so that credit could flow easier. We deregulated the telecommunications industry, which was an extremely difficult thing to get passed. We created a new tax-exempt authority called NIFA [the Nebraska Investment Finance Authority awarded a low-interest loan to the Prairie Life Center, an enterprise headed by Dean Rasmussen, Kerrey's brother-in-law] in the second year, and put about $25 million of block grants out. We had an exceptional success in rural development, in economic development. I think that we made progress in making the taxes fair. We took the sales tax off of food, which was no small task. And in the midst of budgetary problems, we expanded the sales tax base in 1985 to include business utilities and half a dozen other items that were previously exempt, so that we could avoid having to raise the rate of taxation on incomes." Always self-critical, Kerrey also spoke of his failures. "I don't want to overstate the successes against the failures," he said. "There were considerable failures, some of which I would mitigate away by saying that I was green and ignorant and too aggressive and didn't communicate with the legislature enough. I can make a whole list of failings that would fill an entire article."

One of Kerrey's regrets was his dealings with the Nebraska legislature. In retrospect, he said, he should have spent more time creating a more productive atmosphere. And others agree. "If you really wanted to be powerful with the legislature, you would be somewhat hidden because you would be working very effectively with coalitions, you would be sharing credit, you would be putting others in the limelight, you would be giving them credit. That's not what happened with Bob Kerrey," says State Senator David Landis.

Despite Kerrey's self-criticism, he was pleased with his overall performance. And so were Nebraskans. Kerrey became the most popular Governor in Nebraska history. He brought lightness and intrigue to state government during a grim time, and Nebraskans appreciated him for it. He worked hard and challenged critics to find a Governor who worked harder than he did. Few could find fault with his doggedness. Kerrey often remained up until the early-morning hours poring over issues. His favorite time for catch-up reading and speech writing was during traditional holidays, when other aides had gone home to their families. One aide recalls Kerrey at the mansion one evening working excitedly on the draft of an upcoming speech and searching for statistics. "I think it was Christmas and there wasn't another soul around who was working but the Governor."

So it was a shock to Nebraskans when Kerrey announced at a press conference in October 1985 that he did not intend to run for reelection. The scene that day was right out of *The Front Page*, with reporters racing from the room to file the year's biggest story. In a simple statement, Kerrey said, "I look inside myself and do not feel the requisite things which would lead me to seek reelection. In my heart there is lacking the necessary call for 'four more years.'"

The Nebraska public was flabbergasted. Kerrey's approval ratings were in the high seventies, and his reelection would have been a virtual cakewalk. Many Republicans were elated but perplexed, knowing Kerrey's strength in the state.

Some members of Kerrey's administration were also surprised, but his closest confidants were aware of his lack of interest in a second term. For Kerrey, 1985 had been a rough year.

That fall, Debra Winger had broken off their relationship and taken up with actor Timothy Hutton. He wanted to spend more time with his children; he missed his business ventures; he wanted to write and he wanted to explore seriously the possibility of teaching. The only way to realize any of those desires, he decided, was to remove himself from politics. He also sensed that his batteries needed recharging, and he decided the only way to do that was to step out of the political arena for a while. He was tired of accusations that he was doing things for political reasons, and he wanted to be totally free of such considerations his last year in office.

At the time, Kerrey was only forty-two years old. He was in the prime of his life, and the idea of another term struck his restless soul as tedious and unexciting. He knew a second term would require a tremendous commitment—one that he did not feel capable of delivering. "I needed to follow my heart," he said.

In an interview shortly after his announcement, Kerrey said, "I'm not leaving the office of Governor because I've got political ambition beyond this. I'm going to do business in a fairly active way—telecommunications, maybe—in some connection. I'm not going to go to work for anybody. Whatever I do, I'll start it and do it on my own. But I really don't know exactly what I am going to do. I have no concrete plans. I have no road map."

Kerrey scoffed at rumors that he was despondent over losing Winger to another man. He admitted, however, that their breakup had affected him and was one of many factors that influenced his decision to step down. "It was one of many reasons," Kerrey said, "but I'm not bitterly lonely." Kerrey confided that he was dating a Cuban-American woman from Texas and planned to lead an active social life, one that simply didn't include Debra Winger. Later in 1986, a few months before his term expired, Kerrey railed against a *Newsweek* picture caption: WITH WINGER: HAPPIER DAYS. "Happier days!" Kerrey screamed. "Where do they get this stuff?" He was also upset about the text of the same *Newsweek* piece. In it, a writer described Kerrey in ebullient terms but announced halfway through that his critics find him "loopy" because, she said, "he muses on the joys of being able to clean his own toilet after he steps down as Governor." In a telephone conversation in the fall of 1986, Kerrey said the story's author told him that the "loopy" paragraph had been added at the last minute after *Newsweek* editors found the original report too effusive. They asked her to add something grittier to the piece. Thus, a new label was added to Kerrey's repertoire—loopy—a word that Kerrey derides and describes as "a *Newsweek* adjective."

Some Nebraska Democrats immediately called to express their dismay and to try to convince Kerrey to change his mind. Kerrey had been known to vacillate, and some party stalwarts thought that maybe he needed coaxing and pleading. In fact, the track record that Kerrey had laid down as Governor was one of about-faces, and there were those who thought he would consider the pleas of his fellow Democrats and acquiesce. But Kerrey was adamant.

Kerrey's announcement that he was going to pass up a guaranteed second term—for nebulous reasons—triggered considerable national attention. Interest in his decision to forgo a sure thing was so pronounced that he became the subject of scores of print and broadcast profiles. In November 1986, *Newsweek* declared him to be running by not running—for the presidency, no less. Kerrey's decision was a legitimate story, a political development in the man-bites-dog category, because none of the factors that usually compel politicians to step down were present. He wasn't ill or facing a difficult reelection. He wasn't under investigation or indictment. He didn't cite family obligations. And a 1986 Senate bid seemed unlikely given that both Nebraska Senate seats appeared likely to be held for another decade by Democratic incumbents James Exon and Edward Zorinsky. Kerrey said only that he didn't feel like running again. Long before term limits became a hot political topic, Kerrey, in effect, limited his term voluntarily.

Some partisan Nebraska Democrats were supremely disappointed. They felt that Kerrey was letting them down. Many Nebraskans, granting him his newness, were suspending their final assessments of his abilities until his second term—a term Kerrey would have entered as a seasoned politician who could be expected to achieve more. That he chose not to run again led some disgruntled Democrats to conclude that Kerrey was aware of the potential pitfalls in a second term and that he wasn't truly interested enough in governing to stay in it for the long haul. Kerrey dismissed those arguments by saying, "Continuity is vastly overrated."

Don Nelson, Kerrey's chief of staff, later said he always somehow felt that Kerrey would be drawn back into the political arena. Since his arrival on Kerrey's staff, Nelson said people had been urging him to lead the charge for the "education of Bob Kerrey," alluding to the character of Crocker Jarman in the movie *The Candidate*.

At the time, however, nobody could have foreseen the death of Senator Zorinsky. Often forgotten is that Zorinsky's party standoffishness in the Senate—which had him threatening, on occasion, to return to the Republican Party—meant that he would have been vulnerable in 1988. And there were a few hints that either he or Exon might step down when their terms expired, in 1988 and 1990, respectively. Candy Exon said of Kerrey's 1985 decision, "Bob didn't know what my dad was going to do." So while it *appeared* that Kerrey didn't have any political options at the time, there were in fact several, including the presidency. Kerrey's self-confidence was such that he felt he could take a break and return on his own terms. He wasn't worried about a specific office; he felt certain that if he wanted to reenter the political world, something would open for him and he would have a surefire chance of succeeding.

On January 9, 1986, in his final state of the state address, Kerrey began with a narrative about the devastation of the May 6, 1975, tornado that ripped through the state. He paralleled that natural disaster with the farm economy: "As I view our state today, I see the same kind of damage and the same kind of potential. The damage is largely to our agricultural sector and . . . the damage is more widespread and serious. Its cause is not a natural disaster around which we almost instinctively rally with private and public support. Its cause is a combination of federal action and inaction as well as profound changes in both the competitions' capacity to produce and in the consumers' volume and quality of purchases. In short, we find ourselves caught as a casualty of successful federal efforts to control inflation and the insidious ability of that government to sell bonds when it is unwilling to make the taxpayers pay for all of the government they receive."

Kerrey's interest in national issues had heightened during his four years as Nebraska Governor. He understood that he could do little about farm policy except rant and rave, and he admitted that he had focused far too much of his energy in that area when there was so little he could actually accomplish. During his 1988 Senate race, Kerrey pledged to attempt to secure a seat on the Agriculture Committee, and he spoke of his interest in working on the 1990 farm bill.

Federal farm policy, the national debt, and issues of war and peace interested Kerrey far more than state issues. As Governor, he once prevented a trainload of nuclear waste from crossing the Nebraska border after the federal government, contrary to agreement, failed to notify the state of the shipment. Kerrey's order to halt the train was roundly hailed by concerned citizens. Never was Kerrey so animated as when he dealt with issues at that level. When President Reagan sent National Guard troops to Honduras, Kerrey declared that he would not allow Nebraska's National Guardsmen to be activated. The heat Kerrey gave off when discussing these issues foreshadowed the day that he would turn to the national stage. As much as he loved Nebraska, Kerrey was ready for a change and a bigger audience. Nebraska was too small a theater for the restless Bob Kerrey. Longtime Kerrey friend and Lincoln businessman Jack Moors says, "Kerrey was losing interest. He's smart. I think he needed a bigger challenge."

For months after his announcement, Kerrey's decision provided food for conversation for Nebraskans curious about his reasons and future plans. John Cavanaugh, himself a political dropout, expressed the view that Kerrey had never intended to become a career politician. Thomas A. Fogarty, who had covered the Kerrey administration for the *Lincoln Journal*, said, "I can't imagine this guy ever having a future in politics."

Two things occurred in Nebraska following Kerrey's announcement: The accolades started pouring in, and those Democrats who had been frustrated with Kerrey felt comfortable criticizing him. Most believed Kerrey would be involved in politics again some day, but that day appeared far in the future, so Democrats hesitant about expressing honest opinions began to voice their differences more vocally. When Kerrey started in 1982, Nebraskans knew him only superficially. By the end of his term Kerrey remained extremely popular with the majority of Nebraskans, but some Democrats found his administration lacking. In a series of interviews conducted in 1986, several Cornhusker Democrats privately expressed their feelings that Kerrey had reneged on the essence of his campaign pledges.

State Senator David Landis was not one of them. "Much of the dissatisfaction comes from the fact that Kerrey appeared out of the blue," he said of the feelings of disenchantment. "That's the inevitable trap of charismatic leadership—because it is not ideologically oriented, people read into an attractive figure their own ideology. Republicans saw him as a businessman, Democrats saw him as socially liberal, and conservatives saw him as conservative."

Kerrey proved to be none of the above and all of the above at the same time. He was a political chameleon, and that tendency frustrated some Democrats and reporters covering him. Fogarty recalls an incident at the 1984 Democratic National Convention in San Francisco when Kerrey, as chairman of both the Nebraska delegation and Gary Hart's Nebraska campaign, voted for an unsuccessful Democratic platform plank that would have put the Democrats on record in favor of substantial reductions in defense spending. Kerrey was joined in his vote by only one other Omahan, who was pledged at the time to the Reverend Jesse Jackson. Kerrey's yes vote went against Gary Hart's advocated position, for which the rest of the delegation voted. When Fogarty cornered Kerrey and asked him to explain his decision, he told Fogarty that he didn't understand the ramifications of his yes vote. But when Fogarty questioned the delegate recorder, Democratic state chairman David Newell, Newell reported that he had repeatedly told Kerrey what the effect of a yes vote would be and had even told the Governor, "The next time you vote yes, I'm going to write it down." Newell asked again and Kerrey voted yes again, only to insist later—publicly—that he hadn't understood the consequences of his vote. Much of Kerrey's gubernatorial inconsistency and indecisiveness stemmed from his neophyte status. Since he has established himself in the Senate, Kerrey's unpredictable, vacillating nature seems to have diminished considerably. But while he was Governor, stories about his changes of mind abounded. And because of the openness and the accessibility of Nebraska politics, many people had a chance for one-on-ones with their chief executive.

One of the biggest complaints of doctrinaire Democrats was Kerrey's penchant for reneging on promises. Ann Boyle, wife of former Omaha Mayor Mike Boyle, recalls several instances in which Kerrey swore to take one direction and then turned around and took precisely the opposite path. "It's a disappointment," she says. "We hold people to their word, and when they break it, when someone lies, I think it's dangerous."

Kerrey dismisses such criticism by pointing out that in each instance he received new information that prompted him to re-evaluate his position. Kerrey describes himself as flexible, someone who is willing to jettison a plan if it isn't working or if there simply isn't support for it. As for promises, he argues that some are made to be broken. In working closely with Kerrey, Steve Fowler found that his shifting approach to issues stemmed from his background as a SEAL. "I would guess that much of Kerrey's political srategic thinking came from military training," says Fowler. "Kerrey was trained in unconventional warfare, and that does not mean that you attack straight on, that you take a position and hold it. You amend your strategy constantly, keeping in mind a larger goal and not necessarily worrying about short-term strategic objectives." As a SEAL, Kerrey's entire thrust was surprises, and certainly, as a politician, he followed that inclination. It drove some Nebraskans wild, although most learned to accept that facet of his personality and, in fact, were in awe of it.

DiAnna Schimek, now a State Senator from Lincoln, says, "Quite frankly, sometimes the Governor and I were at odds over political kinds of things, but I found myself thoroughly fascinated by him because he is so unpredictable and because he's not afraid to take risks and he puts a real creative touch on things." Again, that "creative touch" drove some Nebraskans crazy, including a handful of the journalists assigned to cover him. Fogarty, for instance, found Kerrey "inconsistent and indecisive. He would go back and forth on issues." Kerrey, who once complimented Fogarty as "the best of the lot" of Nebraska journalists, was infuriated that Fogarty would characterize him that way. In discussing Fogarty's comments with a writer in 1988, Kerrey screamed, "Fuck Fogarty, fuck him! I've never been indecisive. I may be impulsive, but I've never been indecisive."

The Nebraska press had a glorious four years covering Governor Kerrey. They were there at the beginning and they observed him from his early faltering days in 1982 to his emergence as the state's most arresting politician when he stepped down in 1986. Every Nebraska political writer or broadcast journalist has a trove of stories about Kerrey, the most memorable of which stem from his days when he lived at the Governor's mansion. As a Senator, he has always made communication with his home state press a priority; still, his election to the U.S. Congress altered the proximity and the routine casualness that existed in the early days. Highly respected political columnist Kathleen Rutledge says, "Along in 1982, here comes this guy who thinks he's a hotshot. He's going to run for Governor, and you go to all these different press conferences and listen to him give all these long, irrelevant presentations. And we're thinking, 'Who is this guy?' And then all of a sudden, he's Governor. And then you have to go from being disdainful to actually being respectful."

To some reporters, Kerrey will always be remembered for the games that he and Don Nelson delighted in playing with the press. Both Nelson and Kerrey believed there were too many reporters asking questions who didn't have a firm grasp of their subject matter.

As chief of staff, Nelson is best remembered for his verbal games. When a reporter would ask if the Governor was out of state, Nelson would respond, "Define out of state." If the query was, "Is the Governor going to cut the budget?" Nelson would say, "Define cut." Nelson also was fond of talking in a singsong voice, intimating that questioners lacked appropriate understanding of the issue at hand. A reporter might say, "Okay, so you said thus and such," and Nelson would say, "No, I did not say thus and such; thus and such is not what I said. You're assuming thus and such. What I said was, 'So and so.' Okay, shall we go back to square one, boys and girls?"

Both Kerrey and Nelson were extremely competitive verbally. They enjoyed lobbing conversational puzzles, and Nelson, especially, saw humor in twisting people around verbally. Kerrey and Nelson often regaled each other with stories about how they had zinged this or that person and the reaction and response the zingee gave. They regarded themselves as exceptionally bright, and Nelson acted accordingly, especially with regard to engaging in three tasks simultaneously.

Says Nelson: "When you have an IQ that's up there at the level that we've got, then you have this incredible ability. Other people who don't have it don't understand it, and they find it frightening and disconcerting."

Actually, many Nebraskans found Nelson's persona less frightening and disconcerting and more annoying and mean-spirited. Nelson's supporters argue that those Nebraskans who disliked the way he dealt with them are the ones who had the least contact with him. One consensus that emerged about Nelson, however, was that he made a concerted effort to change after examining the effects of some of his actions during his glory days with Kerrey.

Despite Nelson's manner, Kerrey was well served by him; he was dedicated to his boss, and he had no personal political agenda. Kerrey and Nelson often worked together at the Governor's mansion until the early-morning hours. The two men had the same high energy level and they tackled problems as intensely as they did everything else. Working in the administration proved harrowing for some top aides, who were expected to imitate their bosses. Most managed to keep up with the Governor and his chief, but some found the workaholic tendencies disquieting.

The only area where Kerrey did not make great demands

was in the press department. Renee Wessels, who was in charge of Kerrey's press for his primary run, returned to Nebraska to reclaim the job from Kandra Hahn, who had handled Kerrey's general election press but went on to run Kerrey's Energy Department. What both women discovered was that Kerrey only wanted a press person to handle logistics, while he wanted to handle his press conferences, return reporters' telephone calls, write his speeches, and draft all but his most perfunctory press releases. "He was his own best press person," Wessels says. During his 1982 run Kerrey needed to rely more on Wessels and Hahn, but as his visibility and popularity escalated, he wanted freedom to do whatever he pleased.

PART III

Chapter 9

SENATOR KERREY

A few years after Bob Kerrey arrived home from Vietnam, he invited boyhood chum Frosty Chapman to his parents' lakeside home on Capitol Beach for a sailboat ride. It was a sunny day, the sky a rich blue. It was also breezy, and as the wind picked up the two men found themselves racing along, the mast tilting so that it seemed certain the boat would soon capsize. Getting nervous about their predicament, Chapman looked at Kerrey, who was staring fearlessly ahead. Chapman said nothing, but instead waited for a cue from his Navy buddy. Perfectly composed, Kerrey turned to his friend and in an even voice, with just a trace of a grin, asked, "What do you think is going to happen?" "I think when that pole hits the water, we're going to go flying," Chapman replied. And sure enough, he barely got the words out before the pole hit and the men were flung into the lake. "I'll never forget how he just looked at me, so coolly, and said, 'Well, what do you think is going to happen?' He wasn't rattled in the least," Chapman recalls.

That story typifies Kerrey's post-Vietnam personality. Before Vietnam, Kerrey was hell-bent on engineering his life. But after the war, while he still restlessly created opportunities, there was also a sense of fatalism: Kerrey began to believe in letting action take its course, and going with the flow. Sailing with Chapman that day, Kerrey could have intervened and probably steered out of trouble, but there is a strong part of him that says to let life unfold; let nature take its course, and if it pitches you or puts you in a new predicament, well, so be it.

On March 6, 1987, Senator Edward Zorinsky died of a heart attack while performing in a skit at Omaha's Peony Park. At the time, Kerrey was in Santa Barbara, California, lecturing to college students about the Vietnam War. Don Nelson, who was a partner of Kerrey's in an investment banking venture, tracked him down to relay the news, and Kerrey immediately returned to Nebraska for the funeral.

Zorinsky had been hospitalized twice with chest pains, but he was considered to be in good health. (He and his gregarious wife, Cece, played a mean game of tennis, occasionally at the White House and often for benefits.) Senate colleagues flew to Omaha for the services at Zorinsky's synagogue, and Utah Republican Senator Orrin Hatch, a Latter-Day Saints minister and a close friend of Zorinsky's, delivered a moving eulogy. Hatch recalled the time that he and Zorinsky were at a McDonald's in Asia, and Zorinsky inquired whether the beef was from Nebraska. All of Nebraska's political notables were at the funeral, along with hundreds of nonpolitical Nebraskans. A short, roundish man, Zorinsky had riled the Democratic Party hierarchy by making frequent public statements that he was thinking of rejoining the GOP. Many national institutional Democrats had a sort of "go figure" attitude about Zorinsky, but the man was loved in his home state. Throughout his Senate career, Zorinsky was known for being one of that body's most frugal members; he paid his staff comparatively low salaries, and he often made public announcements about how much of his Senate money he was returning to the U.S. Treasury. Zorinsky had been Mayor of Omaha, and before that he ran a family vending machine company. He had signed on as a Democrat shortly before winning in 1976, and his upset victory was viewed as a major blow to the Republicans, who had pushed him from their ranks.

After Kerrey announced he would not seek a second term as Governor, some speculated that he was planning to challenge Zorinsky in 1988. Zorinsky had once publicly declared that he would serve in the Senate for only two terms so as not to grow stale on the job. But he recanted in his second term and let it be known that he planned to win a third time. Still, the talk that Kerrey planned to take him on reached such levels that an irritated Zorinsky finally called Kerrey to speak with him about it. Kerrey blamed the rumors on a luncheon conversation he had had earlier that year in Washington with Senator George Mitchell of Maine, then head of the Democratic Senatorial Campaign Committee. Mitchell asked Kerrey if he would take on Zorinsky if the incumbent returned to the Republican Party. Kerrey claimed that he didn't answer Mitchell's question, but that Mitchell went to Zorinsky and indicated that Kerrey would indeed challenge him if he switched parties again. In a 1986 interview, Kerrey said, "I'm not planning to run against Senator Zorinsky in 1988. I am not taking two years off to organize a Senate campaign. I'm not planning to run for the Senate in 1990 for that matter." Shortly thereafter, Kerrey made a formal announcement that he did not have any plans to run for Zorinsky's seat.

People began speculating about Kerrey's plans immediately after Zorinsky's death, but he shied away from such discussions, which he believed were morbid and in poor taste. Jim Crounse, who had worked in the Kerrey administration, approached his former boss at the close of Zorinsky's funeral and expressed a hope that Kerrey would run for the seat. Kerrey looked at him blankly; obviously, Crounse remembers, Kerrey felt the remark was inappropriate. Crounse said he didn't mean to show Zorinsky any disrespect, but since he might not see Kerrey for a while, he simply wanted to express support for his candidacy. "The fact is, people were talking about Kerrey running at the funeral," Crounse recalls.

Later, Kerrey did begin to mull over the idea. Since leaving the Governor's office, he had been lecturing at the University of California, Santa Barbara, and managing an investment company with Don Nelson. The Vietnam history course, which has been profiled in newspapers and featured on "60 Minutes," was created at Santa Barbara by Nebraska native Walter Capps, whom Kerrey had befriended while he was Governor. Capps was the first person to invite Vietnam veterans to speak about their experiences and to weave a college course around their reflections. The course is widely praised by Vietnam veterans, many of whom used the forum to speak about their own experiences for the first time.

In January 1987, when Kerrey's term as Governor ended, he headed for Santa Barbara for a three-month teaching assignment. Kerrey and Nelson opened their investment banking office just prior to Kerrey's move west, and the ex-Governor periodically returned to Nebraska to take care of business. He moved back home after his teaching assignment ended, and he and Nelson remained business partners for the rest of that year.

During this period Kerrey also lectured at Omaha's premier urban school, Omaha Central High School. Located on the grounds of Nebraska's former territorial capitol, Central is the alma mater of some of Nebraska's best and brightest, including Walter Capps and Robert Spire, both Kerrey confidants. In February and March of 1987, Kerrey lectured before Clyde Lincoln's government class seven times. Because Kerrey was not an accredited teacher, Lincoln always sat in, thereby legitimizing the arrangement in the eyes of Omaha's school board and its teachers association. Lincoln described Kerrey as "an extremely charismatic teacher." He was impressed by how well prepared Kerrey came to his classes and how eager he was to study his students' textbooks for material that might fit into his own lectures. "He didn't try to impress the students with power language," says Lincoln. "He didn't talk down to them. He saw them as developing young adults, and he had their attention the whole time, which is a major coup.

"Kerrey is the epitome of the lifelong student," he adds, "and he is not afraid of controversy."

Throughout this time, Kerrey was beseeched by Democrats eager for him to run for Zorinsky's seat. Among them was Senator Exon, who appealed to Kerrey's sense of duty by telling him that his four years as Governor were not enough service. Kerrey and Exon developed a strong bond during this time—a bond that continues today.

Kerrey rented a house in Lincoln after he stepped down, but later bought a home in Omaha's Memorial Park section. That purchase was interpreted by some to mean that he was planning to run for the Senate, regardless of Zorinsky's plans or fate. In Nebraska, one Senator has traditionally been from Omaha, and since both Kerrey and Exon are from Lincoln, there was talk that the ex-Governor was moving to Omaha to position himself in the right city. On March 20, 1987, *Lincoln Journal* political writer Don Walton speculated that Kerrey was "the only Nebraskan with the clout to abruptly end the tradition of an Omaha seat in the Senate. But even if he decides to run, and ultimately wins, we might never know if that is true. He might become an Omahan himself this year."

Best known for Boys Town, the Strategic Air Command, and the cattle livestock market, Omaha is also the state's financial center: it is the corporate headquarters for Mutual of Omaha, Union Pacific, and ConAgra; the city is also the hometown of Warren Buffett, who became a friend of Kerrey's while he was Governor, and whom Kerrey said he would rely on for economic policy guidance should he become President. Kerrey's Grandmother's headquarters are in Omaha, and he had lived in the suburb of Ralston during his early restaurant days.

In 1986, Governor Kay Orr beat Lincoln Mayor Helen Boosalis in a hotly contested woman-against-woman race for Governor and, one year later, was called on to make an unexpected senatorial appointment. Orr appointed an unknown Omaha Republican, grain agribusinessman David Karnes, to take Zorinsky's place. It was her first major appointment, and it proved to be a disaster for the party. A man who appeared to have all the right stuff, Karnes was chosen by Orr to be a match for Kerrey. Nebraska Republicans had watched Kerrey's house hunting and determined that he would run in 1988, despite his statements to the contrary.

The problem with Orr's appointment of Karnes was that she bypassed Congressman Hal Daub of Omaha, an intensely partisan Republican who had been paying his dues for years. Daub, once labeled "the pit bull of Nebraska politics," ran in 1978 against John Cavanaugh. When Cavanaugh retired from Congress in 1980, Daub ran again and won. A brilliant handler of constituent services, which John Cavanaugh was not, Daub served Omaha well, and he was anxious to step up to higher office. Most Nebraskans figured he would get the nod from Orr, and were shocked when she picked a virtual unknown. Daub was predictably furious. Orr, after little deliberation with party regulars, decided that Daub's quirky mannerisms and high-strung personality would not play well against Kerrey, and that a good-looking newcomer would have a better chance at the spot because the appointee would have nearly two years in office to gain recognition. So she gambled, expecting to be heralded. Instead, she created a civil war within the party, the repercussions of which continue still. Orr's 1990 defeat was primarily due to her handling of tax issues, although there still was resentment toward her by Nebraska Republicans supportive of Hal Daub.

Meanwhile, Kerrey's postpolitical life wasn't as compelling as he thought it would be. He admitted in an August 1987 interview that he missed the political life. He added, "I don't regret not running. I mean, I don't think that I could have run again. I think I've got a much better perspective on politics and I'm much healthier today than I was a year ago." Kerrey said he was healthier emotionally and in "lots of ways," referring to the end of his relationship with Debra Winger in 1985.

Winger told *Vanity Fair* in October 1990 that the breakup was turbulent, that the two did not part as friends. At the time, Kerrey intimates in Nebraska knew the relationship was tenuous, and many were privately pleased. Kerrey's close friends always spoke highly of Winger in public, but off the record they spoke of her as being the only potential baggage he had attached to his career.

Kerrey formally announced plans to run for the Senate in February 1988, and one month later it was announced through publicists that Winger and Hutton were separated. From that point on, Kerrey's Senate campaign was rife with rumors that he and Winger had rekindled their romance. Kerrey did visit her that year in California, but once the campaign geared up, she completely dropped out of the picture. One rumor that gained currency was that while he was living in Omaha during the 1988 race, Winger was staying at the Swanson Tower Hotel. In a December 4, 1988, interview with the *Omaha World-Herald* Senator-elect Kerrey said, "I loved the Swanson Tower rumor.

It was so mature. It made me want to go over and see if she was there."

While Kerrey was Governor, Winger chafed at the artifice of it all and was eager to begin a family. Kerrey was landlocked as Nebraska Governor; he had two young children; and, personal inclinations aside, he did not have the time to consider beginning a new family. But when Kerrey left the Governor's office and was free to travel or move or even think of making personal and family commitments, Winger was married and having a baby. By the time Winger's marriage began to unravel, the couple would have been able to pick up again. But there were complications: Kerrey was planning his run for the U.S. Senate, and Winger was still a touchy subject for those Nebraskans unable to understand off-again, on-again relationships. Winger was interested in Kerrey during this period and contacted him when she felt like it. One Kerrey friend chanted the musical motif from *Jaws* whenever Winger's name came up, so convinced was he that she was a liability. So even though the two remained close throughout his Senate race (Winger contributed money to his campaign effort), she did not return to Nebraska during that 1988 election year. (After Kerrey won, and after Winger's divorce was finalized in the summer of 1990, the relationship was on again. But it was off again by the time he announced his plans to run for the presidency in September 1991.)

With the Winger question resolved, Kerrey's Senate race was ready to roll and the media could focus on a few more paramount issues of the Kerrey campaign. In November, Kerrey told reporters that he did indeed plan to run for the Senate; he said he would work toward that goal throughout the fall, but he would not formally announce his plans until early 1988. During this time, Kerrey flew to Washington to meet with party leaders. Early in 1988, Kerrey, Nelson, and others met at John Cavanaugh's house to discuss strategy. Cavanaugh had been one of the top trusted advisers to presidential aspirant Gary Hart, and he had become close to Hart aide Billy Shore, who later would become Kerrey's chief of staff and presidential campaign aide.

From the outset, Kerrey decided to bring in a group of veteran political professionals to run his campaign; in fact, it was the rare person who had worked in his campaign for Governor who was hired to work for his Senate race.

Kerrey discussed his candidacy with the Democratic Senatorial Campaign Committee and other leading advisers, including his 1982 pollster, Harrison Hickman. He eventually assembled a staff of skillful and seasoned political professionals, who put together what is generally acknowledged as the most well-executed campaign in Nebraska history. His choice of an out-of-state group of pros to run everything caused the usual friction between them and Nebraska's party regulars, some of whom resented not playing a larger role in Kerrey's campaign. Later, however, they grudgingly admitted that Kerrey's Senate race was about as close to being flawless as a political race can be.

At a prekickoff rally at Peony Park Ballroom on February 9, 1988, Kerrey stood before hundreds of eager Nebraskans and launched his campaign with a six-page speech. In it, Kerrey spoke of the concerns he would address as a Senator: a fair federal farm policy; affordable health care; opposition to the arms race; a bloated defense budget; civil and human rights; education; and the economy. "The number-one issue must be our economy," Kerrey said. "Unless our people are working and unless their work results in a product or service which can be sold in the marketplace, we cannot hope for a better world. To increase our standard of living, we must not only apply our technology to products in a way that will add value, but we must be able to add value to our people."

As he had done as Governor, Kerrey spoke of his ambivalent feelings about government and his belief that it was government, coupled with his personal initiative, that allowed an embittered Vietnam veteran to fulfill his dreams. "I stand before you tonight a living, breathing example of what American can do: public education, public health care, public income maintenance combined with the freedom to pursue my private enterprise dreams relatively unencumbered by the heavy hand of government." Remembering his days at the Philadelphia Naval Hospital and his accrued government benefits as a wounded veteran, Kerrey rails against those who generalize about the recipients of government handouts; in his case, Kerrey says, those benefits made him grateful and productive.

Kerrey spent the next month drafting another speech that launched his formal announcement of his candidacy. On March 10, 1988, before a group of more than three hundred fifty supporters in Omaha, Kerrey delivered an address titled, "Not What We Are—But What We Can Be." The room was bedecked with running shoes, which Kerrey used as a metaphor for his campaign, and the topic with which he opened his speech. "Shoes. What a way to start a campaign: with a room full of shoes. . . . Shoes are a wonderful refuge when we are lost or embarrassed. When your question catches me completely off guard or unprepared, I am apt to look at my shoes for the answer. . . . Now, as we begin this campaign, it is time for us to put on our shoes, to start our journey together, remembering that our goal is a moment in time that is much further ahead than November 8, 1988. We must consider the world of our children when they are adults, and our children's children as well. And that's what this campaign is all about—not what we are—but what we can be."

Kerrey's campaign theme focused on the future, and he sounded the generational theme that he would use three and a half years later in his bid for the presidency. Acknowledging that the road ahead would not be smooth, Kerrey said, "A great and glorious future will not happen unless we do the unglamorous work today." He also spoke of Nebraska's plains. "We understand that the paradise of a family farm takes generations to create; that it is not done overnight. We understand that the forces of Nature are a part of our lives; we know the seasons, the flow of the river, the rise of the moon. . . . You are a special people, Nebraska: your roots stretch back to an empty and inhospitable prairie which you have made your home."

Kerrey then embarked on a two-day campaign swing, after which he addressed campaign supporters in Nebraska's capitol rotunda. Although state Democrats had been quietly working for Kerrey since November, they were ready and anxious for his formal announcement so they could officially begin to pound the pavement for him. Most Democrats were confident that Kerrey would win the election; however, because of the strength of Nebraska's GOP machine, no one thought the race would be a breeze.

Kerrey would soon stand before audiences as the most popular and widely known politician in the state. He was able to
choose a staff from among the Democratic Party's top campaign
gypsies. He began the race with close to 100 percent name recognition and broad and deep support. The escalation of Kerrey's
personal popularity had reached such staggering proportions during his race for the Senate that it was doubtful that Republicans
could have fielded anyone capable of winning. Kerrey had become an even more intriguing politician since stepping down as
Governor, and people were eager to make a connection with
him.

State Senator David Landis sums up a general feeling about
Kerrey: "You got the feeling that if you were admitted to Kerrey's inner circle, you would have a marvelous time." Says Dan
Ladeley, "People are attracted to him because he's vivacious and
good-looking and friendly. That is a very attractive set of qualities to possess, and in the case of Bob Kerrey it works doubly
well because he is also a very capable and intelligent person."

Kerrey was opposed in the Democratic primary by an unknown attorney from a small Nebraska town. Daub and Karnes,
however, battled each other daily for more than half a year;
while they were sparring, Kerrey was discussing the issues, raising money, planning strategy, and making appearances. The
Karnes-Daub race eventually became so cutthroat that the two
camps were filled with loathing. Many Daub supporters pledged
their votes to Kerrey should their man lose. Liz Karnes stated
publicly that she too would vote for Kerrey if her husband lost
the primary. And she wasn't the only Republican who delighted
Democrats with that kind of sentiment. At the July state Republican convention in Lincoln, keynote speaker James Thompson,
Governor of Illinois, praised Kerrey at a news conference, calling him charismatic and a hard worker.

Daub's defeat in the Republican primary was more or less
assured when Karnes was endorsed by the *Omaha World-Herald.*
The Karnes-Daub contest was the nation's only primary race in
which an incumbent Senator was challenged by a rival from his
own party, and it was not a pretty fight. Nebraska's Republican
Party was torn asunder that year under the leadership of Kay

Orr. Karnes and Daub became so outrageous in their attacks against each other that Kerrey aides observing the battle were astounded. "There's nothing we could ever say about either man that they haven't already said about each other," Steve Jarding, Kerrey's press secretary, said. Daub had the advantage of eight years of effective service as an Omaha Congressman, but Karnes had the power of incumbency. Polls taken one week before the primary showed the two men neck and neck, but Karnes surged in the final days and won handily.

Two weeks after the May primary, Kerrey's pollster determined that he was leading Karnes by 16 percent, and he would remain ahead until Election Day.

Still, the Kerrey camp was not going to take his lead for granted. They wanted to rack up an impressive win, so they worked as though they were ten points behind. Kerrey often cautioned about getting complacent because of their poll results. The Kerrey campaign also was concerned because of Karnes's surge toward the end of his primary bout with Daub. Nebraska has a well-financed and powerful Republican machine, and with Orr in the driver's seat, Karnes had managed to beat a skillful Congressman.

Karnes, a strapping, handsome, and congenial Omaha native, became the youngest member of the Senate when Orr appointed him at age thirty-nine. Karnes is married to a dynamic and ambitious woman, Liz Lueder Karnes, whose father had been a consistent top-dollar contributor to national Republican politicians, including Ronald Reagan. She had earned a doctorate in education and was an elected school board member of Omaha's wealthiest school district. When her husband's appointment was first announced, many Nebraskans speculated that Orr had chosen the wrong Karnes. Liz Karnes readily agreed that she was a better campaigner than her husband, but she denied all suggestions that she should have been the nominee. Despite her protests, the race could have been called the Karneses against Kerrey. Democrats joked that it would take two to tango with Kerrey, but they weren't laughing in July when they brought in the candidate's younger brother, Bill, to cover the events Kerrey's schedule wouldn't permit him to attend. Kerrey insiders at the time believed that Liz Karnes's ubiquitous presence (she had spoken at hundreds of events in her husband's honor since his March 1987 appointment) would backfire by November. "Look, Liz Karnes's name will not be on the ballot in November," said Jarding, "and Nebraska voters are sophisticated enough that when it comes down to voting, they're going to vote for Kerrey because he is his own man." After all the devastation the Daub bypass caused, however, many disgruntled GOP insiders believed that the Karneses together presented a much tougher challenge to bachelor Kerrey than Daub ever could have mounted with his finger-pointing demeanor. Dave Karnes was considered affable and competent, but he lacked intensity and political astuteness, and he did not generate enthusiasm among his followers. Nebraskans believed Karnes was a nice man; Kerrey was nice too, Cornhuskers felt, but he also possessed a necessary edge. So Nebraska's 1988 Senate race came down to two likable, dedicated, earnest men with wonderful families, lots of friends, and many supporters. They both were interested in representing Nebraska in the 1990s, a decade that many believed would be a watershed period in American history.

The battle between Karnes and Kerrey that summer was conducted in drop-dead, record-breaking heat. But the extremes in temperature accompanying the race were only a footnote to the real headlines. The first was record-breaking cost. Karnes and Kerrey each spent more than $2 million in a state with nine hundred thousand registered voters. In June, Kerrey proposed a joint voluntary agreement to limit spending to just under $1 million but Karnes refused. The second was record-breaking invective. "This will be the dirtiest campaign in Nebraska history," one Republican accurately predicted. The GOP desperately wanted to keep the seat.

At the outset, Kerrey told intimates that he wondered if Nebraskans would accept him back on the political scene. He need not have worried. If anything, the aura that he possessed as Governor intensified during his Senate race, and his personal magnetism seemed to have increased.

As Governor, Kerrey had endeared himself to Nebraskans completely. Literally hundreds of Nebraskans will tell you that they know Bob Kerrey. If they are pressed, often what emerges is a tiny slice of life that is meaningful to the receiver—a conversation at a downtown diner, a greeting at the YMCA, a brief telephone call to talk about a prosthesis, some dialogue in a meeting—small snapshots that people treasure and enlarge. Part of that is the wide-open system that allows a real measure of access and part of it is Kerrey's personality. Long before he ran for public office, he gave rise to those feelings in people.

The great irony is that often the people who spent real time with Bob Kerrey and would be presumed to truly know him will tell you that they, in fact, don't know him but wish they did. Kandra Hahn, director of the Nebraska Energy Office in Kerrey's gubernatorial days, said, "People will tell you that they are close friends of Bob's but I question whether they know him well."

There were people who would remain opposed to Kerrey—forever alienated by Debra Winger or the Commonwealth crisis—but they were in the minority. Nebraskans welcomed Kerrey back with open arms, open pocketbooks, and unlimited time—his campaign offices in Omaha and Lincoln were deluged with volunteers.

Kerrey engineered his own campaign, a state-of-the-art, sophisticated operation. But there was one major glitch—personality conflicts between Kerrey's out-of-state staffers and Nebraskans who felt they were being underutilized. Many Lincolnites, especially those who had played critical roles in Kerrey's first campaign, found that they simply weren't needed the second time around. Much of the work they had performed earlier was not necessary, and Kerrey's invited carpetbaggers would not delegate duties to the Nebraskans.

The Karnes campaign was woeful in comparison. He was unfamiliar with politics, nor was he a natural at the game. Trouble appeared for Karnes soon after he was nominated, and he spent much of his time playing catch-up. One Senate staffer who watched Karnes in the beginning observed that he seemed to be in a daze. Karnes and his wife attended scores of meetings in which GOP operatives, eager to hang on to the Nebraska seat, gave them crash courses in every conceivable subject. This reliance on GOP professionals in Washington gave Karnes a reputation of being a scripted candidate. The Kerrey camp decided to focus on the difference between the two men by highlighting Kerrey's independence and by portraying Karnes as a tool of the Republican Party. They repeatedly ridiculed him as an ineptly dependent and murky-on-the-issues GOP machine appointee. In speeches, brochures, position papers, and commercials, Kerrey stressed the fact that he wrote his own speeches, directed his campaign, and decided the issues he would address. That theme resonated easily with disgruntled Daub supporters, who resented the enormous amount of Republican support Karnes had received in their ferocious primary slugfest.

Kerrey's first major opportunity to show his enhanced speechmaking skills and discuss important campaign issues came at the state's annual Democratic convention, which was held that year in Grand Island, birthplace of actor Henry Fonda. Kerrey's address, which he wrote himself, was to be the keynote speech, and he was eager to inspire the crowd. In a rousing, tub-thumping speech, Kerrey moved his exuberant fellow Democrats to cheers with an impassioned declaration of the differences between himself and Karnes. "Senator Karnes supports aid to the Contras and I say no. He supports funding for the deployment of the Strategic Defense Initiative and I say do not. He voted against the trade bill with the plant-closing provision and I would have voted for it. He was strongly opposed to the Civil Rights Restoration Act and I would have strongly supported it. He is uncertain about affirmative action and I strongly believe in its need." That weekend, Kerrey emerged as a politician with a clear, coherent vision and a strengthened ideological backbone. He exhibited none of the rambling, nebulous outlines of his first campaign. The matured Kerrey sounded simpatico to the Democratic Party, and the feeling was clearly mutual.

In a state with sixty-seven thousand more registered Republicans than Democrats, being a Democrat usually means having to say you're sorry. But with Kerrey, the Democrats realized they need not make any apologies. Kerrey's track record as Governor was proof he could not be pigeonholed by the Republicans. He balanced the state budget, he vetoed raises for state employees, he appointed a Republican to the post of attorney general—all actions for which any Republican chief executive would delight in taking credit. But after his forceful declarations in Grand Island, no one could argue that Kerrey was anything other than a devoted Democrat.

Twelve days earlier, Kerrey had been buoyed by the news from his pollsters that 55 percent of Nebraska voters preferred him and 39 percent favored Karnes.

After the Grand Island convention, Kerrey turned his attention to debates, the first of which, by tradition, was to be an agriculture-oriented debate at the Nebraska state fair in early September. Karnes and Kerrey spent the summer bickering over the format of their debates—so much so that eventually their haggling became known as "the debate over the debates." For most of July and August, Nebraska newspaper readers awoke to articles about debates in which the candidates accused each other of debate transgressions. Kerrey declared that he wanted substantive debates that resembled the celebrated Lincoln-Douglas nineteenth-century debates, and Karnes pushed for a more restrictive format. In early July, Kerrey sent Karnes a detailed letter proposing ten debates without questioners or rules. "Let us not drive our political discourse through the mathematical function of one-hour television, where sound bites are the rule. Let us stand face to face, each with his opportunity to present a lengthy and thoughtful analysis of his philosophy, beliefs, and solutions," Kerrey wrote. When Karnes countered that they be questioned on specific topics by a panel of reporters, Kerrey wrote back that Karnes's counterproposal was, in essence, a rejection of his own idea of one-to-one debates. "The uniqueness of what I am offering may have been lost on you and your advisers. The pressure should be on us to describe what we believe the government's role should be in our lives instead of preparing answers for questions that are relatively easy to predict. . . . The typical political debate where the press writes and asks the questions does not connect with the lives of the individuals and families," Kerrey wrote.

The great irony about the brouhaha over the Kerrey-Karnes debates is that they ended up having only one—at the Nebraska state fair in early September. Before that, the two sides had agreed to eight ninety-minute debates with four of the meetings outlined to resemble Kerrey's plan and the other four to follow the structure proposed by Karnes. Although Karnes and Kerrey had often appeared at the same forums, this was to be their first serious exchange. With both candidates' families seated in the front row, Karnes and Kerrey took the stage before a rowdy, capacity crowd made up mostly of partisan campaign workers and farmers. Held in an open-air auditorium, the debate was the traditional general election kickoff and was covered by Nebraska's Educational Television Network and a phalanx of state media representatives. For Karnes, the meeting turned out to be a bona fide disaster: Midway into the debate, he was roundly booed when he said, "We need fewer farmers at this point in time."

The Kerrey camp was overjoyed. Kerrey had spent long hours preparing for the debates, and his campaign packed the audience to assure that his remarks received warm responses. From the beginning, Kerrey and his followers believed that Karnes would somehow stumble during the debates, but no one had imagined a gaffe of such proportions. One Kerrey staffer said that when he heard the remark, he immediately saw visions of dynamite commercials; unfortunately, both sides had agreed that neither could use excerpts from the debates for campaign commercials. Still, Karnes's remark was so often repeated by the media that, years later, he was still remembered more for his farmer faux pas than for anything else.

Karnes's statement—that technology has advanced to the point where fewer farmers are required to do the work performed in decades past—may indeed be true; however, he framed his remark in such a way that it came across as a suggestion that the country should have fewer farmers. Karnes initially had no idea why the audience was booing him; only later would he realize the extent of his blunder, and his press secretary would soon issue an apology and admit that Karnes was "inarticulate."

Karnes never recovered from the state fair fiasco. For the next ten weeks his campaign sputtered along, with Karnes struggling to overcome his image as a scripted candidate who lacked the skill to be an effective member of the Senate. The Karnes campaign tried just about every political tactic: They distorted Kerrey's record, they planted scurrilous rumors, they sent out vicious fund-raising letters, they ran what Omaha columnist Warren Franke called a "simpy photo" of Kerrey and ran it every hour on every TV station, and they tagged him with unfair political labels. For a while, everywhere they went the Karneses told audiences that Bob Kerrey and Ted Kennedy were soul brothers. "Kerrey is just like Ted Kennedy," Liz Karnes said, "but what's good for Massachusetts is not necessarily good for Nebraska." At the end of June, in North Platte, David Karnes said, "When the voters know the *real* Bob Kerrey, they are going to decide that he's just too liberal."

In truth, both Karnes and Kerrey are typical Nebraskans. Each man—in style and in ideological orientation—embodies a distinct kind of Cornhusker. Kerrey, with his verbal facility, embodies the Irish who settled Nebraska; Karnes, in personality, is more representative of the Germans and Swedes who, in the words of one comedienne, traversed oceans, rivers, mountains, and forests to settle down in the same godforsaken climate they left. Kerrey is the quintessential Irish charmer, a profile that turns off those voters who have become so jaded about charm that they don't believe it exists. Yet, in our television-obsessed, sound-bite society, where the principal means of communication rewards candidates' rehearsed one-liners, it is bracing to listen to a politician who is authentically clever. Critics call him flip, but his detractors will admit that his sharpness is impressive.

During a July thank-you rally, Kerrey stepped up to the microphone and began a salute to one of Omaha's most celebrated musicians. Kerrey toasted "Nuncio and his band" and called him one of the finest musicians "in this era—I mean, area." Realizing instantly that he had reduced the scope of Nuncio's contributions, Kerrey added deftly, "Nuncio is one of the premiere musicians of this era, as well." Even when Kerrey makes mistakes, he is extremely resourceful in how he recovers and in turning his error into advantage, usually by some self-effacing remark.

Karnes possessed the kind of deliberative reserve most commonly associated with a Scandinavian heritage. Karnes did lighten up in one-on-one situations, but he came across as unsure of himself in large groups. Goaded into entering the Nebraskaland Days hog-calling contest, Karnes bellowed out a priceless pig imitation. However, returning to his table, flushed and nervous, he told aides he should have done something similar to Nebraska State Senator Dave Bernard-Stevens, who simply screamed into the mike: "Here, pig, c'mon, pig . . . dammit, pig, get the hell over here!" Bernard-Stevens's porcine call received big laughs, but the audience enjoyed Karnes's hog shouting just as much. Yet Karnes shook his head as he sat down and assessed his actions with aides, one of whom suggested, "You should have said something about wanting to stop the pork barrel efforts in Washington, D.C." Karnes replied, "That's good. But why didn't you give me that line *before* I went on?"

The irony is that a pork barrel remark would have come across as just another artificial ad-lib, whereas Karnes's nonpolitical performance bordered on endearing. The crowd truly appreciated his spirited spontaneity. Yet Karnes dismissed his instincts and complimented the contrived one-liner of a youthful aide. Kerrey, on the other hand, even during his 1982 gubernatorial campaign, exhibited tremendous self-assurance and did not second-guess himself in unchartered situations. Such seemingly trivial incidents epitomize the contrasting confidence levels and temperaments of Kerrey and Karnes. Throughout the campaign, Kerrey was quick to delineate his views off-the-cuff while Karnes was hesitant, always more at ease with a script. "Wouldn't you be?" one Karnes supporter questioned. "Imagine one day you're an ordinary guy and the next day you're a member of the most exclusive political club in the country. He's got a lot of catch-up to do." Democrats were more brutal: "He's out of his league."

But for all their ideological and stylistic differences, Karnes and Kerrey had strikingly similar formative years. Both were raised in Protestant, middle-class neighborhoods where afternoons were filled with sports. Both their mothers were raised on farms, moved to the city for marriage, and were homemakers who returned to work as their children matured. Karnes attended Omaha's Benson High School, whose student body makeup closely resembles that of Lincoln's Northeast High School. Both young men were active in sports. They graduated from the University of Nebraska–Lincoln, Kerrey with a degree in pharmacy in 1965 and Karnes from law school in 1974. Both joined popular fraternities and are remembered as affable. Both were grooming themselves for careers in business.

Two men, parallel lives. And then, Vietnam. Karnes was not involved in the war, nor did he protest against or actively support it. Were it not for Vietnam, Karnes and Kerrey might have been opponents in a Republican primary. As it was, the Vietnam War, which had not been discussed in the Kerrey-Karnes bout, was highlighted when Dan Quayle was chosen as the Republican Vice Presidential nominee. From the time of the Republican National Convention on, Vietnam became an overt and an under-the-surface issue in Nebraska's 1988 Senate race. The Vietnam War had virtually been ignored before Quayle's selection, but discussion of it at the top of the ticket quite naturally trickled down to the state level, and as might be imagined, Kerrey benefited from it. Although he chose never to exploit his military service, the fact remains that being a veteran has always been a political advantage, and to be a combat veteran provides even more of a boost.

But Kerrey's wound is not visible to the voting public—it is noticeable only to the few who have seen him jog with his prosthetic foot braced to his leg and knee—and therefore, his injury is often overlooked and sometimes forgotten. With Quayle as the Vice Presidential nominee, Nebraskans were forced to reflect on war, service, and heroism as they had not been before Quayle's Vietnam history became an issue. Rightly or wrongly, some Nebraskans viewed Kerrey and Bush in a favorable light and judged Karnes and Quayle unfavorably because of their glaringly contrasting service choices. Karnes and Quayle also drew comparisons because of their tendency to make verbal gaffes.

It didn't help the Karnes-Quayle comparisons that Omaha was chosen as the site of the 1988 vice-presidential debate—the one in which Democratic candidate Lloyd Bentsen eviscerated

Dan Quayle with his "You're no John Kennedy" remark. Had the issue of Kennedy's personal character been as controversial as it is one presidential term later, Quayle could have quipped, "Thank God!" and he would have found some sympathetic listeners. At the time, however, Quayle's poor October 1988 debate performance did little to help Karnes and in the end it turned out that the Bush-Quayle team provided no coattails for Karnes.

Kerrey, meanwhile, was unimpressed with the Dukakis campaign and provoked a small furor among Democrats when he announced that he couldn't think of one overriding reason to vote for him outside of the obvious fact that he was the nominee. Kerrey was infuriated with the insularity of Dukakis's campaign staff and the standoffish personality he projected while discussing issues. On more than one occasion, Kerrey questioned Dukakis's appeal and he expressed concern that should the Democratic nominee lose in a landslide, Kerrey's own vote tally would be affected. Kerrey was, however, impressed by Dukakis's July Democratic convention speech and he thought for a time that maybe the Massachusetts Democrat could pull off a formidable effort after all.

Kerrey spoke at the 1988 Democratic convention, giving a speech in which he used the summer Great Plains drought as a metaphor for America's social climate. "While our leaders all seem to be aware that there is a drought in America's agriculture sector, we as a people are often blind to the drought in other sectors of our society. There is a comparable drought in children's nutrition programs; in education; in programs for women; in care for the elderly; in jobs; and in opportunities for small business," Kerrey declared. Throughout the convention, Kerrey was approached by delegates and politicians who expressed interest in him as a future presidential aspirant. That same week, Kerrey announced that he had been assured by Senate Agriculture Committee Chairman Patrick Leahy that, if elected, he would receive appointment to that body.

A Federal Election Commission report released right before the Democratic convention showed that Kerrey had raised approximately $825,000, compared to $145,000 for Karnes. During the 1988 season, Senator John Kerry of Massachusetts, chairman of the Democratic Senatorial Campaign Committee, announced that Kerrey's race would be given top priority by his organization. Both parties considered the Republican hold on Nebraska's Senate seat to be fragile, and Kerrey's campaign was promised the maximum amount allowed by the federal campaign law.

In the meantime, Nebraska's Supreme Court was considering whether to allow a third-party candidate on the ballot. Ernie Chambers, the legislature's lone black member and a strident critic of Kerrey, had recently positioned himself as the head of the New Alliance Party (NAP), a controversial party headed by Lenora B. Fulani. The NAP did not field a candidate for the primary, but was able to be on the ballot because more than five thousand Nebraskans signed an NAP petition that allowed the group to qualify as a party. Since by its own admission the NAP had only fourteen members statewide, many of the rest of the signers penned their names unwittingly to the petition. *Omaha Metropolitan* editor John Boyd wrote, "Had there been an NAP candidate on the ballot, or had Senator Chambers campaigned as a write-in candidate and won the nomination (ironically, Kerrey received the highest number of NAP write-in votes but he refused the nomination), there might be some room to argue that Chambers should be fully included in the general election campaign process. Instead, Chambers was nominated after the primary at the famous NAP convention in a restaurant booth." Democrats cried foul, asserting that Chambers was not a legitimate candidate and had only attached himself to the NAP as a means of inserting himself into the race to siphon votes away from Kerrey and to champion his personal causes. The Karnes campaign and Nebraska Republicans argued that Chambers should be granted entry into the November race. Some Democrats saw the strange alliance of the right-leaning Karnes campaign and the radical NAP with Chambers as its spokesman as a spectacle that was being presented simply for the intention of eroding Kerrey's support in Omaha's sizable black community, where Chambers was adored. Says Associated Press writer Ed Howard, "I'd subscribe to the oft-stated theory that if God were to run against Ernie Chambers in his district, God would need a lot of money."

No one expected Chambers to garner many votes, but if the race turned out to be close, he could take enough votes away from Kerrey to do damage. Kerrey, personally, wasn't worried about votes; he genuinely believed the NAP with Chambers at the helm to be a farce. Still, Kerrey supporters were concerned about a potential vote drain-off. In addition, should Chambers be granted legitimacy as a candidate, he would be able to partici-pate in campaign debates. Both the Karnes and Kerrey camps were well aware that the nature of the debates could be dramati-cally altered by Chambers, given his oratorical skills and his ten-dency to hog the stage. When Chambers wanted to make points, he was relentless, possessing an overwhelming capacity to domi-nate. Chambers had tangled with Kerrey while he was Governor, and Republicans were convinced that the presence of the incen-diary State Senator during debates would irritate and possibly rattle Kerrey, thereby making Karnes the beneficiary. At that time, Chambers had been a member of Nebraska's legislature for eighteen years, and his reputation was that of the ultimate antiestablishment crusader; for Chambers, Kerrey was the epit-ome of that establishment. To Chambers, Kerrey is part of the clique of white men in suits who run Nebraska. Despite his om-etimes-inflammatory statements, the political warrior is roundly hailed as a beacon for the disenfranchised of Nebraska, espe-cially the state's suffering minorities. Always clad in a T-shirt and jeans, the muscular Chambers is a formidable debater whose no-holds-barred approach creates consternation among oppo-nents. When really riled, he occasionally suggests to opponents that they step outside and settle their arguments like men.

Throughout the summer, the issue of whether the NAP should be—and legally could be—on the ballot simmered. In the fall it was finally determined that the NAP could take a place on the ballot against Karnes and Kerrey. Democrats were incensed, especially at the sight of Karnes and Chambers speaking out in tandem in support of the rights of the NAP and Chambers's candidacy. The Kerrey campaign viewed the NAP as insidious, and at one point they alluded to the fact that Chambers was representing an organization whose platform advocated terrorist tactics and that stood for principles unacceptable to the Ameri-

can public. Although the Kerrey campaign was careful not to tar
Chambers with the radical brush of the NAP, they nonetheless
argued that he would be carrying their banner. It was well understood that Chambers accepted the NAP nomination to use it as
a vehicle for addressing social issues, since he was far more well
known than the radical party, with which he was not truly affili-
ated. Kerrey had been telling aides all along that if the NAP and
Chambers made it to the ballot, he would refuse to enter debates
with Chambers. One Kerrey confidant argued that a refusal to
debate might backfire and become a political hot potato. Kerrey
was unswayed. He would not legitimize Chambers's candidacy
by debating him. Immediately upon the announcement in favor
of Chambers, the Kerrey campaign scheduled a press conference. Kerrey announced that he did not believe the NAP to be
legitimate, and therefore he would not recognize it as such by
debating Chambers. "A party of fourteen that holds its nominating convention in booth number two at Denny's Restaurant
does not deserve to be on the ballot," Kerrey said.

Kerrey campaign workers and state Democrats collectively
held their breath. Nobody at the time was certain how Kerrey's
position would play out. His gambit was a risky one, given the
historical tradition of open and accessible debates and the possibility that Nebraska voters might be upset that Kerrey would not
recognize a candidate sanctioned by the state. It was entirely
conceivable that Kerrey's move would create a political mael-
strom and jeopardize his strong lead. Some Democrats predicted
that the absence of Kerrey at the upcoming debates would benefit Karnes by making him appear to be receptive to Chambers
and his minority concerns. Kerrey remained steadfast in his refusal to debate Chambers.

So after the summer-long "debate about the debates," the
eight planned debates were pared down to only one. After the
Karnes-Kerrey state fair debate, Chambers and Karnes participated in one lifeless debate, and then Karnes backed out of the
commitment, just as Kerrey had. Kerrey's popularity increased.
Both the Republicans and Chambers tried to stroke Kerrey's
opting out of the debates into a major issue, but were not successful. Democratic critics of his position later conceded that his

bold move was a wise one, and he received across-the-board accolades for his adroit handling of the sticky issue. More money
came rolling into the Kerrey campaign coffers.

The Karnes campaign, on the other hand, was not having
an easy time raising money. Earlier in the summer, Karnes had
sent out an ill-conceived fund-raising letter to Republican supporters that had backfired and pumped up his negative ratings
in the polls. In it, Karnes labeled Kerrey an embarrassment to
Nebraska and said, "The people of Nebraska cannot trust Bob
Kerrey to represent them in the Senate." The Karnes letter also
criticized Kerrey for accepting money from Democratic activists
in Hollywood who, the letter stated, view him as similar to
"Jerry Brown, their own erratic, left-wing former Governor."
The letter went on to state that the "Democrats in Washington
have targeted me for defeat and Bob Kerrey is their 'fair-haired
boy.' They want to replace a pro-Reagan Republican vote with
a pro-Kennedy Democrat vote in the Senate. Believe me, Bob
Kerrey will give them what they want."

The extent of Kerrey's bipartisan support became apparent
in July, when an outcry followed the sending of the letter, with
hundreds of Nebraskans from both parties offended and incensed over comments about a man "who lost a leg for our country . . . a distinguished Nebraskan," as one farmer put it. The
letter ended up haunting David Karnes. Patently nasty, the four-
page fund-raising letter combined an Oral Roberts–type appeal
for money ("I must raise $121,750 in the next ten days to pay
for the food and room expenses for this event, or I may have to
cancel the entire evening. . . . Unless I have your immediate
help, I have to cancel it altogether") with vicious characteriza-
tions of Kerrey. The Republican speaker of the legislature, William Barrett, publicly chided Karnes, reminding him that voters
in the third district soundly rejected Hal Daub in the primary
because he was perceived as "mean-spirited." Democratic insiders who read the letter called it the work of campaign consultants. Some Republicans labeled it likewise. And as it turned
out, Brent Bahler, Karnes's press secretary, admitted in a late-
July telephone conversation that Karnes did not have a hand in
writing it. When asked to explain the folksy postscript which be-

gan, "P.S. Liz just walked into the room," Bahler responded, after a pause, that come to think of it Karnes had, in fact, written just that one last paragraph. Bahler stressed, however, that Karnes had approved the piece—as if that information were reassuring rather than troubling.

Karnes's vitriolic fund-raising letter marked the point at which his momentum clearly stalled. Before the letter Karnes had windows of opportunity, but the windows were slammed shut. Seldom has a Nebraska candidate accrued negatives as quickly as Karnes did after his summer fund-raising letter. A great many Nebraskans believe in the old-fashioned textbook campaign philosophy in which candidates wrestle over ideas, issues, and vision but in which impugning motives and character is considered below the belt. The tactic backfired.

Paul Johnson, Kerrey's campaign manager, said, "I think it was a mistake for David Karnes. He's not that well-known, and until you have established a high positive rating, it's very hard to throw mud without having it stick to you. On a personal level, what's difficult about the letter is that it belittles the whole process. . . . He hurt himself on that letter, significantly, I'm convinced."

Johnson, who in the fall of 1991 was chosen to head Kerrey's New Hampshire presidential campaign drive, accurately forecasted the effect of the Karnes letter. Karnes lost support, and Kerrey's fund-raising, then on schedule, surged. Kerrey did receive a great deal of out-of-state money, including contributions from the likes of Ed Asner, Julie Andrews, Abigail Van Buren, and Oliver Stone. Debra Winger contributed two thousand dollars and singer Willie Nelson performed at a Kerrey fund-raiser in May. More than half of Kerrey's time was spent fund-raising; often he sought support on the telephone while he was being escorted from one engagement to the next.

Despite how well fund-raising was going in the summer, Kerrey did not feel entirely comfortable with his Washington fund-raising arm. He was unhappy with the turnout and the atmosphere of one Washington political event in his honor, and he mentioned that fact to campaign aides. In the meantime, enter Billy Shore, Kerrey's personal aide and overall right-hand man in his 1992 presidential bid.

Shore had been policy and political director for Gary Hart's U.S. Senate staff and presidential campaigns. When he signed on with Kerrey as a volunteer, he was the director of Share Our Strength, a Washington, D.C.–based hunger-relief organization that he founded and headed up with his sister. Since Hart's political demise, Shore had been searching for a suitable candidate with whom to connect. Like many other Hart staffers, Shore had long been impressed with Kerrey, and they had a mutual friend in John Cavanaugh, who encouraged Shore to reach out to Kerrey. Shore had first met Kerrey in 1984, when he was one of only two Governors to endorse Hart's presidential bid (the other being Colorado's Richard Lamm). In the course of Hart's campaign in Nebraska, the two men, along with Cavanaugh, had traveled the state together. After Hart's downfall, Shore heard that Kerrey was going to run for the Senate and he sent him a note saying, "Let me know if there is any way I can help you." Kerrey called him to say there were areas that needed tending to, and by late June 1988 Shore was named national finance director.

Throughout the rest of the campaign, Shore used his volunteer position to rally the vast network of disenchanted former Hart supporters and financial contributors into the Kerrey camp. Kerrey and Shore quickly developed a strong rapport, and soon Shore became the point man for his Senate race. Shore's selection signaled to many Nebraskans that Kerrey had aspirations beyond the Senate, as Shore's presidential campaign experience had been so high-profile in Nebraska with Hart. The Kerrey campaign was extremely sensitive to charges that he planned to use his Nebraska Senate seat as a stepping-stone to higher office. Repeatedly, Kerrey spoke of his paramount desire to represent the state of Nebraska. Because Kerrey had walked away from the governorship after one term, Republicans contended that Kerrey did not possess a commitment to public service; Karnes often stated that, if elected, he would remain a Senator "for thirty years." Kerrey countered that it was ludicrous to announce a plan to stay in office—that it would be up to Nebraska voters to "make that determination every six years." Even with fundraisers headlined by both President Reagan and Vice President

Bush, the Karnes campaign could not erode Kerrey's broad support.

In the final weeks of the campaign, both sides began the heavy artillery of television advertising. As he had done for his Governor's race, Kerrey again used Joe Rothstein to create his media campaign. And as Rothstein had done in 1982, he portrayed Kerrey as the quintessential Nebraskan. One especially powerful commercial had Kerrey discussing his Vietnam War experience ("No one knows war like those who have been there"). Other commercials emphasized his gubernatorial triumph in eliminating the state deficit and his opposition to the elimination of crop subsidies for farmers. Karnes's commercials stressed values and family; his campaign believed that if they presented their candidate's traditional family unit often enough, the contrast with Kerrey's life-style would be highlighted. Again, however, Nebraska voters did not respond to the comparisons.

And so it was that on Election Day, November 8, 1988, Kerrey easily wrestled the Senate seat away from Karnes, winning the contest by more than ninety-seven thousand votes. Despite the fact that President Bush carried the state by a sweeping margin, Karnes could not manage more than 42 percent of the vote against Kerrey's whopping 57 percent. State Senator Ernie Chambers received nearly ten thousand votes, a figure that would have been significant only in an extremely close race.

Nebraska Republicans, who had been expecting Kerrey's win, were furious that they also lost the second congressional seat, which Hal Daub had held, to Democrat Peter Hoagland, a fifth-generation Omahan, Central High School alumni, and Stanford University honors graduate who had served as a State Senator from 1978 to 1986. Hoagland and Kerrey staffers worked well together on Election Day, and Hoagland's candidacy benefited from the remarkable efficiency of the Democrats' coordinated campaign that year.

Kerrey's get-out-the-vote effort in Nebraska was unprecedented. Hundreds of Kerrey workers manned phone banks, pounded the pavement, and monitored polling places; they did not plan to take their huge preelection lead for granted; yet, most Nebraskans could sense even before the returns were in that Kerrey, again, was a winner. Kerrey, whose children had traveled to Lincoln from Texas, spent half the day making last-minute rounds in Omaha, and then headed to Lincoln, where he briefly addressed an excited throng of supporters early in the evening at Lincoln's Hilton Hotel. Kerrey returned to Omaha for his final victory celebration at Peony Park.

Thousands of Nebraskans gathered at the city's cavernous ballroom to await Kerrey's entrance. When he finally stepped onto the stage, the jubilant crowd roared their approval. Democrats especially were ecstatic because they had just been handed their fifth straight senatorial victory in a state where Republicans dominate. Lined up beside and behind Kerrey were members of his family and his Navy SEAL buddies, who had spent the day electioneering for their comrade. After the scene had calmed down, Kerrey hesitated for a moment and then began singing "And the Band Played Waltzing Matilda." The audience was stunned. Everyone had been expecting some kind of a rah-rah speech, and quickly it dawned on supporters that, instead, he was singing of the horrors of war, a mournful tale written in 1972 by Scotland native Bogle after witnessing an Australian–New Zealand Army Command Day parade that included Gallipoli veterans. A staple in the repertoire of folksingers, "And the Band Played Waltzing Matilda" long has been the anthem of antiwar protesters throughout the world but is one that is still relatively obscure in the United States. That both Kerrey and the subject of the song, a young soldier from Australia who served at the World War I Battle of Gallipoli, had lost legs in misunderstood and tragic conflicts made Kerrey's rendition all the more poignant. When he finished, a reflective crowd, some wiping away tears, cheered. There was a palpable sense among observers that they had been witnesses to history. Kerrey quickly brought the crowd back up by encouraging them to "waltz tonight" because work beckoned in the morning. Later, Kerrey told members of the media that he sang the song because "the blues cheer me up." After attempting to make his way through hundreds of Nebraskans who wanted to make contact with him that night, Kerrey was deluged by members of the state and national press, all eager to describe his unusual Election Night "victory speech."

If there was ever any question that Kerrey is a rare politician he put it to rest that evening. Kerrey transformed the evening from the standard to the extraordinary; he lifted politics from the mundane to the magnificent; he allowed a jaded electorate to witness truth in politics. Politics, for one brief shining moment, became a vehicle for great and real drama to spectators aching for a chance to participate in classic political theater, the kind that history tells us has moved our nation in decades past, the kind that has become nearly extinct in contemporary politics. Driven to conformity by fear of the media frenzy that follows any risky move, as Kerrey's victory song certainly was, most politicians have quite understandably given up trying to be who they are and, instead, seek out and follow the advice of media-savvy handlers who tell them who they should be for TV. What political consultant would ever have okayed a triumphant senatorial candidate singing an aching story about the cost of war at a victory rally? "And the Band Played Waltzing Matilda" is not a sound-bite kind of song—it is long, it is decidedly downbeat, it is not the type of song that fits easily into the evening news. But Kerrey didn't consult anyone before he went on; he had made a promise to his fellow SEALS that if he won the election, he would sing it for them. And in so doing, Kerrey forced observers to contemplate the dark side of his personal political victory. From that night forward, a new layer was added to the already thick Kerrey legacy. Two months later he entered the United States Senate to justifiable fanfare.

On Tuesday, January 3, 1989, Robert Kerrey, along with just three other select newcomers, joined our country's most exclusive political club. Facing President-elect Bush with his family looking on, Kerrey strode down the hisoric Senate chamber aisle near noontime, answering Bush's call: "Mr. Kerrey, from Nebraska." (Of that year's thirty-three inductees, Kerrey was the only man singled out by state, to distinguish him from Senator John Kerry of Massachusetts.) As the Vice President reached out to shake Kerrey's hand, the World War II combat veteran greeted the Vietnam combat veteran with "Governor" and then, smiling, Bush corrected his salutation to "Senator." Kerrey solemnly repeated the oath, signed the registry with his left hand,

and walked back down the aisle an official U.S. Senator.

Kerrey was subdued at the Tuesday evening reception at Union Station's elegant Adirondack Club. More than eight hundred fifty people attended the three-hour bash, including Debra Winger's parents, who flew in from California to attend. Kerrey mingled with the masses but declined to speak formally, and it was clear he was exhausted. In addition, he was saddened that his children had to leave early so that they could catch their flight back to Texas and make it to school the next morning. His son, Ben, pleaded to stay, and his fruitless entreaties contributed to Kerrey's tempered manner. (At this time, Kerrey's former wife's marriage was in trouble. By the summer of 1990, she would divorce her second husband, Gary Higby, and move Ben and Lindsey back to an Omaha suburb. Kerrey bought a house for her, gave her credit cards to buy furniture, and enrolled his son in Omaha's most prestigious Catholic prep school, Creighton Prep.) Half of the nighttime crowd consisted of Washington lobbyists, transplanted Nebraskans, and even résumé-carrying political groupies who tried to corner on to anyone in a position of power within the Kerrey camp who might help them land a job. Since announcing his candidacy, Kerrey had received more than seven thousand résumés from aspiring Senate staffers, the most in Senate history, according to one Senate personnel employee. Since November, Kerrey had stated repeatedly that he planned to take his time staffing the office. As he had when he was Governor, he asked Bill Hoppner to help him set up his Senate office and stay on as chief of staff. Kerrey was relieved that the long and winding road he had traveled to arrive at the Senate door had finally ended. He was eager for the festivities to end and to get on with the business of Congress.

Chapter 10

THE BIG BATTALIONS

n George Bernard Shaw's classic, *Saint Joan*—the story of an inspired individual in conflict with ineptitude and apathy of leadership—Saint Joan is warned that she is naive, that even God can be on the side of the big battalions. But true to an inner voice, she stays on course, undeterred by the might or odds against her. Similarly, Bob Kerrey has exhibited a consistent pattern of being undeterred by the mighty or by overwhelming odds. When Kerrey entered the Senate, he challenged the leadership of some of the country's biggest battalions.

From the beginning, Kerrey and his staff made health-care assessment a priority. Traveling the country, he consulted experts, analyzed data, and mastered the issue. After two years of analysis, in the spring of 1991, Kerrey introduced a bill to provide national health insurance for all Americans. Entitled Health USA, Kerrey's plan proposed to streamline the system and make it more financially efficient. Breaking with tradition, Kerrey chose to focus on a subject outside the bailiwick of his Senate committee assignments.

While some suggested that the introduction of a national health-care plan showed Kerrey positioning himself as a presidential contender, those close to him know that his concern about the issue dates back to his time spent at the Philadelphia Naval Hospital. That experience fueled his beliefs that recipients of government health care usually feel gratitude, and that the assistance provides them a chance to become more productive citizens. Kerrey framed his argument for national health care from the standpoint of cost containment, universal need, and health benefits independent of employment. He believes that breaking the link between health care and employment is a crucial step. He argues that America can build a more financially efficient system, enabling the nation to provide health care to all its citizens. With his plan, Kerrey was able to fuse his strong sense of fiscal responsibility with his belief that health care is a basic right. He stresses that his plan does not mirror the Canadian, German, or other systems; instead, it relies heavily on the private sector, it promotes innovation in the organized delivery of health care, and it provides Americans with complete choice among competing private and public health plans. In essence, the proposal has the dual purpose of extending health care to those Americans not covered and containing the rising costs of health-care insurance for families and individuals.

As originally proposed, Kerrey's bill would provide health-care coverage for all Americans, replacing Medicaid for the poor, Medicare for the elderly, and veterans' care with coverage purchased through private insurance companies.

In Nebraska, as in other states, the idea of universal health care conjures images that run afoul of traditional American individualism. The fear of national health care is expressed in many forms by various interest groups—such big battalions as the American Medical Association and its state counterparts; the various state health-care associations representing long-term-care facilities that provide for the elderly under the Medicaid program; Blue Cross–Blue Shield; the state hospital associations; and the insurance companies that provide health insurance or serve as contract processors for medical and hospital claims.

Despite the counterattacks he knew would be hurled his way, Kerrey pressed ahead. On October 30, 1991, he presented his Health USA plan in testimony before Congress. "Reforming our nation's health-care system is no longer only a humanitarian issue, it's a vital economic issue," he said. "It's eroding our standard of living and threatening our ability to compete in an aggressive international marketplace." It was time, he added, to head off "a disaster in the making."

Soon after being elected to the Senate, Kerrey began criticizing government regulation of savings and loan institutions and the handling of the bailout overseen by the Resolution Trust Corporation (RTC). Given the fleecing the American public had suffered, Kerrey believed it imperative not to mismanage the bailout. At every opportunity, he stressed his belief that the structural inadequacies of the RTC were setting the scene for a second rip-off as the organization disposed of the assets. It is unusual for a freshman Senator to tackle and address subjects not within his jurisdiction. (Kerrey was not appointed to any banking-related committees.) But this freshman Senator had been following the S&L debacle since Nebraska's Commonwealth disaster in 1983, and he had spent considerable time examining the steps that had led to the nation's most severe fiscal nightmare.

Beginning in the mid-seventies, soaring inflation caused large numbers of S&L depositors to move their funds into higher-yielding investments such as money market funds. At the time, S&Ls were largely confined by law to investing in safe but low-yielding home mortgage loans, and therefore could not pay high rates to depositors. As a result, the industry lobbied for permission to move solely from the home mortgage lending business in order to become more competitive.

In 1980, the Depository Institutions Deregulatory and Monetary Control Act expanded the array of savings accounts and loans S&Ls could offer—legislation considered helpful but inadequate. Two years later, more comprehensive legislation was enacted that purported to remedy the underlying cause of the S&L earnings squeeze by providing institutions new powers: It allowed up to 10 percent of an S&L's assets to be put in speculative commonweal loans; it allowed large consumer loans to be held by the thrifts; and it provided new—and riskier—powers relating to S&L liabilities by allowing thrifts to pay more competitive rates. These new asset and liability powers made it possible for S&L managers, who were inexperienced in the new lending mediums, to quickly get overextended in risky loans. It also gave crooked S&L managers a license to steal, a situation exacerbated by a dearth of experienced regulators.

The die, then, was cast for the S&L debacle. The rationale was that S&Ls were headed for bankruptcy and that the institutions would be salvaged by a closer tie to economic growth. But subsequent events showed that the cure was worse than the anticipated illness. The new approach was a long leap from the days when S&Ls loaned money almost exclusively on residences and limited real-estate projects by requiring down payments of 20 percent. The stability and security of loaning to families gave way to such risky ventures as fast-food outlets, novelty shops, speculative shopping centers, and motel developments. With a one-hundred-thousand-dollar guarantee by the Federal Savings and Loan Insurance Corporation, promoters began to see S&Ls as an accelerated trip to new money by buying in, then selling out, with accompanying perks and hefty salaries along the way. The stigma of failure was minimal; there would be no irate depositors to ride an owner out of town on a rail—in this era, he could leave quietly in his Mercedes. Such risk-taking investments were tempting even to honest promoters and financial managers. Most of the failed S&Ls had operated under procedures that were technically in accord with existing laws and regulations, but it was also paradise for crooks who specialized in the promotion of fraud and deception. The eighties saw legalized rip-offs by those who operated within the parameters of the regulations and swindles by those who were in direct violation of even the more relaxed and permissive regulations.

Early on, the Bush Administration focused on rectifying the damage done to the S&L industry, the result being legislation that created the RTC. Within months of taking office, Senator Kerrey began railing against the RTC. In an April 1989 floor speech, Kerrey charged that giving the RTC board power to deal with the failed institutions amounted to "putting a fox in charge of the henhouse." In June, Kerrey said, "The potential for abuse is enormous. People are going to make millions of dollars on these assets; there is going to be a feeding frenzy out there. I am concerned that the RTC, as currently structured, will not provide the trust that we need. I believe there is potential for scandal in the RTC."

Claiming that the board responsible for policy "was dominated by five men who were too busy to give any meaningful time to the task," Kerrey introduced the Resolution Trust Corporation Reorganization Act on February 7, 1990. The Bush Administration had asked Congress for an additional $30 billion to bail out the industry, but Kerrey believed that the RTC's structure needed to be addressed before Congress voted to provide the agency any additional funds. Kerrey's approach to the request for money was not unlike that he used with former University of Nebraska head Ronald Roskens: Show us that the structure of the university system is sound and efficient before you ask the legislature for more money. He declared that the Administration's S&L bailout plan had failed to protect American taxpayers, that the President's solution simply was not working. "Decisions are not being made," Kerrey argued. "The agency is supposed to be accountable to the taxpayer but is so cumbersome that it is fair to describe its services as nonexistent. The best that can be said for the President's plan is that he swept it under the bureaucratic rug so that blame will now be directed at people who run new alphabet agencies." Kerrey maintained it was ludicrous to believe that part-time board members could provide meaningful review of the many failed institutions.

From the outset of his crusade, Kerrey was blasted by Administration officials, Democratic members of the Senate Banking Committee, and political writers who dismissed his railings as those of a naive freshman violating a strict tenet of Senate protocol: Don't dig into issues that do not directly emanate from your assigned committees.

But Kerrey kept up his attacks. "I am on the floor today to talk about the President's performance. One year ago, he asked us for $167 billion to save the nation's thrifts. He asked us to hurry because we were losing $10 billion a day. He insisted that we pass the legislation in forty-five days. . . . However, in this case the President just wanted to spend some money and hope that perhaps the problem would go away. He trusted the industry-regulator alliance, which devised what I believe is a much-too-clever plan which buries most of the critical decisions deep within the bowels of government."

Kerrey's concern about the government's handling of the

S&L scandal grew as investigative reports showed flaws in the policies and procedures of the organization created to handle the assets of the failed institutions. From its inception, the RTC had trouble accounting for the property that had come within its jurisdiction and control, and Kerrey believed that was due, in part, to the fact that the RTC oversight board and the board of directors could not operate as a single governing entity. At every opportunity, Kerrey insisted that the RTC's structure was inherently unsound and ill conceived. He complained that the two boards caused conflict and accountability problems and, as a result, were unable to respond quickly to pressing problems. He pointed out that of the 296 institutions taken over, fewer than 50 had been sold; in addition, more than 600 were waiting for review.

On March 14, 1990, Kerrey introduced a bill to restructure the RTC. He proposed eliminating RTC's board in favor of creating an expanded but streamlined board that would include nongovernment members who would be shielded from political influence.

The third issue of prominence Kerrey dealt with in his first two years in the Senate was that of our nation's flag, a sacred symbol to many of his constituents.

Some days on Nebraska's isolated farms and ranches, the loudest sound is that of the plains wind whipping the American flag against the backdrop of a wide, blue sky. Like lonely church steeples, red barns, and working windmills, Old Glory dots the Nebraska landscape—symbols of Cornhusker commitment to God, work, and country. Some Nebraska restaurants compete to fly the largest American flag in deference to the expansive sky that swallows small symbols of America's freedom. Flags at Nebraska's pristine rest stops along Interstate 80 alert America's travelers in much the way the U.S. flag beckons patrons to post offices.

"The bombs bursting in air gave proof through the night that our flag was still there." The salient line from the Star-Spangled Banner is the most forcefully sung line by more than a few of the seventy-six thousand Big Red fans who sing the anthem every fall before game time of the University of

Nebraska–Lincoln football team, the Cornhuskers. It is not surprising, then, that Nebraskans would rate a flag-burner right up there with a cattle-rustler.

So, when a young man named Johnson burned a flag at the 1984 Republican convention, Nebraskans began to pay attention. He was arrested and charged with desecration and the general sentiment in Nebraska was something akin to "They burn the flag and we burn them." The whole incident was familiar to Americans who had followed flag-burning protests during the Vietnam War. Burning or desecrating the U.S. flag has been an issue in this country for a long time, but it was an act that reached its peak during the Vietnam War when protesters tore it up, stomped on it, wore it on the seat of their pants, and burned it to make the point that our armed forces were in the wrong war in the wrong place at the wrong time. While there have not been any flag-burning confrontations in Nebraska, the issue has been hotly debated since television in the sixties and seventies brought the incendiary act into the living rooms of the American public.

Johnson appealed his conviction and the average Nebraskan rooted for the state of Texas. Like most Americans, Nebraskans did not delve into the niceties of the First Amendment. The idea that preventing someone from burning Old Glory throttled the fundamental right of free speech was foreign. As Johnson's attorney appealed to the circuit court and then the U.S. Supreme Court, the prediction in Nebraska was that the court would uphold the Texas statute. But in 1989, the Supreme Court held the Texas statute to be unconstitutional in abridging the right of free expression. The Court reasoned that the right of free speech encompassed more than just the uttering of words, that in certain contexts, such as a protest against questionable government activity, the destruction of a symbol could be a legitimate manner of protest.

Congress immediately followed with a bill to make such acts a violation of federal law, and polls showed overwhelming support by the American public for either legislation or a constitutional amendment to prohibit flag-burning. President Bush was a supporter of the bill, as was Senator Robert Dole, a veteran wounded in infantry combat in Italy in World War II. Nebraskans assumed their junior Senator would join the President, and at first Kerrey did. Then, as he later explained in a Senate floor statement and *Washington Post* editorial, after examining the decision closely, he changed his mind. Kerrey said: "I was surprised to discover that I found the majority argument to be reasonable, understandable, and consistent with those values that I believe make America so wonderful. Further, I was surprised to discover that after reading this decision, my anger was not directed at Justices Brennan, Scalia, Kennedy, Marshall, and Blackmun, who joined in the majority. Rather, it was with the language of the dissent, particularly that of Chief Justice Rehnquist, whose argument appears to stand not on two hundred years of case law supporting greater and greater freedom of speech but on a sentimental nationalism that imposes a functional litmus test of loyalty before expression is permitted."

But Bob Kerrey didn't stop with criticizing Rehnquist; he castigated President Bush. "President Bush did not stand before the angry and distressed mob to stop us in our tracks before we did something we would regret. He did not offer words that calm us or give us assurance that the nation is not endangered. Instead of leading us, President Bush joined us." A line Kerrey would frequently use in defending his position in Nebraska and on national talk shows was: "There is simply no line of Americans queuing up to burn our flag. On the face of the evidence at hand, it seems to me that there is no need for us to do anything." Toward the end of the editorial, Kerrey personalized his defense. "Chief Justice Rehnquist, in his disappointing dissent, asserts that men and women fought for our flag in Vietnam. In my case I do not remember feeling this way. I remember that my first impulse to fight was the result of a feeling that it was my duty. My nation called and I went." At the end of the editorial, the *Post* wrote: "The writer won the Medal of Honor in Vietnam." Enough said.

Many of Kerrey's congressional colleagues expressed envy that Kerrey, insulated by his Medal of Honor, would take a position that they wanted to take but felt emotional constituents would not accept. Given the flag hoopla that had occurred during the 1988 presidential election, most Democrats were skittish about casting a vote that could easily haunt them in future elections. Still, they were thrilled that someone as convincing and tailor-made as Senator Bob Kerrey was willing to lead the better angels of their nature in opposing all flag-related measures.

Kerrey did not have an easy time convincing his fellow Nebraskans. Many Nebraskans were outraged and expressed the view that, once again, Bob Kerrey was out of step with the people he represented. On his first trip back to Nebraska after his Senate speech, Kerrey was repeatedly cornered by citizens baffled about his position. Veterans in Nebraska were livid but still were willing to listen to Kerrey explain his position. Bill E. Williams, chaplain of Nebraska's Department of American Veterans, found himself so hurt by the ruling that he penned an essay entitled "Our Flag" that was passed out to Nebraska vets at their annual Vietnam Veterans Reunion. Williams wrote: "I am terribly upset and cannot understand just how the Supreme Court could rule that it's all right to burn the American flag, Old Glory. . . . I see the flag as an extension of my brother [who served in Vietnam], and it stands for all that he held dear to his heart." Nonetheless, Williams remains an ardent Kerrey supporter.

Williams's sentiment was expressed in varying themes by countless Americans who viewed the issue through an emotional prism and who simply did not want to look at the far more complicated big picture. Kerrey stuck to his position, calmly explaining his feelings to anyone who challenged him. By the time Congress voted on the measure, Democrats had mustered enough courage to defeat it handily with the help of a few Republicans. Despite his neophyte status in the Senate, Kerrey is acknowledged as the Senator responsible for its defeat. Often Kerrey expressed dismay that the whole issue got so much play. "When it's all over, have we accomplished anything?" he would ask Nebraska audiences who continue to question him on the subject. "Have we built a house or educated a child?"

A few Nebraskans will never forgive Kerrey for his views. That became apparent in the summer of 1990 at the state's Vietnam Veterans reunion at the Holiday Inn Motel. During Kerrey's introduction of the keynote speaker, a table of disgruntled vets kept up a visibly disruptive patter of talking and laughing. Later, one vet at the table said they were showing their disapproval of Kerrey's vote on the flag-burning issue. And as recently as the July 4, 1991, Desert Storm Independence Day parade, a group of vets was overheard commenting on a T-shirt that showed an American flag and the words JUST TRY AND BURN THIS ONE, with "I wonder what Senator Kerrey would say to that."

Bethany native Jaime Obrecht reported that the American Legion in Nebraska said they would see Kerrey defeated in his Senate reelection bid because of his flag-burning stance.

Of the five new Democratic Senators elected in 1988, Kerrey received the choicest committee assignments. He landed a plum spot on the Appropriations Committee, a coveted position that presented him with the opportunity to quickly become a political insider. By giving the seat to Kerrey over Senator Herbert Kohl of Wisconsin, who wanted the assignment badly, Democratic Party leaders were saying, in effect, that Kerrey showed potential and was entitled to a head start over the rest of his colleagues. From the outset, Kerrey's goal was to become an effective player by dint of hard work rather than by socializing and personal chumminess. He befriended a handful of legislators including Senators Don Reigle of Michigan, Bill Bradley of New Jersey, Daniel Patrick Moynihan of New York, and Tom Daschle of South Dakota, but most of his senatorial relationships remained professional and cordial. So much so that when Kerrey announced his intentions to run for President, Nebraska's senior Senator, James Exon, found himself fielding questions from colleagues who wondered if they could feel comfortable with Kerrey at the top or, in a more likely scenario, at the bottom of the Democratic ticket.

Despite Kerrey's desire to be a dutiful member of the Senate, he has always felt like an outsider and was a bit uncomfortable jockeying to join the ranks of insiders. All his life Kerrey had acted the part of the outsider. He grew up in a community outside Lincoln. He joined a commando group outside traditional Navy operations. He was an outsider in the anti–Vietnam War movement because the insiders seemed so antiveteran and anti–service oriented. He was an outsider in Nebraska Democratic politics when he staged his surprising 1982 gubernatorial upset. Only a true outsider could dismiss party pleas to make an easy reelection bid and instead announce a self-imposed term limitation, as Kerrey did in 1986.

Yet, in 1989, Kerrey was positioning himself as an insider in the U.S. Senate, the biggest insider's club of them all, and he felt a great measure of ambivalence. Kerrey possesses in part a Jerry Brown–like irreverence toward institutions such as the Senate, and at the same time a part of him feels deep and overriding respect for the institution. In a sense, Kerrey's feelings toward the Senate and the city of Washington, D.C., mirror his post-Vietnam love-hate feelings toward the government as a whole.

Seven months after Kerrey's arrival, a young Nebraskan, newly transplanted to Washington, D.C., was murdered a few blocks from Capitol Hill. Daniel Hotz, the victim, was one of ten children of a close-knit Omaha family and his death hit Kerrey hard. Weeks later at a gathering of Nebraskans in Washington, Kerrey announced that he used to feel safer in Vietnam than he does in D.C., where he bought a townhouse on Capitol Hill. He railed against the city's violence and the corruption of then-Mayor Marion Barry's administration. To friends, Kerrey expressed his deep distress over the economic disparity in Washington and how depressing it was for him to drive through poverty-ridden sections of the Capital. "I wonder with some weariness," Kerrey said, "if anything can be done to reduce the level of violence in this country I love so much . . . our black neighborhoods are too run down, personal income and job skills too low, and families too shattered to expect a reversal without a major investment of capital."

Kerrey often confided that he missed Nebraska's sunsets and vowed that he would return to his homestate whenever possible because he trusted his instincts more when he was on Nebraska soil. He told interviewers that he felt half the folks in Washington were on the take. He summed up his cynicism toward the city's power brokers in a *Wall Street Journal* interview with the line "Just be sure you know when you're pretending."

A decision was made at the outset of Kerrey's election to the Senate to limit his press coverage so that he would not be viewed as someone with open ambition. First impressions in the Senate are long-lasting and Kerrey wanted a reputation as an assiduous legislator. While he received scores of requests for in-depth interviews, he turned down most of them his first year. So Kerrey and his advisers were looking forward to his first major cover story in *The New Republic* magazine written by Jake Weisberg for the December 18, 1989, issue. However, instead of being pleased with the piece as he thought he would be, Kerrey was angered by many of Weisberg's assessments. In it Weisberg said, ". . . he's a quick study, but lacks an analytic bent," and "where his experience doesn't guide him, Kerrey seems lost. Nothing he has done in his ten months in the Senate has shown much sophistication about the Soviet Union, Eastern Europe, the European Community, China, the Mideast, or South Africa." Kerrey and his top aides derided Weisberg's statement as thoroughly naive given the fact that it is next to impossible to do anything in the Senate in ten months, let alone make an impact on foreign policy as a freshman Senator. They also were disturbed by Weisberg's crude statement "All this makes Bob Kerrey—despite his limited exposure to the key issues of foreign and domestic policy—a Democratic political consultant's wet dream." Many Nebraskans told Kerrey staffers they were offended by Weisberg's not-so-subtle put-down of the state. In discussing the similarities between former California Governor Jerry Brown and Kerrey, Weisberg wrote, "Just as Brown left to get real with Mother Teresa in Calcutta, Kerrey felt compelled to look for genuine experiences again. But Kerrey's version of what's 'real' is more that of a Nebraskan druggist than a California monk." The Kerrey camp would find themselves overjoyed down the line when another of Weisberg's articles in which he villified the New York publishing world was roundly criticized by opinion makers. Kerrey regretted granting Weisberg access and he continued to scoff at the title of the account, "Senator Perfect."

With that mantle over him, Kerrey settled into Washington.

From the beginning, his work on the Appropriations Committee received praise from its chairman, Senator Robert Byrd, Democrat of West Virginia, who repeatedly told interviewers that he "just stood out from the start." In his three years there, Kerrey has secured funding for several major projects for Nebraska, including substantial research money for his alma mater, the University of Nebraska. To avoid criticism that his success suggests pork-barrel politics, Kerrey stresses that "all of my requests for Nebraska projects fall within the budget limits set forth in the Budget Enforcement Act."

Much of Kerrey's energy in the Senate has been devoted to agriculture, an area in which he has worked hard to become an expert. While Kerrey became well-versed in agriculture issues as Governor, it was not until his 1988 election that he focused feverishly on farm policy, prompting Nebraska observers to declare that he had matured greatly and grown deeper as a policymaker. They began to express faith that Kerrey would be a strong agriculture advocate. Kerrey's leadership on farm issues is a natural evolution given that he could actually make a difference as a federal legislator, something he could not do as Governor.

During the first week of April 1990, Kerrey and four fellow farm-state Senators, in a nontraditional move, unveiled what was termed flagship legislation for a 1990 farm bill after weeks of gathering testimony in Nebraska, South Dakota, Iowa, and North Dakota. In the subsequent debate on the farm bill, Kerrey called for greater flexibility in planting decisions and higher loan rates for American farmers. Kerrey championed the farm cause to such a degree that he received across-the-board accolades from Nebraskans for his efforts. And while many Americans believe that well-off farmers are getting away with bloody murder as far as subsidies go, Kerrey speaks of agriculture with near-reverence.

"Politically, our agricultural policy is often referenced as having only economic value and it has, in fact, great social value," Kerrey says. Quoting Bush Administration Secretary of Agriculture Clayton Yeutter, Kerrey called the Reagan years "a reign of error" for American farmers, and he decried Yeutter and company for also failing the American farmer. Kerrey tangled often with Yeutter, taking issue with him repeatedly and once even ripping into him at a committee hearing. When Yeutter said that the federal deficit "would double or triple, just based on agricultural requests alone," Kerrey fired off a letter to Yeutter stating that "this is the sort of thing [Yeutter's statement] that misleads the public into thinking that farmers are to blame for our budget deficit. The statement is wrong."

Kerrey spent many weeks in his first year in the Senate as an appointed Senator at the impeachment trial of Federal Judge Alcee Hastings from Florida, the first person ever to be convicted by the Congress after being acquitted in a criminal trial on related charges. In his subcommittee work, much of Kerrey's time also was spent deliberating over District of Columbia appropriations, and Kerrey routinely criticized then-Mayor Marion Barry's performance in office.

In the spring of 1990, Kerrey intervened in Nebraska's closely contested gubernatorial primary after pledging that he would remain neutral until the primary battle was over. Kerrey's longtime chief of staff, Bill Hoppner, was locked in a fierce three-way battle for Governor with Ben Nelson, a wealthy insurance executive and Mike Boyle, Omaha's former Mayor who by then had a decidedly cool relationship with Kerrey. The weekend before the Tuesday vote, Kerrey announced his support of Hoppner, the candidate originally favored to win but who found himself slipping in the last weeks of the race. The vote turned out to be the closest in Nebraska history with Nelson eventually winning by forty-odd votes. Although it is roundly agreed that it was Kerrey's last-minute decision to publicly support Hoppner that created such a close race, surprisingly, Kerrey did not suffer any political fallout. Most institutional Democrats wanted Hoppner and wished only that Kerrey had expressed his preference earlier. Boyle, on the other hand, was furious that Kerrey reneged on his pledge to stay out of the race and he used Kerrey's change of heart as evidence of what Boyle called Kerrey's propensity to break his word.

After the election, Kerrey again turned his attention to Washington, where it became clear that, despite his dislike of the city, he was enjoying the Senate. Some Nebraskans did not expect Kerrey to fit in well in an institution where persuasion, cajoling, and coalition-building is the norm—arts Kerrey had never before shown a preference for. However, he quickly developed his own agenda with health care being at the top of his list, and rather than feeling uncomfortable, he relished the environs, albeit somewhat restlessly.

One of Kerrey's primary goals in his first term has been to develop expertise in the foreign-policy arena. During the second week of April 1990, Kerrey returned to Southeast Asia for the first time since his 1969 SEAL deployment for a nine-day fact-finding tour of Vietnam, Cambodia, and Thailand. In a March 9, 1990, floor statement, Kerrey said, "My trip is motivated by a deep desire to help the people of Indochina. The people of Vietnam, Laos, and Cambodia have suffered greatly from centuries of war and occupation. My interest in helping construct American policy toward Indochina also derives from the experiences of the Vietnam War, including the still-unresolved questions concerning American prisoners of war. The genocide that occurred in Cambodia after the war also deepens my conviction on the importance of focusing attention in this area of the world." Before his trip, which was authorized by Senate Majority Leader George Mitchell, Kerrey consulted with the Department of State, the American intelligence community, and other experts with firsthand experience in the region. Kerrey's Senate office received several calls from members of the media eager to travel with Kerrey, but he declined, saying he didn't want any hoopla surrounding his visit. While there he met with governmental and nongovernmental leaders in all three countries, arguing at one point in Hanoi with Foreign Minister Nguyen Co Thach over the legacy of the Vietnam War.

The following year in April, Kerrey made his second trip to the region, where he met with many of the same leaders he had earlier visited. But in between his two trips to Southeast Asia, Kerrey turned his attention, as did other Americans, to the foreign-policy situation developing in the Persian Gulf. On August 1, 1990, Saddam Hussein of Iraq invaded Kuwait. The United States and the rest of the world community, stunned by

Hussein's flagrant violation of international law, responded with general condemnation.

President Bush "drew a line in the sand" and asked the Congress for authority to use whatever force necessary to drive Iraqi forces from Kuwait. Kerrey spoke out against the use of force immediately after the invasion and his voice and vote in opposition to war continued up to the actual commitment to ground battle. On November 27, 1990, in testimony submitted to the Senate Armed Services Committee, Kerrey said, "The Administration simply has not answered the fundamental question that must precede any use of American force: What is the principle for which we are ready to die? Oil is not a sufficient rationale. Nor are jobs. . . . In this case, the Administration has neither made a clear, compelling case for the use of force . . ."

One and a half months later, on January 11, 1991, Kerrey spoke on the floor of the Senate and submitted six pages of testimony he wrote himself arguing for caution in the Gulf and expressing his support for a resolution offered by Senator Sam Nunn, Chairman of the Armed Services Committee, that called for an alternative strategy of military containment and economic sanctions.

"For most of the past five months we hoped that Saddam Hussein would withdraw from Kuwait," Kerrey said. "As U.N. security council resolution followed security council resolution, we expected a reversal but got instead a rebuff. Today, after moving from a defensive to an offensive posture—after increasing our troop strength so as to have the capacity to launch an offensive strike—Saddam Hussein seems willing to take our blow. So, as we stand here debating this resolution, the smell of battle is in the air. Notwithstanding the constitutional arguments over who has the authority to declare war and the important question of whether or not economic sanctions will work, I cannot shake the conclusion that it would be a mistake for us to launch a war against Iraq."

On January 16, 1991, President Bush initiated Operation Desert Storm, and despite Kerrey's opposition to military action, since it was initiated, he supported the Administration and the troops completely. Like many other Americans, Kerrey was surprised by what he called "the smashing forty-two-day victory." Kerrey praised President Bush's handling of the war and declared that he planned to "participate in the prideful sense that America has just done something good even if I am not invited by the Republican National Committee to do so."

In a statement on the floor of the Senate on March 7, 1991, Kerrey said, "For me the syndrome of skepticism about the wisdom and efficacy of American intervention in the internal affairs of other nations had been fading rapidly long before this success. When the Berlin Wall came down and the people of Eastern Europe rushed to embrace freedom, I saw our patient cold war much differently than I had before. . . . When Nelson Mandela, Vaclav Havel, and Lech Walesa addressed joint sessions of Congress to thank Americans for their willingness to fight for their causes, I knew I had been wrong to doubt the moral cause of Vietnam."

Throughout the Gulf War debate, Kerrey invoked the memory of Vietnam and suggested there were parallels between the two situations. Later, he would say his experience in Vietnam had "influenced my judgment on what we should do, perhaps too much."

Of his Vietnam experience, Kerrey said, "I grew to distrust anyone whose call to arms appeared insincere. That distrust has not disappeared. I remain deeply skeptical whenever I hear we have no choice but to send our troops into battle. And while I know there are times we must use force, I do not apologize for my cynicism. I believe it can be constructive."

Shortly thereafter Clayton Yeutter, newly appointed as chairman of the RNC, told a Lincoln, Nebraska, audience that the Democrats would be politically vulnerable in the 1992 elections if "they picked the wrong side" on the Persian Gulf Resolution. Kerrey was livid and in a Senate floor statement castigated Yeutter for politicizing the war. "Those of us who have actually stood for elective office already understand that our job is to state our opinions, vote our consciences, and take the electoral consequences."

Kerrey's voting record in the Senate has proven to be basically a liberal one and he once commented after voting to raise the minimum wage, "I guess I'm a real Democrat now." Nonetheless, he has exhibited a willingness to display an independent streak, as evidenced by his refusal to vote in favor of the savings and loan bailout bill and the 1990 budget reconciliation act that implemented that year's budget summit agreement.

He voted against the nominations of the late Senator John Tower as Secretary of Defense and he opposed the nominations of Judges Robert Bork and Clarence Thomas to the Supreme Court. He voted in favor of the nomination of Judge David Souter to the high court because of his "distinguished judicial record." Kerrey also voted against funding for the Strategic Defense Initiative and he supported canceling funding for the B-2 Stealth bomber.

Kerrey voted to table an amendment requiring parental notification forty-eight hours before an abortion for a woman under eighteen in the case of rape or incest. His position on abortion evolved from his gubernatorial days. At the beginning of his 1982 race Kerrey seemed firmly positioned on the issue of abortion, but after the primary was over, he met with prominent pro-life advocates in Omaha and later announced, in a nebulous statement, that he was pro-life. In the Senate, however, Kerrey declared he was pro-choice and admitted in an *Omaha World-Herald* interview that he'd been "all over the map" on abortion during his 1982 campaign.

Throughout the first half of his first term in the Senate, Kerrey repeatedly was cited as a potential presidential candidate. Although he did little to encourage such speculation, a review of Kerrey's press from 1989–91 reveals scores of suggestions from citizens, members of the media, polltakers, and national Democrats that he run for the presidency.

Chapter 11

BORN TO RUN

On September 30, 1991, Bob Kerrey announced he was ready to run again—this time for the United States presidency. When Kerrey ascended the platform in Lincoln's Centennial Mall on a windy, blue-sky day, he was surrounded not only by familiar faces—his children, his supportive ex-wife, Nebraska politicians, Navy SEAL buddies, and friends—but by places he had known all his life. No matter which direction he looked, he could see landmarks of his past: the campus where he had walked as a college student; the capitol building on whose steps he had protested the war in Vietnam and later treaded as Governor; the production set where he had visited Debra Winger.

As the sun peeked over the federal building and began spraying the gold capitol dome three blocks south, Kerrey stepped into a building to change his shirt. As friends soon realized, he had inadvertently entered an old office of his late friend, Donna Karnes, who had felt all along that he was destined for the day that was about to unfold.

College students and families with babies in tow blended with women and men in suits, farmers and factory workers. The Boys Town choir and the Crete High School band shared the stage; the speakers pumped out the sounds of John Cougar Mellencamp and Bruce Springsteen, who titled his acclaimed acoustic album *Nebraska* and who wrote "Born to Run," Kerrey's theme song. Kids wore old KERREY FOR SENATE T-shirts with SENATE crossed out and replaced with PRESIDENT in black Magic Marker. High-tech mixed with the homemade, and the atmosphere was part business, part family festival, part rock concert, and part Democratic reunion.

Kerrey surveyed the crowd of more than five thousand who had skipped work and school to be on hand and hesitated before he began, overcome by the moment and the memories that no doubt tumbled upon him. Half a lifetime earlier, a wounded, embittered Vietnam vet hitchhiked home to Lincoln from the Philadelphia Naval Hospital; that "unpleasant young man" was now standing before the nation asking for the honor to serve his country as the Democratic presidential nominee. Kerrey began a speech that made it clear why he was running: "To lead America's fearless, restless voyage of generational progress." Kerrey's speech, which was drafted with the help of former staffer Jeremy Rosner, contained as its centerpiece his belief that "my generation is uniquely positioned to understand what must now be done. . . . It is time for leadership in America that focuses its attention on posterity rather than on popularity, on the next generation rather than the next election."

Kerrey's emphasis on generational change was not missed by Nebraskans who remembered his focus on that theme a decade earlier when he wrestled the Republican governorship away from a popular establishment candidate. Editors for the *Lincoln Star*, the city's morning paper and the only major daily to consistently support and endorse Kerrey in his political races, wrote the following on the day after his presidential announcement: "Kerrey has a decent chance to win the nomination and the opportunity to face a popular President. His candidacy is a long shot. That, too, is a Kerrey legacy. This weekend a reporter asked some college students at the Phoenix airport if they had ever heard of Bob Kerrey. None had. Almost ten years ago, on the marble murals of the Capitol Rotunda, Bob Kerrey made another formal announcement in his opening shot for the Governor's race. And back then, in his home state, nobody knew his name."

The major difference was that back then Kerrey picked up

the Democratic nomination with ease; in 1991, he positioned himself against a pack of strong Democratic candidates, half of whom could rightfully and forcefully stake out their own claim to generational leadership.

Kerrey's presidential announcement speech differed from those given by other Democratic contenders in that he praised President Bush and his World War II generation. "I am proud and grateful for the effort made by the architects and implementers of the policies of containment. . . . America heard President Bush—a proud man who has been fighting cold war battles for most of his thirty-five years in public life—take the first concrete step beyond containment." That Kerrey would single out the opposition for praise was not campaign rhetoric intended to endear himself to President Bush supporters; Kerrey believed Bush deserved praise for his foreign policy accomplishments. Politics, as with life, Kerrey has often maintained, is rarely black and white. He is inherently opposed to the dogmatic Democratic approach of "GOP bad—Demos good." Earlier in his speech, Kerrey said, "This campaign is grounded in the belief that we can and should trust again. As such it's not so much a fight against George Bush as a fight for what America can be. . . . The year 1992 offers a chance to end the feeling that our economic future is impaired. President Bush simply has not done all he could or should be doing. . . . Still, President Bush is not the enemy. A more difficult enemy for us to defeat is our own pessimism—particularly in the Democratic Party."

Some pundits immediately declared that Kerrey had been too easy on the Bush Administration, and indeed a few months later he sharpened his attack considerably, calling the President a "witch doctor."

Kerrey stressed that the legacy left to future generations of Americans would not be the rich one he inherited unless the issues of health care, fair trade, infrastructure rebuilding, and education were addressed quickly and comprehensively. Kerrey delivered the speech powerfully and without any stumbles. Later, he would tell confidants that appearing before his fellow Nebraskans for his presidential announcement was the most gratifying political event of his life. He paid homage to Nebraska's pioneers and their resounding tenacity: "Just look at what they did. They built this building [the Nebraska state capitol] with cash. They built it to last and to be enjoyed beyond their lifetimes. They were not motivated by a depreciation schedule or the desire to brag about their accomplishment on their campaign brochures. They built this building for generations yet unborn. And they did something else we should notice and emulate—they built it to inspire.

"This building turns our eyes and spirits upward. It should occur to us that if God gave the Nebraskans of our past the strength and courage to overcome pessimism and build for greatness, then we ought not doubt our capacity to do the same."

Kerrey concluded his speech and remained onstage, flanked by his son and daughter. Finally he worked his way off the platform and into the adoring audience of Nebraskans, who hadn't witnessed a native son posing a serious bid for President since William Jennings Bryan's final push for the presidency in 1908. As if to emphasize both Kerrey's roots and his sixties-generation candidacy, the music he chose to conclude his rally was John Cougar Mellencamp's "Small Town."

Meanwhile, the team Kerrey had assembled to put the event together toasted its success. Kerrey's announcement speech went off without a hitch, and the Kerrey camp was overjoyed. Kerrey himself was elated, and he let everyone know. He eagerly read press accounts and later watched the television coverage. Kerrey, who had at one point vacillated about how prominent a place his former wife should have in the event, agreed that her presence was a major plus. Debra Winger was a conspicuous no-show. Kerrey officially states that his relationship with Winger is one of friendship, and that her being an asset or liability is a moot question, because they're not married or otherwise germanely connected. Kerrey aides, however, knew that the presence of Winger would have presented a decidedly different Kerrey image—one that he has worked hard to distance himself from, despite pronouncements to the contrary. There is little question in the minds of most Nebraskans that while Winger is well liked, she was not welcome in Lincoln for his announcement.

By mid-September Kerrey had signed on a group of political aides culled from past Democratic presidential campaigns, the exception being novice campaign chairman Bill Hoppner. However, Kerrey's Lincoln event attracted scores of campaign gypsies who volunteered to lend their expertise in the hopes of landing real jobs down the line. Nebraska locals were somewhat amazed by their naïveté; many traveling to Lincoln that day were intrigued by Kerrey but able to offer only one reason for their support of his candidacy: They believed he could get the country moving.

It had been only six weeks since Kerrey decided he wanted to make America's ultimate political journey. He made up his mind swiftly and without angst after a number of things happened. Deciding against running were Senators Albert Gore, Jay Rockefeller, Bill Bradley, and Sam Nunn—all men whom Kerrey believed had good shots at the nomination. Among those entering the race were Tom Harkin, Jerry Brown, and Paul Tsongas—men whom Kerrey greatly respected, but, he believed, couldn't garner broad support. (Harkin and Kerrey have many similarities, but Kerrey believes that many Americans view Harkin as a liberal retread. Kerrey also shares one paramount similarity with Tsongas—they both have looked death square in the eye and exhibited courage in the face of it. But he believed Tsongas would not be appealing nationwide. Kerrey felt he could mount a more effective challenge than either man.) He thought the race would come down to Governor Bill Clinton and himself.

Aside from consideration about the competition, Kerrey was increasingly frustrated with the state of the economy and other aspects of the Bush Administration, including the fact that the President had expressed a willingness to work with the Russian coup leaders. Home for vacation with his family in August, he started to float the idea of running. One asked him, "What are you going to do—how are you going to feel if you lose?" Kerrey responded, "No, the question is, What if I win?" Kerrey said he knew he was ready to run when he felt supremely confident answering that question to himself. Then, much to his listener's surprise, Kerrey started talking about the kind of team that he would put together and how he felt Americans were finally ready to accept sacrifices for the future, for their kids.

One subject Kerrey didn't discuss with friends—and that irritates him intensely—is that he was considering the run because he was personally restless. He becomes irritated when Nebraska critics contend that his political chafing is less a sign of sincere eagerness for challenge and more a sign of a short attention span. Kerrey was always challenged by being a U.S. Senator, but he is always looking for a newer and greater challenge. When criticized for being too quick to move up to higher office, the Kerrey camp becomes frustrated. They believe the American public and the press get politicians coming and going: On the one hand, people are frothing for term limitations; on the other hand, they question politicians who impose their own term limitations or who desire to move on to different or more imposing challenges.

An examination of Kerrey's life shows a distinct pattern of restlessness every three or four years. He was in the SEALS for three years. He was married for four years. He was Governor for four years. He was a Senator for three years before he announced he wanted to run for President. And Nebraskans would not be surprised if Kerrey, should he ever win the presidency, remains on the job voluntarily for only one term.

There are those who are impressed with how much Kerrey has accomplished and who like his flexibility and forward motion. There are those who look at Kerrey's history and don't like or understand his movement. They see a man like Kerrey and call him unfinished, evolving, incomplete. These conclusive descriptions follow accolades on his background and the intensity of his dedication. But descriptions of Kerrey as unfinished and incomplete imply that since he is evolving, he would be more suitable to shadow a so-called finished politician, such as Mario Cuomo, and that somehow Kerrey's governorship of Nebraska doesn't count because the state is so small. Kerrey addresses that by saying, "I'll take you out and have you spend an evening with Waldo Haythorn in Ogallala, and if you're from Manhattan, you may snicker and sneer about Nebraska before you have that experience. But after you've spent that night on Waldo's ranch, you'll go back and say, 'I understand something that I didn't understand before.'"

And though Americans glorify youth, it is not surprising now that President John Kennedy's legacy has been revised, that there is coming a backward swing toward equating age with wisdom. But the unfinished politician summary is not based just on chronological age, it is also based on the number of years spent in the public eye. The theory permits a viable candidate to be relatively young so long as he or she has had enough years in the process—enough being ten, or perhaps fifteen or twenty.

Kerrey's brief career as a Senator makes him an easy target for those who believe he has not spent enough time in elected office. Not long after Kerrey won his 1988 Senate race, talk centered on a presidential run. In response, Nebraska's senior Senator declared that Kerrey needed seasoning. What kind of seasoning was Exon alluding to? Has there been some format, series of job positions, or ideal résumé developed over the years that especially prepares one for the presidency?

Exon may have been referring to his own environs—the U.S. Senate, where he is serving his third term—as the academy or "finishing school" for politicians. The Senate did produce Lyndon Johnson, Richard Nixon, and Gerald Ford, but given the chicanery, deception, and mediocrity that surfaced in their administrations, it is doubtful that the American people are ready to consider longevity in Congress as a singular guarantee of honest, visionary leadership. To recall the careers of many Congressmen and Senators is to be reminded that lengthy service there does not in itself create a dedication to serve others, nor does it somehow provide politicians with vision or courage.

Since Franklin Roosevelt—with the exception, perhaps, of Kennedy—all our Presidents were considered finished, mature politicians when they were elected. (Kennedy was considered unfinished, and critics now point to his tenure as an example of youth run amuck in the White House.) Still, each one of them, in many ways, came up to the job despite the great diversity in their backgrounds and experience. Perhaps there are some positions that are actually beyond training or experience.

If so, then the presidency, like the Supreme Court, is one of them. No experience in a law firm or tenure on a U.S. district court bench completely prepares one to sit as one of the nine individuals deciding the direction of a multifaceted democracy for the next half century. The test and qualifications for the presidency should not be based as much on longevity of experience as on how an individual has performed in the experiences he or she has had. Has a vision been articulated? Has the person been able to lead by taking a position and convincing others to follow? Does the person show a concern for others, compassion for the needy and the unfortunate? Has the person shown the courage of conviction in standing up to opposition? Without question, Kerrey has.

And he has taken some major chances in the course of his many journeys. Kerrey risked his life for his country in Vietnam when he agreed to head up the commando mission near Hon Tre Island. His selflessness and fearlessness were similar to that of President Bush during World War II, when he continued on in the *Avenger* in the face of heavy antiaircraft fire to take out a radio tower in the Bonin Islands near Iwo Jima. The President's war experience was part of his maturation, and the continuation of a journey such as Kerrey's would be one-quarter century later in the jungles of Vietnam. Kerrey has proven himself to be a journeyman, to be a true passage-seeker.

Seasoning and passage-seeking are not the exclusive criteria for leadership, even among those citizens who prize it highly. In deciding upon a candidate, voters don't just look at voting records, positions on issues, and life experiences; they look at the candidate as an individual and all of the facets of personality come into consideration—appearance, voice, stature, and demeanor. In all this, the citizen is looking for leadership, and in leaders Americans look for the qualities found in heroes. And though the search rarely focuses on the soldier-hero, people do look for candidates with traditional qualities of the central characters of history and mythology. Americans feel a need for heroes, society demands them and establishes criteria for the roles they play.

The Greek conception required that heroes possess heroic valor and individual aspiration for excellence, but through time all cultures have passed down standards as to what a hero should be. Since its beginnings, the United States has produced heroes who have exhibited unusual valor; and like all nations, America has honored its heroes. Usually, however, heroic figures return to the routine of private life and are not public figures.

Most leaders in the public eye must, by necessity, display their valor not by acts of physical courage but by taking stands at the risk of reputation. Kerrey is unusual in that he even meets the Greek standard. He has performed heroically in battle. He has constantly propelled himself in the pursuit of excellence—as an amputee jogging, as a successful businessman, as a student of national and international affairs, as a speaker and campaigner. All these pursuits have little or nothing to do with seasoning or longevity in public life. They are pursuits, however, that define a finished politician.

What a leader is, then, becomes a salient question. As we move to the record, we find that Kerrey, in his first three years in the U.S. Senate, has been willing to take stands consistent with the virtue of moral courage. Kerrey was one of nine Senators willing to cast a vote against the 1989 savings and loan bailout bill. That vote by a freshman Senator was, at a minimum, a statement of independence, a willingness not to go along with the crowd and endorse a popular idea.

Certainly, his Senate speech and vote against the flag desecration constitutional amendment was an example of his nonconformism. Many of his constituents like to keep their symbols intact, and it was a stand that cost him some popularity. In a state where a few residents question the loyalty of football fans who refuse to wear the color red at Cornhusker games, it is easy to see how Kerrey might have trouble making his point.

Only time and history will be able to fully assess the magnitude or the isolation of Kerrey's stand against the 1991 Gulf War. Although there wasn't any rush of Nebraskans to volunteer for hazardous duty in Vietnam, as Kerrey did, there were plenty of young men who served and served well. Many of them had the same doubts about becoming bogged down in what they believed could have become a Middle East counterpart to the Vietnam War. Kerrey's stand ran afoul of the militarism still prevalent in Nebraska. Many Nebraskans did not readily accept their junior Senator's recommendation for a thoughtful approach of sanctions before direct assault. Letters to the editor castigated him, and Kerrey was chastised by constituents who disagreed vehemently with his position, not granting that his own war experience gave him a perspective not available to the average citizen.

Republican National Committee Chairman Clayton Yeutter hit Kerrey hard with a statement that implicitly questioned his patriotism—one that infuriated Kerrey and that he lambasted Yeutter for. Still, Kerrey stood his ground and voted against the resolution to support the war.

In just three years in the Senate, Kerrey has proved that he is willing to take on the country's big battalions. Many Americans view him as an impressive candidate. And yet, before his September announcement Kerrey was still confused by most Americans with Senator John Kerry of Massachusetts. The Kerrey campaign, with its late start, determined that their man would have to make a respectable showing in New Hampshire to generate the necessary monetary contributions. Kerrey's campaign strategy had him campaigning heavily there from October right up to the February 18 primary. During October and the first two weeks of November everything ran smoothly—even more smoothly than would reasonably be expected, given the late start the Kerrey campaign encountered. As in his 1988 Senate race, Kerrey's campaign had a healthy measure of infighting that led to reshuffling.

Kerrey's first major address to delegates at the New Hampshire state Democratic convention was successful, despite an off-the-cuff opening remark that fell flat. The introduction Kerrey received was a masterful one that took more than five minutes, and by the time he made his way through hordes of New Hampshire residents, excitement was high. Because of the sustained ovation Kerrey received on his way to the stage, the sense of anticipation was palpable; as a result, there was a letdown when Kerrey offhandedly remarked as his first line, "Wow, what a way to make a living." He then laughed slightly, but stopped quickly when he realized that the remark was out of place in a region with such high unemployment. Kerrey is used to his offhand remarks being well received; this one wasn't, but he didn't let his opening stumble affect his performance. A few weeks later, however, New Hampshire would be the venue for a serious Kerrey slipup. On November 15, at a political roast, Kerrey privately told an off-color joke to fellow candidate Bill Clinton. Unbeknownst to either man, their conversation was picked up and recorded by C-SPAN. Democratic candidates had gathered in Manchester to speak at a roast for Representative Dick Swett, and Kerrey later explained, "During a private conversation last weekend there were a lot of inappropriate jokes being told and repeated. I made a mistake in repeating one I shouldn't have. If it offended anyone, I apologize." The *San Francisco Examiner* broke the story the Monday after the event, and by midweek it dominated Democratic political coverage, with Kerrey working furiously to contain the fallout. Coincidence had it that the day after his mistake made national headlines, Kerrey was scheduled to appear at San Francisco General Hospital to visit AIDS patients, a time when he had been planning to push his national health-care proposal, Health USA. Instead, Kerrey found himself apologizing repeatedly and promising to reevaluate his behavior. That evening Kerrey attended a fund-raiser that drew Northern California heavyweights and prominent gay activists, who were receptive to Kerrey in part, they announced, because of his strong voting record in the Senate as determined by the National Gay and Lesbian Task Force. Kerrey told California writers later that week while he believed his gaffe bruised an otherwise unsoiled campaign and temporarily damaged it, he did not see himself giving up. The issue dogged him for several weeks but gradually abated as the media feeding frenzy ended. For Kerrey staffers the whole period was a nightmare, and for former Hart supporters there was a whiff of déjà vu. The major difference, however, is that Hart's peccadilloes were roundly perceived to be part of a disturbing and potentially dangerous pattern. Most Americans considered the coverage of Kerrey's joke to be overblown.

After the fact, Kerrey was wise and forthright in issuing a statement that admitted he had told salty jokes before. If he had tried to pass himself off as someone who had erred for the first time, it wouldn't have played in Nebraska. Kerrey confidants know that he can, on occasion, be raunchy. It is not a revealing feature of his personality that masks deeper and darker secrets. It is simply that Kerrey came of age around strong environmental influences that dismissed crudeness as long as only men were involved. Kerrey was reared in a decidedly working-class neighborhood, and the Navy SEALS have never put a high priority on politically correct jokes. Kerrey critics argued that at forty-eight Kerrey is a big boy and should have known better. Kerrey agreed and said that the exposure the joke received required that he stand back and see "an unpleasant side" of his personality. Kerrey analysts and Nebraskans know that while Kerrey bravely admitted having an "unpleasant side," that he possesses an extremely pleasant and sensitive side passed down to him by his gentle and loving mother, Elinor. Kerrey never considered fudging on the subject. In California, Kerrey said, "I've told jokes like this in the past and didn't give it a second thought, and the fact that it's public today I think merely opens up a problem of my insensitivity. It's time for me to evaluate my own behavior." Some opinion writers lambasted Kerrey for what they labeled his effusive apologizing.

Candidates have learned from watching enough of their comrades fall that politicians routinely get in more trouble with their handling of mistakes than they do with the actual mistake itself. And so Kerrey felt relieved when the *San Francisco Examiner* reported after his day touring the AIDS outpatient ward that "Kerrey wasted no time trying to put the gaffe behind him, and he offered no excuses. He admitted everything, denied nothing, and said the experience changed him."

It would have had to. For the first time in his brief political career, Kerrey, who has always had strong rapport with the national media, was on the receiving end of negative press. He was caught off-guard. Before his remarks were caught, Kerrey enjoyed an untarnished reputation, most especially with the national media.

Kerrey, who while governor made a point of encouraging the media to get tougher on politicians, once said of a Nicholas von Hoffman *Esquire* profile, "There's no question the national press comes in and does fluff pieces. Hoffman came in with a story already written—with Whigs and Tories, et cetera. He really didn't even need to interview me."

Receiving negative press was completely new to Kerrey and could have been potentially disastrous. He was exceedingly fortunate that a few weeks later *Parade* magazine featured him on a December cover and that the January issue of *Vanity Fair* served up a flattering profile. The timing of those two could not have been more perfect for Kerrey to recover the momentum he lost with the joke episode.

Meanwhile, the Kerrey camp was humbled and overjoyed that Americans seemed willing to allow him a mistake and let him move on. Kerrey enjoyed a cartoon that showed Abraham Lincoln looking frozen as Stephen Douglas brings a VCR onto the stage for the debates and announces, "Instead of debating the issues, I thought you might like to see this videotape of a few off-color jokes my opponent told at dinner last night." The Kerrey camp believed the cartoon put his joke in perspective—that with all the problems facing the country, Americans should be discussing issues. They were disheartened that those who disseminated the joke and those who quickly accepted it as meaningful were willing to cast aside the substance of a man and the vision of a leader to dramatize a lapse of decorum.

The joke marked the moment when Kerrey's presidential campaign stalled. Small signs were evident in late November that Governor Bill Clinton was ready to break out of the pack, and it is likely that he might have overtaken Kerrey even without the joke misstep. But Kerrey's short-term freefall gave Clinton an edge at a crucial period. By the beginning of 1992, Clinton, a powerful campaigner, had surpassed Kerrey by a wide margin in the New Hampshire polls and the Arkansan was poised to overtake the acknowledged front-runner, Paul Tsongas.

Kerrey reacted to his lackluster placing in the polls by firing his longtime media adviser, Joe Rothstein, and hiring the Washington firm of Doak, Shrum, Harris, Sherman, Donilon. This new team scrapped thousands of dollars' worth of ads and hastily put together a new series, which included one of Kerrey standing at an empty hockey net and talking tough about trade with Japan. A short time later, Kerrey criticized the ad in an interview, acknowledging that it did not accurately reflect his free-trade philosophy.

January and February were not easy months for Kerrey and his campaign. They were shaken by his inability to move up in the polls despite the fact that his debate performances were roundly praised by voters and opinion makers.

Kerrey and his aides had entered the race convinced that he would be the front-runner, a status he had yet to achieve by March.

Just about the time a Clinton victory seemed assured in New Hampshire, campaign winds shifted again when he was battered by allegations of marital infidelity and draft dodging. The Kerrey camp and political pundits alike waited for the Nebraskan to become the beneficiary of Clinton's drop in the polls. A Kerrey surge never came and he finished a distant third in New Hampshire's February 18 primary, barely two percentage points ahead of crusader Jerry Brown, who spent a great deal less money than Kerrey, whose media costs were the highest of all candidates. Kerrey tried to put the best possible spin on his poor showing by declaring that New Hampshire had breathed new life into his campaign. "I didn't get the gold," Kerrey said to an audience who had been captivated that week by Olympic performances in France, "but bronze ain't bad."

Five days later, Jerry Brown would come within one percentage point of Tsongas to nearly beat him at the Maine caucuses. And one week after the New Hampshire primary, on February 25, Bob Kerrey won the South Dakota primary. After his first win, Kerrey urged the nation's Democrats to give his candidacy a chance and he further declared himself to be the strongest contender against President Bush.

Clearly, the possibility loomed in early March that no one candidate would have a majority of delegates by the time of the Democratic convention in New York from July 13 to 16. The idea that Clinton, who survived New Hampshire with a strong second showing and who billed himself as the most electable candidate, was the only candidate at the end of February who had not yet won a primary or caucus made his future all the more fragile.

Campaign '92 has proven that politics is about as predictable as a prairie twister. That's what makes it so fascinating. Four months before the Democratic convention, nobody was certain who would end up leading the charge against the Republicans in the fall. Despite his weak early start, Kerrey supporters believed he would be the eventual nominee on the strength of his call for national health insurance and his proven track record as a veteran, businessman, Governor, and Senator.

Walter Lippman wrote that a man's philosophy is his biography—that we "may read in it the story of his conflict with life." Some observers who dismiss Kerrey's life still demand precise packaged plans and position papers as if the economy, world events, and even life were somehow predictable. Certainly, future leaders must be brilliantly insightful about the economy and know the painfully exacting requirements of global competition. Yet, in reality, situations in business, economy, and international relations change so rapidly that a plan or policy that claims to have all the answers is engaging in smoke-and-mirror imagery. Ideally, citizens look for leaders whose lives match their rhetoric.

This year, as always, citizens want the question of character answered, just as they want to examine candidates' records. And although it would be impossible for every voter to have every question answered, many can be. In examining Kerrey, what emerges is a portrait of a complicated, determined man who chooses to live life fully. He is, notwithstanding political pundits' descriptions of him as incomplete, a finished politician. Kerrey's character was completed during the months he spent in the Philadelphia Naval Hospital. The record he has achieved since then is reflective of his basic conservatism tempered by a catastrophe that made him a more compassionate man.

In 1988, during the middle of his intense Senate race, Kerrey took time out to address students at Boys Town. Before his speech, Kerrey met with Father Val Peter, director, to hear some background on the kids he would be facing. "These kids have suffered," Peter said. "Not only are they hearing-impaired, but most are from broken homes with abusive parents. They are all exceptionally bright and interested in learning, but they have really suffered." Peter then recounted for Kerrey a story about Michelangelo, who was once presented with a painting by a student smug about what he believed was a flawless picture. He waited anxiously for the great master's opinion. Michelangelo studied it and then told the student that the painting was technically perfect, but worthless, and said, "You haven't suffered and it shows in your painting."

Men and women who have battled illness, risked reputation, and seen the real face of war and its aftermath have suffered. Bob Kerrey emerged from the suffering that was Vietnam a hero for exhibiting courage in the heat of battle. But whether courage is displayed in war, in the give and take of daily government, or as Shakespeare wrote, "against the slings and arrows of outrageous fortune," it is a cornerstone of leadership, a quality that cannot, and should not, be ignored.

Epilogue

Just one week after Kerrey struck "gold in the hills of South Dakota," in February of 1992, he came up completely empty-handed in all the March 3, 1992, Democratic primaries and caucuses. Nebraska's junior Senator placed at the bottom in Georgia, Maryland, Washington, Idaho, Utah, and Colorado, where he finished fourth to Jerry Brown's first. The Colorado loss was particularly painful for Kerrey, as he had campaigned there heavily and had once been favored to win the state that shares a border with Nebraska. While Kerrey knew that polls showed him behind, he was surprised and saddened by the shutout.

Kerrey met with aides the next day and rumors immediately began circulating that he planned to withdraw. He listened to campaign strategists and fundraisers who cautioned that continuing would be futile and that he risked the goodwill of contributors whose help would be needed to reduce his six-hundred-thousand-dollar campaign debt. Some advisers urged him to stay in the race, so convinced were they that candidate Clinton would again stumble on the road to the nomination. But Kerrey knew it was over and he decided that day to drop out.

On Thursday, March 5, 1992, just five months and five days after Kerrey's exuberant entrance into the race, he appeared before hundreds of supporters, reporters, and Senate colleagues in the Hart Office Building and announced his withdrawal. In a gracious, candid, and reassuring thirty-minute speech, laden with winning self-effacing humor, Kerrey thanked his well-wishers for their "confidence, idealism, money, time, and effort," which he compared to the Jamaican Olympic bobsled team. "We had a lot of spirit, but unfortunately we didn't get a lot of medals." More than a few in the audience felt they were witnessing the exit of the Democrats' most electable politician in 1992. Many seemed stunned that the compelling candidate before them had not caught on with the electorate.

With characteristic intensity, Kerrey vowed to move his fight for fundamental change in health care, education, foreign policy, and government infrastructure to new arenas, specifically, the U.S. Senate.

"These were the reasons for my running for President, and they will always be my compass to guide me in the fight ahead. This is the end of a single presidential campaign, unfortunately my own," Kerrey said to laughter. "As I look back on my campaign, difficult though that might be to do, I feel neither regret nor disappointment."

Later, however, Kerrey admitted that he did feel a supreme sense of letdown and he said so Thursday evening at Omaha's Peony Park Ballroom, where he addressed Nebraskans, some of whom interrupted his remarks with cries of "Ninety-six." "I was concerned that perhaps I'd disappointed the team," Kerrey said.

Kerrey's failure did not so much disappoint participants and political observers as it baffled them. After all, Kerrey, more than any other candidate, had the media stamp of approval. And therein lies a factor in his failure. His overwhelmingly flattering pre-announcement reviews meant that he really had nowhere to go but down. For Kerrey's primary performance to have matched early expectations would have been almost impossible. Paul Tsongas and Jerry Brown, who were virtually ignored early on by what the former California Governor correctly calls "the media elite," literally had nowhere to go but up, which is the direction they both went. Bill Clinton also did not receive the level of pre-announcement press buildup that Kerrey enjoyed. By the media's yardstick, Kerrey was expected to dazzle as he broke out of the pack in the fall of 1991. When he didn't, the standard story adopted by the journalistic pack was that he was an unfinished and unprepared politician. That spin on the Kerrey story is half right. Unfinished he is not.

But Kerrey was unprepared for a presidential nominating system that has evolved to the point where a genuine dark horse, as he most certainly was—media hype aside—really does not have a prayer. Politicians have to seek the nomination, strive for it, and strenuously organize for years before they are well positioned to have a serious shot at securing it. The only reason Kerrey, his staff, or anyone in the press believed that he could actually win the nomination is because they had all read all of his press clippings, suggesting that there is a widespread feeling that the press controls the election. National writers wrote a great deal about Kerrey being of presidential timbre and nothing about a Byzantine and unfair nominating process that guarantees doom for late starters who don't have carefully cultivated organizations. Kerrey did not begin to consider the process until the fall of 1991. He had been too busy embracing life.

Bill Clinton, on the other hand, had been planning a run for the presidency since his teenage Boys State days and had been actively courting delegates for at least one decade or more. Paul Tsongas spoke to confidants back in his early Senate days about his interest in the presidency, and the 1992 race heralded the third presidential try for Jerry Brown. It is no coincidence that the man who jumped into the race last was the first to jump out. Kerrey never really had an exploratory period. He did not have time to mount an aggressive campaign to win over those who are instrumental in the presidential sweepstakes. And yet many political analysts and Kerrey aides expressed shock that he did not take the nomination by storm.

The real story is how well an unknown freshman Senator from an obscure state actually did. If expectations for Kerrey had not been unrealistically high, placing third in New Hampshire behind Tsongas and Clinton would have been considered a good showing, given the reality that he had been in the race a mere eighteen weeks and had not spent the prime of his life planning for the presidency.

Some members of Kerrey's family and a few staffers warned him about the pitfalls of a late-starting campaign, but Kerrey felt confident. His brashness had served him well one decade earlier in Nebraska's 1982 gubernatorial race and he saw perfect parallels between his first run and the 1992 presidential race. Back then conventional wisdom had it that Republican incumbent Charley Thone would be reelected, so better-positioned Democrats who had paid their dues in the party sat on the sidelines. Kerrey was audacious enough that he took the plunge and ended up winning by a few thousand votes. He figured the same scenario could be played out on the national stage.

What Kerrey overlooked in the comparison is the precariousness of his first victory. He won in Nebraska as much because of Thone's missteps as for preparedness or insightfulness on his own part. With a slight change of reality, he would have been an also-ran in Nebraska politics, which he became in 1992 in national politics. His luck, if you will, ran out.

Stanford University professor James March, in a lecture on leaders, said, "Since most of our leaders have been promoted because they are successful, they have this wonderful illusion of control. They believe that they can beat the odds because they've always won. It's called the gambler's fallacy in the trade. If you take one hundred people and put them in a casino, the ones who lose tend to disappear. The ones who win tend to stay and a small number of them will win a whole series of bets. Those people have a very powerful sense that they can beat the odds, that they have a system. They have a sense that they know what they are doing. Those are the people we let be leaders—people who have been successful all along the way—and being successful leads them to believe they can beat the odds. They don't notice the luck component in their own success."

Several political pundits attributed Kerrey's failure in the primaries to what they labeled his tendency to shift personas, campaign disarray, and lack of a defined message. All are off-the-mark explanations.

First, all candidates change personae. In 1992, Bill Clinton moved continuously from what one *Washington Post* writer called his good ol' boy side to his policy nerd side. In fact, Clinton has shown more personas to the public than any politician in memory. Paul Tsongas repeatedly vacillated between his St. Paul side and his Greek warrior side.

If candidates were lauded for evenness, Michael Dukakis would be a hero today for maintaining his tightly controlled demeanor during his answer to 1988 debate moderator Bernard Shaw's hypothetical question about rape. Instead, Dukakis was crucified for not stepping out of his normal reserve and summoning a different one when the occasion demanded it.

Second, all campaigns have disarray, most especially national ones. To be sure, some have more than others, but the idea that successful campaigns are seamless is simply a fantasy. Anyone who has ever worked on a national campaign knows that infighting, staff overhauling, and a certain measure of "admired disorder," as Cicero called it, is a part of the game.

Third, Kerrey had as powerful a message as any Democrat in the race and a more comprehensive one than several of his competitors. He did not articulate that message as effectively at the outset of the campaign as he did later on, but that fact does not mean he did not possess a vision. What will no doubt gnaw at the Kerrey camp for many moons is how its man began to hit his stride too late in the race to make a difference. Toward the end, Kerrey put in masterful performances, prompting observers to declare he had finally found his voice.

Not long before the New Hampshire primary, Kerrey received counsel from former Kennedy speechwriter Theodore Sorensen, now a prominent New York attorney. On February 16, 1992, at the final debate before the primary, Kerrey was roundly acknowledged as the most impressive of the five candidates. The *Washington Post* singled out Kerrey as displaying the "most vivid language" when he called President Bush "massively indifferent" to the plight of ordinary Americans.

Pundit praise notwithstanding, Kerrey came in third in New Hampshire and two weeks later he would be gone from the race. Kerrey, his aides, Nebraskans, and others will be debating why for many months.

Kerrey undoubtedly will look back on some of the matters he worried about initially and recast them as inconsequential. Before his formal announcement on September 30, 1991, Kerrey called several of his siblings and said, "Okay, here are the rules." He then proceeded to outline how they were to deal with media questions, especially ones about his personal life. The biggest fear the Kerrey campaign harbored in the beginning was that his relationship with Debra Winger would somehow become an issue. Later, when Bill Clinton's alleged philandering made headlines, Kerrey came across as a choirboy in comparison—a development nobody ever imagined.

Kerrey also did not benefit from the revelation that Clinton dodged the draft during the Vietnam War. That fact, more than any other aspect of the campaign, is the most puzzling to political analysts and Kerrey supporters. *Baltimore Sun* associate editor Ernest B. Furgurson wrote in the fall, "If the height of one's heroism determined who would win and who would lose in politics, Bob Kerrey of Nebraska would be the next President of the United States.

Instead, for the first time in American history, an outstanding record in war did not give a political candidate a major boost. By like token, a record of having wavered and waffled through calculated draft avoidance was not something to sink a candidate.

Observers declared that Vietnam was the wrong war. Kerrey found himself in the unbelievable position of defending his Vietnam experience. In New Hampshire, Kerrey said that he sensed his war history, in essence, troubled voters. He seemed to remind America of a time and a place that most people wanted to forget. It is easy to see how Kerrey's unique war record might be off-putting to his peers in the press. Certainly most of the media were more comfortable with Clinton's Vietnam-era résumé because it more clearly resembled that of the establishment press. But it was unexpected that average voters, including World War II veterans, would find Kerrey's service unsettling and dismiss his valor so easily.

In his Gettysburg Address, President Abraham Lincoln did not distinguish between a right war and a wrong one when he honored those who had served on both sides, men and women who "gave the last full measure of devotion." Lincoln paid tribute to Northern and Southern veterans who had no voice in the decision to go to war.

Bob Kerrey was in a canoe the last time he came in last in a race. Two decades ago, an excited Kerrey called Bethany buddy Frosty Chapman, urging him to be a partner in a Memorial Day weekend ten-mile canoe race down a Nebraska river. "Bob, neither of us have spent a lot of time canoeing," Chapman reminded him, "and you want to enter a race?" Amused and intrigued, Chapman agreed and the two rented a canoe. They camped out the night before, drinking beer and playing cards in their tent past midnight.

On the morning of the race, the two discovered they had rented the wrong kind of paddles; another team loaned them the right kind. As they were going through makeshift preparations, Kerrey and Chapman realized they were surrounded by extremely serious canoeists.

The race started below a bridge with participants holding on to ropes that had been thrown down. After a signal, racers were to let go of the ropes and begin. "The first thing we did," Chapman recalls, "was ram the canoe of the guys who had given us their paddles. They ended up coming in second by just a minute, so we probably cost them the race. We finished dead last. It nearly killed us. But we had such a great time. It didn't matter that we were last. We laughed all the way. We were going from bank to bank and everywhere but straight down the river."

One week later, Kerrey asked Chapman to meet him at Capitol Beach. "He had bought a yellow racing canoe," Chapman said, "and he was very serious then. All of a sudden we had to win—that competitive spirit. Kerrey continued practicing until he was forced to stop because of grenade fragments in his hand that had caused an infection and required that he undergo further surgery. But oh, he wanted to compete again."

More than likely Kerrey will one day run again for the presidency. He enjoys the journey. As a gubernatorial candidate in 1982, Kerrey often allayed the fears of political friends who worried about what they perceived as his futile crusade against an incumbent. "What most politicians don't realize," Kerrey would say, "is that there are a lot of things worse than losing an election. I know there are worse things." Kerrey once told Chapman that when he used that line, he thought of the two most painful events in his life—the loss of his leg and the loss of his kids in divorce.

In keeping with his character and resilient nature, Kerrey has put his presidential loss in perspective. He might even recall the response he gave to the commanding officer who screamed at him after a less-than-skillful parachute performance. "At least I jumped."

Bibliography

Austin, Anthony. *The President's War.* Philadelphia: Lippincott, 1971.

Beitzinger, A. J. *A History of American Political Thought.* New York: Dodd, Mead & Co., 1972.

Bennett, Mildred. *The World of Willa Cather.* Lincoln: University of Nebraska Press, 1961.

Bonham, Barbara. *Willa Cather.* Philadelphia: Chilton, 1970.

Boye, Alan. *The Complete Roadside Guide to Nebraska.* St. Johnsbury, Vt.: Saltilla, 1989.

Brown, E. K. *Willa Cather: A Critical Biography* (completed by Leon Edel). New York: Alfred A. Knopf, 1953.

Brown, Peter. *Minority Party.* Washington, D.C.: Regnery Gateway, 1991.

Cather, Willa. *My Antonia.*

———. *O Pioneers!* Boston: Houghton Mifflin, 1913.

Creigh, Dorothy Weyer. *Nebraska, Where Dreams Grow.* Lincoln, Neb.: Miller & Paine, 1981.

Crosby, Robert B. "Dedication of the George W. Norris West Legislative Chamber." *Nebraska History* 66 (Spring 1985): 1–6.

Davidson, Lieutenant General Phillip B. (USA). *Vietnam at War: 1945–1975.* Novato, Calif.: Presidio Press, 1979.

De Benedetti, Charles. *An American Ordeal.* Syracuse, N.Y.: Syracuse, 1990.

Dionne, E. J., Jr. *Why Americans Hate Politics.* New York: Simon and Schuster, 1991.

Editors, Boston Publishing Company. *Above and Beyond: A History of the Medal of Honor from the Civil War to Vietnam.* Boston: Boston Publishing Company, 1985.

Editors, Time-Life Books. *World War II: The Aftermath.* Alexandria, Va.: Time-Life Books, 1983.

Faulkner, Virginia, ed. *Roundup: A Nebraska Reader.* Lincoln: University of Nebraska Press, 1957.

Federal Writer's Project of the Works Progress Administration. *Nebraska: A Guide to the Cornhusker State.* Lincoln: University of Nebraska Press, 1979.

Fenno, Richard F., Jr. *The Making of a Senator.* Washington, D.C.: Congressional Quarterly Press, 1989.

Filley, H. Clyde. *Their Hopes Were High.* Chicago: Johnson Publishing Co., 1969.

Fitzgerald, Frances. *Fire in the Lake.* Boston: Little, Brown, 1972.

Flexner, Stuart B. *I Hear America Talking.* New York: Simon and Schuster, 1976.

Fonda, Henry. *My Life,* as told to Howard Teichman. New York: NAL Books, 1981.

Grand Island Daily Independent, July 1982.

Harper, Ivy. "Bad Good Press." *American Politics Magazine,* January 1988.

Hutchinson, Duane. *Exon, Biography of a Governor.* Lincoln, Neb.: Foundation Books, 1973.

Johnsgard, Paul A. *The Platte, Channels in Time.* Lincoln: University of Nebraska Press, 1984.

Karnow, Stanley. *Vietnam: A History.* New York: Viking Press, 1983.

Kennedy, John F. *Profiles in Courage.* New York: Harper & Brothers, 1955.

King, Patricia. "Running by Not Running." *Newsweek,* November 3, 1986, p. 26.

Kovic, Ron. *Born on the Fourth of July.* New York: McGraw-Hill, 1976.

Lee, Hermoine. *Double Lives.* New York: Pantheon, 1989.

Lee, Wayne C. *Wild Towns of Nebraska.* Caldwell, Idaho: 1988.

Lincoln Journal, 1976–1991.

Lincoln Star, 1982–1991.

Manley, Robert N. *Nebraska: Our Pioneer Heritage.* Lincoln, Neb.: Media Productions and Marketing, 1981.

Martin, Ralph G. *The Wizard of Wall Street.* New York: Morrow, 1965.

McKee, James L. *Lincoln: The Prairie Capital.* Northridge, Calif.: Windsor, 1984.

McKinnon, E., O. Koehle, and S. Valentine. *Looking at Lincoln.* Lincoln, Neb.: Media Productions, 1983.

Meyerson, Joel D. *Images of a Lengthy War: The United States Army in Vietnam.* Washington, D.C.: U.S. Government Printing Office.

Miewald, Robert D., ed. *Nebraska Government and Politics.* Lincoln: University of Nebraska Press, 1984.

Neihardt, John G. *Lyric and Dramatic Poems.* Lincoln: University of Nebraska Press, 1913.

Norris, George. *Fighting Liberal.* New York: A.M.S., 1945.

O'Brien, Sharon. *The Emerging Voice.* New York: Oxford University Press, 1987.

Omaha Metropolitan, 1987–1989.

Omaha World-Herald, 1976–1991.

Pedersen, James F., and Wald, Kenneth D. *Shall the People Rule.* Lincoln, Neb.: Jacob North, 1972.

Perkey, Elton A. *Perkey's Nebraska Place Names.* Lincoln: Nebraska State Historical Society, 1982.

Pound, Louise. *Nebraska Folklore.* Lincoln: University of Nebraska Press, 1947.

Puller, Lewis B., Jr. *Fortunate Son.* New York: Grove Weidenfeld, 1991.

Reeves, Thomas C. *A Question of Character.* New York: Free Press, 1991.

Sabato, Larry J. *Feeding Frenzy.* New York: Free Press, 1991.

Sorensen, Theodore. *Kennedy.* New York: HarperCollins, 1988.

———. *Let the Word Go Forth.* New York: Delacorte, 1988.

Steel, Ronald. *Walter Lippman and the American Century.* Boston: Little, Brown, 1980.

Teal, Alison. "At Home With Bob Kerrey." *Denver Post Magazine,* July 13, 1986.

Toner, Robin. "The Unfinished Politician." *New York Times Magazine,* April 14, 1991.

Von Hoffman, Nicholas. "A Basic Introduction to Bob Kerrey." *Esquire,* November 1985.

Weisberg, Jacob. "Senator Perfect." *The New Republic,* December 18, 1989.

INDEX

About the Author

Ivy Harper, a native Nebraskan, was raised in Grand Island and Lincoln. She graduated from the University of Nebraska–Lincoln College of Journalism in 1975. After reporting for the *York News-Times* newspaper, she signed on with the campaign of Omahan John J. Cavanaugh, moved to Washington, D.C., and worked on Capitol Hill after his successful election to the U.S. Congress. Her work has appeared in the *Washington Post, Regardies* magazine, *American Politics* magazine, the *Lincoln Journal,* and the *Omaha Metropolitan* newspapers. She is married and lives with her husband and two children in Bethesda, Maryland.